Collaborative Teaming

Teachers' Guides to Inclusive Practices

Collaborative Teaming

Second Edition

by

Martha E. Snell, Ph.D.
University of Virginia
Charlottesville

and

Rachel Janney, Ph.D.
Radford University
Radford, Virginia

with contributions by

Maria Beck, M.Ed.
Kenna M. Colley, Ed.D.
Johnna Elliott, M.Ed.
Christine C. Burton, M.S.

·P A U L·H·
BROOKES
PUBLISHING Co ®

Baltimore • London • Sydney

Paul H. Brookes Publishing Co.
Post Office Box 10624
Baltimore, Maryland 21285-0624

www.brookespublishing.com

Typeset by Barton Matheson Willse & Worthington, Baltimore, Maryland.
Manufactured in the United States of America by
Edwards Brothers, Inc., Ann Arbor, Michigan.

All of the vignettes in this book are composites of the authors' actual experiences. In all instances, names have been changed; in some instances, identifying details have been altered to protect confidentiality.

Library of Congress Cataloging-in-Publication Data

Snell, Martha E.
    Collaborative teaming/by Martha E. Snell and Rachel Janney; with contributions by Maria Beck...[et al.].—2nd ed.
        p.   cm.—(Teachers' guides to inclusive practices)
    Includes bibliographical references and index.
    ISBN 1-55766-711-X (layflat)
    1. Inclusive education—United States.   2. School support teams—
    United States.   3. Home and school—United States.   I. Janney, Rachel.
    II. Elliott, Johnna.   III. Title.   IV. Series.
    LC1201.S64 2005
    371.1'48—dc22   2005002210

British Library Cataloguing in Publication data are available from the British Library.

Contents

     Purpose of This Book
     Inclusive Education
     Collaborative Teaming
     Delivering Special Education Support
     Team Members
     Team Interactions
     Components of Collaborative Teamwork
     Benefits and Challenges of Collaborative Teaming

     Administrative Leadership and Negative Staff Attitudes
     Phases of Policy Development and Administrative Support for Teams
     Define Team Purpose and Focus
     Establish Team Membership
     Time Needed for Teams to Meet
     Finding the Time to Plan
     Support Teams and Teamwork

     Listening and Interacting Well
     Establishing Shared Values
     Defining Roles and Responsibilities
     Establishing a Team Meeting Process and Schedule
     Preparing for and Conducting Team Meetings
     Giving and Receiving Information
     Making Decisions by Consensus
     Teaming Effectively On-the-Fly
     Reflecting on the Team Process

About the Authors

Martha E. Snell, Ph.D., is Professor in the Curry School of Education at the University of Virginia, where she has taught since 1973. Her focus is special education and, specifically, the preparation of teachers of students with mental retardation and severe disabilities and young children with disabilities. Prior to completing her doctoral degree in special education at Michigan State University, she worked with children and adults with disabilities as a residential child care worker, a provider of technical assistance to school and residential programs, and a teacher. In addition to teaching courses at the undergraduate and graduate levels, she currently directs the graduate program in severe disabilities and coordinates the special education program, serves on the boards of several community agencies serving people with disabilities, and is an active member of the American Association on Mental Retardation and TASH.

Rachel Janney, Ph.D., is Professor in the Special Education Department at Radford University in Virginia. She has worked with, and on behalf of, children and adults with disabilities in a number of roles, including special education teacher, educational consultant, researcher, and teacher educator. She received her master's degree from Syracruse University and her doctorate from the University of Nebraska–Lincoln. Dr. Janney now teaches coursework in the special education teacher preparation program at Radford University, specializing in the area of cognitive disabilities. She also supervises student interns and student teachers in a number of schools that have a firm commitment to the inclusion of all students. Dr. Janney serves as Co-director of Radford University's Training and Technical Assistance Center, which provides a variety of services and resources to special education teams in school divisions throughout southwest Virginia.

Drs. Snell and Janney have conducted several research projects in inclusive schools and classrooms. These projects have studied the ways that special and general educators work together to design and implement modifications and accommodations for students with disabilities in inclusive settings. Both authors frequently present workshops on topics related to successful inclusive education.

ABOUT THE CONTRIBUTORS

Maria Beck, M.Ed., was an elementary school inclusion specialist and a provider of technical assistance to teachers of students with disabilities. She currently works on a deaf-blind project at Virginia Commonwealth University.

Kenna M. Colley, Ed.D., was an elementary school inclusion specialist and is the co-director of the Training and Technical Assistance Center (T/TAC) at Radford University. She currently is Assistant Professor in Special Education at Radford University.

Johnna Elliott, M.Ed., and **Christine C. Burton, M.S.,** are consulting teachers in a school division that serves all students in their neighborhood schools and provides individualized support to students with disabilities in general education classrooms. As consulting teachers, they provide and coordinate an array of supports for students across all disability categories.

Acknowledgments

Many colleagues, parents, and students deserve our recognition and praise for their contributions to what we know about team collaboration. Some of these individuals whose work we have learned from and built on include Michael F. Giangreco, Lynn Cook, Anita DeBoer, Susan Fister, Janet Freston, Marilyn Friend, David Johnson, Bev Rainforth, Jacque Thousand, Rich Villa, and Jennifer York-Barr.

We would also like to acknowledge our colleagues at Paul H. Brookes Publishing Co.: Rebecca Lazo for her ongoing support and guidance and Janet Betten for her excellent editing and persistence in completing this second edition.

To those who are working to establish
meaningful inclusion in schools
so that all students have membership,
enjoy interactions with peers, and
receive the needed supports to learn
what is important for them to be
successful in life

Chapter 1

Overview of Collaborative Teaming

Student Snapshot

Ms. James begins her first-grade class by asking her 23 students to gather in a circle to share class news and review what's in store for the day. Two classmates help the teaching assistant, Ms. Johnson, get Daniel situated in his floor sitter as the other children squirm and maneuver into a spot on the floor. Ms. Johnson places Daniel's scrapbook on his lap along with his communication device. Daniel shares some news about a puppy that his family has just acquired. His classmates eagerly examine photos that he has brought in, and they laugh at the "facewash" photo of Daniel being licked by the puppy.

Student Snapshot

Sam, a 14-year-old who attends the local high school, takes general education classes and attends a one-to-one resource period. While Sam's classmates like the noise and chaos between every class, they understand that Sam may need support to make the transition between classes without "losing it." Some of Sam's peers have known him since middle school; although they recognize his talents, they also know his feelings about between-class noise and confusion. Tom, one of Sam's best friends, directs Sam to walk with him along the wall that has no lockers in order to avoid the chaos.

Daniel and Sam are both students with disabilities who receive special education support in general classrooms from collaborative teams. Their teachers work closely with family members and other school staff to plan and implement programs that have been individually designed to suit their needs. The responsibility for teaching and monitoring progress is shared by the team members.

PURPOSE OF THIS BOOK

This book describes how teachers can collaborate with each other and with other school staff, students, and families to individualize and deliver special education supports in general education classrooms and activities. The focus of this book is groups of people organized to address the learning needs and priorities of individual or groups of students, known as *student-level teams* (York-Barr, 1996). This book is written primarily for general and special educators who are serving or planning to serve students with disabilities in inclusive classrooms. In addition, it can be a useful resource for anyone working with a team (e.g., related services staff, administrators, family members).

Collaborative teams act to include students with disabilities—both academically and socially—in general education settings. In schools where inclusion is practiced, several standards are valued by staff:

- All students are members of general education classrooms in their neighborhood schools alongside their peers.

- Educational programs and special education supports are individually defined and implemented by teams.

- Special education supports follow students as they move through their daily school routines.

To reach these high standards, administrators must provide strong support. They need to work cooperatively with teachers while drawing family members and other school staff members into their decision making. With team planning, students are not merely placed into general education, they are actively *involved and learning*.

The range of supports that teams can plan for and provide is not limited to schoolwork. Team-generated supports can have many different functions: to reduce barriers to participation in school activities, to facilitate social interactions between students, to build peer support, to encourage family members to contribute ideas, to embed related services into the school day, to replace problem behavior with skills, and to design plans to ease students' transitions between grades and schools and into jobs or college. Likewise, teams take many forms to address these functions. This book primarily addresses teams that focus on students who use special education support; however, many of the principles of collaborative teaming that apply to these student-centered teams also apply to other types of teams that are formed within schools, such as teams to revise curriculum, select textbooks, promote inclusion, and implement a new literacy program. Effective communication and trust are relevant whether a team is addressing a student with disabilities or designing a math curriculum.

The five students described in this book are composites of student characteristics and personalities we have encountered over the years:

- *Daniel*, a first-grade student with severe disabilities, including cerebral palsy and mental retardation

- *Melanie*, a fourth-grade student with autism

- *Vanessa*, a middle school student with a learning disability

- *Sam*, a ninth-grade student with a behavioral disorder and Asperger syndrome

- *Walter*, a high school junior with mental retardation

Their stories provide realistic examples of collaboration in an inclusive environment.

INCLUSIVE EDUCATION

Although inclusive education affects staff and students, many educational procedures, and core educational outcomes, it is not defined or practiced consistently within most schools, districts, or states. For example, statistics from the U.S. Department of Education's web site (http://www.ed.gov/offices/OSERS/OSEP/Research/) show that states differ widely in their placement of students with disabilities in general education classrooms, resource classrooms, self-contained classrooms, and separate educational settings serving only students with disabilities.

In this book, we use the following definition of *inclusive education*:

- Students attend neighborhood schools or the school they would attend if they did not have a disability.

- All students are based in general education classrooms.

- General and special educators collaborate to pull services and supports into the general education classroom.

- Decision-making about students is flexible, individualized, and not based solely on disability categories.

- Students are taught what is important for them to learn, which may vary from one student to another.

Inclusive education is individually defined for each student with disabilities; that is, the individualized education program (IEP) team defines the supports and services needed to enable a given student to learn what he or she needs to learn. This approach is not the same as *total inclusion*—an approach that operates on a "one size fits all" philosophy. Just as all students with disabilities must first be provided with an IEP, the services and supports that follow students throughout the school day must also be tailored to their needs.

Key Elements

Six elements are essential to the successful functioning of inclusive education:

1. *Inclusive program model*—staffing arrangements and delivery methods that enable students to receive appropriate services within inclusive environments, along with administrative support and involvement

2. *Inclusive culture in the school*—a vision of a diverse community that is put into practice within classrooms and at the school level

3. *Collaborative teaming and problem solving*—
   general and special educators who have
   skills and strategies for productive co-
   planning, communication, problem solving, and teaching

4. *Curricular and instructional practices that accommodate diverse learners*—teaching strategies
   that are known to be effective for most
   learners, with and without disabilities

5. *Strategies for making individualized adaptations*—agreed-on methods for planning,
   implementing, and evaluating the adaptations needed by specific students

6. *Strategies to facilitate peer relationships and supports*—formal and informal ways to foster
   age-appropriate interactions and relationships among students

This book is part of a series, *Teachers' Guides to
Inclusive Practices*, that addresses these elements. The third element, collaborative teaming and problem solving, is the focus of this
book. (For more in-depth information on the
inclusive program model and inclusive culture in school, see also Bauer & Shea, 1999;
Downing, 2002; Lipsky & Gartner, 1997;
Villa & Thousand, 2000; Vitello & Mithaug,
1998). For most schools, these key elements
are highly dynamic and require ongoing attention. Although it would be nice to work on
an element and then check it off the list, potential exists for ongoing growth in each element and linkage between the elements.

Inclusive education requires a focused, systematic effort among administrators, general
and special educators, parents, and support
personnel. The teachers involved will need
professional development to increase their
skills in collaborative planning and delivery of
instruction to diverse groups of students.
Many other variables, however, are interrelated (e.g., staff attitudes, school culture, school
and district history of change efforts, the existing program model) and can inhibit or facilitate inclusive education (Weiner, 2003).
Schools should expect to find one or more elements that need work and aim for complementary attitudes, knowledge, and practices.

Most schools have some type of school improvement or action plan that has been developed through a self-study process. These
plans often focus on the accountability requirement of the No Child Left Behind
(NCLB) Act of 2001 (PL 107-110)—high academic standards and participation in the
general curriculum for all students. An ideal
approach to promoting and improving a
school's inclusive practices is to incorporate
goals and strategies related to the elements of
inclusive education into the existing school
improvement plan. Assessing inclusive practices can also take place on a smaller scale by
a grade-level, departmental, or classroom
team. To obtain meaningful improvement,
among other things, means careful planning
by a group that represents all of the stakeholders who will be affected by the change.

The Team Survey of Inclusive Practices
(see Figure 1.1) is a tool that can be used to
develop action plans for improving a school
system's inclusive programming. Before completing the survey, a team should be sure that
its members have some background information about the current state of affairs in the
school and knowledge of what constitutes an
effective inclusive program. The survey addresses the six elements listed previously.
Completing the survey requires making a
judgment about the extent to which each of
these key elements is in place in the school.
After discussion and reaching consensus on
the rating for each item in the survey, the
planning team then identifies which of the six
elements should be action priorities at this
time. One strategy for selecting action priorities is to begin where the teacher can have the
most impact. Another is to set a goal, such as
reaching a score of 2 on all six elements. The
survey includes room for the status and priority to be reevaluated later in the year.

For a school to make changes, each individual who is implementing the change must
develop a new map of his or her job. Teachers, as practitioners who care deeply about
students' success, can gain motivation for a
new program by seeing positive results for
children. Therefore, starting small with a

Team Survey of Inclusive Practices

School:_____ Team:_____ Year:_____

Team members/roles:

_____   _____

_____   _____

_____   _____

Status key: 3 = We have done it well.   **Action priority:** Indicate "high" or "low."
               2 = We have tried, but it needs   Complete Issue-Action Plan for high-
                   improvement.   priority items.
               1 = We have not done it.

Practice	Status (1, 2, 3)		Action Priority (high/low)	
	Date 1	Date 2	Date 1	Date 2
1. **Inclusive program model:** Do all students start from a base in general classes? Do services and supports follow the students? Does the special education model facilitate teaching?				
2. **Inclusive culture in the school:** Is diversity valued? Are we a community? Do we expect excellence and equity for all of the students?				
3. **Collaborative teaming and problem solving:** Have we identified team members' roles and responsibilities? Do we have strategies for making and communicating decisions? Do we evaluate team functioning and celebrate our successes?				
4. **Accommodating curricular and instructional practices in the classroom:** Is the curriculum meaningful? Do we use active learning; multiple modalities; and small, flexible groupings?				
5. **Strategies for making and evaluating individualized adaptations:** Do we use explicit, agreed-upon strategies for planning, delivering, and evaluating adaptations? Do adaptations facilitate social and instructional participation, and are they only as special as necessary?				
6. **Strategies to facilitate peer relationships and supports:** Do we teach social interaction and problem-solving skills? Do we facilitate social and helping relationships for all students?				

Figure 1.1. Team survey of inclusive practices. (From Ford, A., Messenheimer-Young, T., Toshner, J., Fitzgerald, M.A., Dyer, C., Glodoski, J., & Laveck, J. [1995, July]. *A team planning packet for inclusive education.* Milwaukee: The Wisconsin School Inclusion Project; adapted by permission.)

pilot focus and building on success can be a very effective way to generate momentum for change. For example, middle school teachers focusing on the inclusive program model (Element 1) and accommodating curricular and instructional practices (Element 4) might "start small" by targeting the provision of pull-in services and supports for all students with IEPs in the sixth grade. Teachers and staff will need to make adjustments in the way they practice their jobs so pull-in services and supports can be delivered instead of removing students from classrooms.

COLLABORATIVE TEAMING

The simplest definition of *collaborative teaming* is two or more people working together to-

ward a common goal (Rainforth & York-Barr, 1997), but teaming is hardly simple! *Working* can mean setting goals, identifying problems, assessing students' needs and skills, exchanging information, brainstorming, problem-solving, reaching consensus, making plans, and implementing and evaluating plans. Working *together* means that positive interdependence exists among team members who agree to pool and partition their resources and rewards and to operate from a foundation of shared values. Team members help each other and lend support (Rainforth & York-Barr, 1997). A team's *common goals* are the goals on which all members have reached mutual agreement. Figure 1.2 elaborates the key characteristics of collaborative teaming.

Much of the energy that can be observed in and around collaborative teams is pro-

---

What the Research Says

DeBoer and Fister (1995–1996) defined six core characteristics of collaborative teaming:

- "Collaboration is based on mutual goals" (p. 55): The team's short- and long-term goals are determined by the entire team. Having mutual goals builds team commitment from the beginning.

- "Collaboration requires parity among participants" (p. 55): When there is equality among team members, each member's contributions and role in decision making are valued and add to the team's outcomes. Parity among members makes team consensus more probable.

- "Collaboration depends on shared responsibility for participation and decision making" (p. 56): Although all team members actively engage in deliberations and decision making, participation is not identical for all members. How a team shares its tasks depends on the team members' particular skills, work and team roles, and available time. Shared responsibility plus parity among team members contributes to both the achievement of team consensus and interdependence.

- "Collaboration requires shared responsibility for outcomes" (p. 57): The team's success and its failure are shared by all team members. If individual members take credit for team success or blame others for team failure, then participation and decision making have not been shared responsibilities. When teams take time to celebrate successes, they also are celebrating their cohesion.

- "Collaboration requires that participants share their resources" (p. 57): Teamwork means that each team member is responsible for sharing his or her particular resources, including information, skills, equipment, and materials, with the rest of the team.

- "Collaboration is a voluntary relationship" (p. 57): No one can be mandated to engage in a collaborative relationship with a team. Collaborative skills have to be learned and then practiced in order to be effective.

Figure 1.2.   Six key characteristics of collaborative teaming (*Source:* DeBoer & Fister, 1995–1996).

What the Research Says

Is Collaboration for the Birds?

Apparently so! Researchers from University of California, Davis (Stamps, Anda, Perez, & Drummond, 2002) studied pairs of Blue Footed Boobies in Mexico to determine whether the dual concern model applied to birds making joint decisions about where to build their nest. This model suggests that "when two parties have very broadly overlapping interests, they may need to exchange extensive amounts of information about their levels of preference for various options, in order to make the joint decision that is best for both of them" (Stamps et al., 2002, p. 1391).

Stamps and her co-investigators found that pairs of Blue Footed Boobies made their nest selection only after exchanging extensive specialized communication signals in the form of pointing their bill at the preferred spot with the bill tip close to the ground and bobbing while also vocalizing. Higher rates of mutual nestpointing at a particular site were associated with the pair selecting that site. When pairs disagreed about a site (one nestpointed and the other did not), they "expanded the pie" by investigating additional sites together. Another collaborative tactic observed in these birds was the "feeling out procedure," by which one bird decided whether a nest site option was acceptable to its mate before signaling a preference with high rate billpointing for that same option.

Finally, each partner had "veto power" over particular nest sites, in that sites that did not yield nestpointing from both members of a pair were rarely selected. Even though females made the final choice, they seemed to make their selection from a "short list" of possible sites that were acceptable to both. There was no evidence for decision making by contentious tactics—birds did not try to persuade a reluctant mate by nagging (intensive bill pointing) or using aggression. Instead, one partner was free to ignore the other who was energetically pointing at a particular site and did so in many cases. In using collaborative tactics, Blue Footed Boobies avoided win-lose outcomes and achieved either compromise or win-win outcomes for both partners.

Thanks to Emilie Snell-Rood for sharing this cross-species example of collaboration!

Figure 1.3. Collaboration among Blue Footed Boobies (*Source:* Stamps, Anda, Perez, & Drummond, 2002).

duced from their operating philosophy: If we work together, we can solve whatever problems we have (Talbert, 1993). Collaborative tactics are not simply a set of procedures that allow humans to work together productively; biologists have found evidence that some animals use collaborative strategies to resolve disputes that occur when shared decisions must be made (see Figure 1.3).

Unfortunately, two traditions operate against a team structure in schools: 1) teachers are accustomed to working alone, and 2) schools provide few incentives and little support for teamwork (Brownell, Yeager, Rennells, & Riley, 1997). Collaboration is greatly needed, but often misunderstood. It is an interpersonal style that is independent from the activities/goals in which it is used. Figure 1.4 clarifies several misunderstandings educators hold about collaboration. Keep these in mind as we examine the components of teamwork in inclusive schools.

Transdisciplinary Philosophy

Many collaborative teams for students with disabilities include members other than those from the teaching profession or students' families. In addition to general education and special education teachers, other *professional* members might include physical therapists, occupational therapists, speech-language pathologists, guidance counselors, school psychologists, vision consultants, orientation and mobility specialists, adapted physical education specialists, counselors, interpreters for students with hearing impairment, nurses, and program administrators. Besides family members, other *nonprofessional* members may

Myth or Misunderstanding	The Reality of Collaboration
Everyone is doing it	Saying that every shared effort is collaborative diminishes the effort required. Collaboration cannot be mandated but requires ongoing commitment from every team member, careful attention to sharing goals, communicating with care, and maintaining parity.
More is better	Collaboration is time intensive and must be kept at a "doable" level. Special educators and related services staff may have so many classroom teachers to collaborate with, students to support and follow, and planning meetings to attend that they have no time for direct service. Schools must set priorities on collaboration that put students and families first. Collaboration effort (time and number of staff) and outcomes (documented results) should be monitored to assess what is worth collaboration.
It's about feeling good and liking others	"Collaboration is the conduit through which professionals can ensure that students receive the most effective educational services to which they are entitled" (Friend, 2000, p. 131). Feeling good at the end of a teaming session gives no guarantee of reaching this goal. The success of collaboration is measured only by what it yields for students. If one teacher can achieve this goal as well alone, then collaboration is not worth its cost in time, despite the fact that team members may have liked it. Collaboration is about respect. Having respect for one another means that team members are more willing to take on the risks involved in teaming.
It comes naturally	The skills needed to collaborate are often viewed in contradictory ways. Some complain that teaming is difficult and they did not have coursework on it, whereas many claim they know all about communication skills and problem solving. It seems that some professionals equate collaboration with conversation, whereas others think that teaming skills come along with caring for children. Professionals are often "lazy" with co-workers they know well and use poor interaction skills. This contributes to being unprepared and out-of-practice for adversarial interactions that require extensive skills. Staff who gossip about others' noncooperative style, operate by under-the-table agendas, and adopt a blaming attitude to parents are exhibiting symptoms that cry out for staff development! Collaboration without the skills threatens the outcomes for students.

Figure 1.4. Myths and misunderstandings about collaboration in schools. (From "Myths and Misunderstandings About Professional Collaboration" by M. Friend, 2000, *Remedial and Special Education, 21,* 130–132. Copyright 2000 by PRO-ED, Inc. Adapted by permission.)

include paraprofessionals working with the student, a family advocate, the student, and friends of the student.

As illustrated in Figure 1.5, *core* teams work together most frequently to achieve the team goals, while a student's *whole* team includes other team members who participate less frequently in the team meetings (Giangreco, Cloninger, & Iverson, 1998). Teams that are collaborative and include members of multiple disciplines are called *transdisciplinary teams*; their approach involves agreement that the

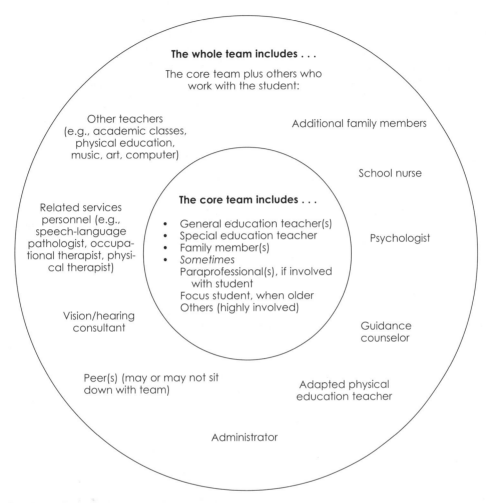

The whole team includes . . .

The core team plus others who work with the student:

Other teachers (e.g., academic classes, physical education, music, art, computer)

Additional family members

School nurse

Related services personnel (e.g., speech-language pathologist, occupational therapist, physical therapist)

The core team includes . . .

- General education teacher(s)
- Special education teacher
- Family member(s)
- *Sometimes* Paraprofessional(s), if involved with student
  Focus student, when older
  Others (highly involved)

Psychologist

Vision/hearing consultant

Guidance counselor

Peer(s) (may or may not sit down with team)

Adapted physical education teacher

Administrator

Figure 1.5. The core team and the whole team.

multiple needs of students are interrelated (Rainforth & York-Barr, 1997) and their coordination of effort is essential.

Student Snapshot

When Daniel shares his morning news with classmates, he uses skills that have been shaped by the efforts of his team members. He sits upright with support from a special "legless" chair. He then touches symbols on a Cheaptalk communication device (Enabling Devices) to activate a corresponding message. Six of Daniel's team members—his classroom and special education teachers; his mother; and his occupational, physical, and speech-language therapists—worked together to design and refine this arrangement.

Role Release

Role release is an important concept for collaborative teamwork. At the simplest level, role release means that team members step out of their usual roles to become either teachers of other team members or learners taught by other team members. This concept results not only in mutual learning but also in professional roles being combined so that one or several team members learn to deliver a variety of interventions to a student (Friend & Cook, 2003; Stanovich, 1996).

To be a *teacher* of another team member requires sharing the knowledge and expertise of one's position as a teacher, parent, therapist, and so forth 1) at times when this information is relevant to the team's goals, and 2) in ways that will yield learning from team members. To be a *learner* and benefit from other team members' experiences requires 1) the belief that each team member's knowledge and perspectives are valuable to other team members and will assist the team in reaching their goals, and 2) the opportunity to receive instruction and feedback from the teaching team member. Two instruction and feedback strategies that have been found to be effective with teachers are *praise and simple prompts* given to the learning teacher during his or her use of the new skill and *brief 3- to 5-minute discussions* of how the learning teacher or the student actually performed during an observation (Noell, Witt, LaFleur, Mortenson, Rainer, & LeVelle, 2000).

Student Snapshot

Sam's classroom teachers are eager to learn how to prevent his disruptive behavior. When he becomes anxious, Sam can change quickly from being a talented student to being so disruptive that an entire class session is lost! During team meetings, Sam's classroom teachers learn new methods of behavior management from the special education teacher and the school counselor, including redirection, behavior rehearsal, peer support, organizational support, and social stories. Because the methods are new to them, the classroom teachers share their expertise to help shape these new methods into strategies that will work in their classrooms. They role-play using the methods on each other, while getting feedback from the special education teacher. Then, they discuss their performance as a group.

Role release enables Sam's classroom teachers to implement the team's behavior plans with Sam even when the special education staff are not present. For example, Mr. Sailor, Sam's world history teacher, has learned to redirect Sam when the bell rings for class change and to rehearse his routine for staying calm. In order to work, role release involves sharing and recognizing the expertise of fellow teammates. It is most likely to occur when teams are operating in a cooperative atmosphere of trust and support and working toward achieving a common goal (Thomas, Correa, & Morsink, 1995). Role release allows the team to move together with a uniform understanding of the rationale for their decisions and the techniques for implementing them.

DELIVERING SPECIAL EDUCATION SUPPORT

Delivery Models

Traditionally, schools have provided special education apart from the general education classroom by either pulling students out of general classrooms into tutoring sessions or resource rooms or by teaching students in self-contained classrooms that only serve students with disabilities. Special education was viewed as a place where special education services were delivered. These approaches generally have not been coupled with sharing of information or ideas between general education and special education teachers. Traditional approaches contrast with the collaborative practices of

1. Pulling in special education services or supports to the general education classroom

2. Collaborative teaching or co-teaching of general and special educators

3. Pulling students out of the classroom using collaborative teaming, which translates into moving the student for a short period to another classroom for special education services (Figure 1.6).

Team support approaches			
Student	Collaborative planning with pull-out	Collaborative planning with pull-in	Co-teaching
Daniel	*Every 6 weeks: PT checks Daniel's movement and equipment.* *M–F: All staff use pull-out for bathroom skills.*	*M–F: OT, PT, speech-language teacher and special educator are scheduled to be in second-grade classroom.*	*M–F: Special educator teaches with Ms. Scott during language arts groups.*

Figure 1.6. Teaming approaches used with Daniel by team members.

According to DeBoer and Fister (1994), one can better understand how these approaches operate by assigning phrases and speakers:

- Self-contained classes = "I do it all by myself" (says the special educator).

- Resource or pull-out = "I do the special part by myself" (says the special educator).

- Pull-in, co-teaching, and collaborative teaming = "We do some or much of it together" (say the general education and special education teachers).

Teams' goals in inclusive education settings center on facilitating student learning and membership within general education classes, school activities, and peer groups. Teams plan ways to "deliver" special education that maximize learning and membership. Thus, the most frequently used "delivery approaches" involve pulling in supports and teaching collaboratively and less often involve pulling the student away from class activities. Use Figure 1.6 as a guide while reading about Daniel's delivery of services.

Student Snapshot

Daniel's team members designed an individual plan for supporting Daniel that suits his IEP objectives and meshes both with his first-grade schedule and with the staff schedule. Pull-out is used only for 6-week assessment checks by the physical therapist and for Daniel's daily personal needs. Pull-in instructional support and co-teaching occur daily and involve Daniel's special education teacher, his therapists, and the teaching assistant. Co-teaching occurs during language arts groups when his special education teacher instructs one small group of students each morning. Daniel's physical therapist also co-teaches but with the entire second grade when a science unit on the body and movement is taught; she teaches the students about Daniel's positioning equipment and his needs for physical support.

Dual Focus of Teams

To deliver special education supports to students, teams need to maintain a dual focus, keeping one eye on the goal and the other on themselves. A collaborative team must direct its attention and effort both toward the student and toward the team itself. Examples of student-centered efforts include

- Developing a student's schedule or program to fulfill his or her IEP

- Designing needed accommodations and adaptations for particular students

- Finding ways to ensure consistency and quality among school staff implementing a team's support plan

- Problem-solving about specific issues that arise (e.g., Why isn't Vanessa passing her math tests? Why has Walter been forgetting to do his homework? What precedes Sam's tantrums?)

- Planning for successful transitions within and between schools, as well as successful transitions out of school

To address student needs, team members must work in synchrony and be team-centered. They interact by consulting, planning, problem-solving, reaching consensus, and "touching base" with other team members throughout the school day. Team members carry out team-generated plans that provide support to students within the context of scheduled class activities and as they work alone with focus students. Examples of team-centered efforts include

- Understanding other team members' roles and talents
- Getting over the "I have to know everything" phenomenon
- Exploring team member values in order to identify values common to the team
- Learning to communicate effectively among team members
- Identifying and resolving concerns
- Learning how to reach consensus on decisions
- Developing trust among members

To address team needs, members should take time to celebrate their successes; to relate to each other as individuals and teammates; to process their teaming skills by self-reflection, self-assessment, and observation and by monitoring skills that are weak; and to discuss and use skill-building strategies.

TEAM MEMBERS

The core members of most collaborative teams are general and special educators and family members. The general and the special educators primarily share the responsibility for teaching the student; however, other professional or paraprofessional team members sometimes contribute by teaching or by monitoring the student's performance during a teaching activity or routine.

The contributions that family members make to the core team are equally important. The family's perspective on the student may differ from that of the school and, therefore, provides a more complete picture of the student's abilities and needs. Also, the family's perspective, along with the family's outlook on their child's educational priorities, is often rich with implications for instruction and should influence team decisions about goals and programs.

Family members are part of the core team because they are the "historians" of what has occurred and the observers of what is current in their child's life beyond school (Salisbury & Dunst, 1997). Limiting family members' involvement to attending formal meetings (eligibility and IEP meetings) or to giving consent for decisions means that their input either is too little or comes too late. In addition to being listened to, understood, and respected by the other team members, family members should influence their child's program development (Soodak, 1998). Because family members are not available for face-to-face interactions as often as teachers are, many team discussions will only involve a small cluster of two or more people. Family members are, however, a part of the core team, so their input needs to be ongoing. They need to be involved in decision-making, and they should receive regular updates on how the team is implementing any decisions regarding their child. Teachers need to work with family members to identify how communication will occur and how much and what types of involvement the family wants to maintain. There is no "right" formula or frequency for participation by family members; instead, participation is determined with each family member and is allowed to change over time.

When students reach adolescence, they should also participate as members of their own team. They may learn to be more self-determined and feel more in control of their lives if they directly participate in planning their educational programs and offer their perspectives. Typically, students should participate in meetings during which key decisions are made, but they usually do not participate in all team meetings. A few students will readily participate, but others will require encouragement. Some students will need family and/or staff support in order to have their say.

TEAM INTERACTIONS

Team interactions occur both during sit-down meetings and during spontaneous, "on-the-fly" exchanges. Sit-down meetings involve two or more team members. These meetings are held apart from students and usually outside of scheduled class time, though not necessarily before or after school. The time, location, and agenda for a sit-down meeting are planned, even if only minimally. The meeting may be formal or informal and may involve many team members or only those members who are on the agenda or available.

For students who receive special education services, more formal collaborative team meetings may center on planning a student's IEP, whereas less formal and more frequent team meetings address specific student needs, classwork modifications, and teacher concerns. The more complicated the student's needs are, the greater the need for structured meetings with a set agenda, even when informal in nature. Over the course of the school year, meeting frequency may decline as the team becomes more efficient and better understands the student's needs.

Informal, on-the-fly interactions among a subset of the team take place frequently during the school day. During on-the-fly communication, members touch base in the hall, lunch room, or other familiar areas on the

implementation of team plans and student progress and make adjustments to those plans. Interaction times may be planned or spontaneous and may occur during or after school. Students are often around when team members are talking, but they should be out of hearing range. If class activities are going on, then students are occupied (e.g., reading with partners, time in between classes, recess, lunch time, rest time in kindergarten) while team members talk. Problem-solving is typically spontaneous. Therefore, team members need to feel comfortable delaying decisions when more information is required by saying to each other, "I need to think about this and get back with you" or "Let's put this on the agenda for the next meeting."

Although family members often participate in formal sit-down meetings, they are less likely to be a part of on-the-fly interactions during school hours. Family members and teachers often take advantage of any spontaneous opportunities to quickly update each other and exchange information. These informal meetings with family members might happen when parents drop off or pick up their child from school, attend PTA meetings and school events, or have chance encounters with teachers in the community.

COMPONENTS OF COLLABORATIVE TEAMWORK

Collaborative teamwork is a set of different, yet overlapping, components. The six components pictured in Figure 1.7 occur somewhat sequentially as a team forms and develops; however, each component maintains its importance even after its implementation. For example, in addition to an initiative from the principal to get the team underway (Component 1), most lasting teams rely on some administrative support to organize and sustain themselves over time. Once a team is organized and operating (Component 2), its members will problem-solve repeatedly (Component 3), make numerous decisions

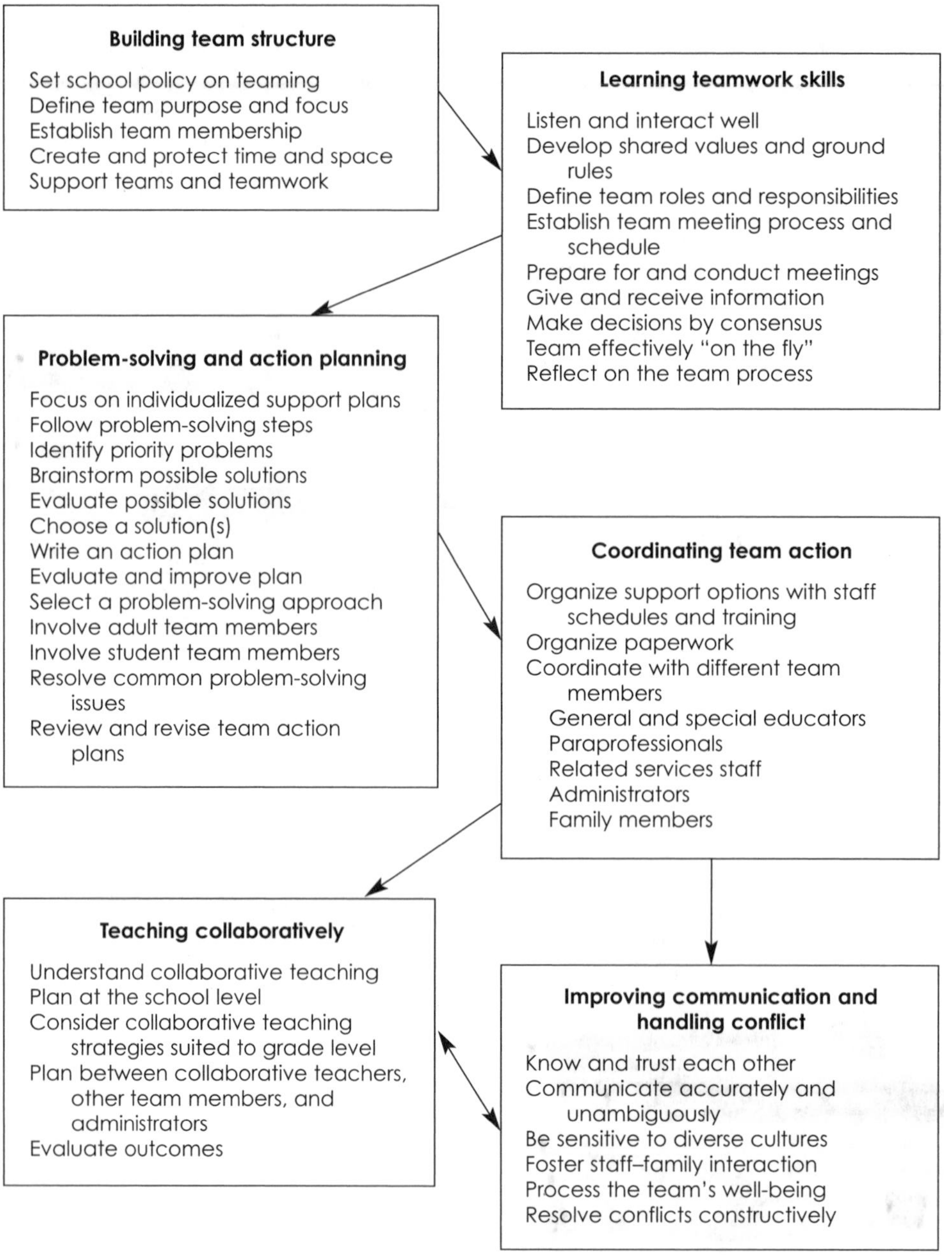

Building team structure

Set school policy on teaming
Define team purpose and focus
Establish team membership
Create and protect time and space
Support teams and teamwork

Learning teamwork skills

Listen and interact well
Develop shared values and ground
 rules
Define team roles and responsibilities
Establish team meeting process and
 schedule
Prepare for and conduct meetings
Give and receive information
Make decisions by consensus
Team effectively "on the fly"
Reflect on the team process

Problem-solving and action planning

Focus on individualized support plans
Follow problem-solving steps
Identify priority problems
Brainstorm possible solutions
Evaluate possible solutions
Choose a solution(s)
Write an action plan
Evaluate and improve plan
Select a problem-solving approach
Involve adult team members
Involve student team members
Resolve common problem-solving
 issues
Review and revise team action
 plans

Coordinating team action

Organize support options with staff
 schedules and training
Organize paperwork
Coordinate with different team
 members
 General and special educators
 Paraprofessionals
 Related services staff
 Administrators
 Family members

Teaching collaboratively

Understand collaborative teaching
Plan at the school level
Consider collaborative teaching
 strategies suited to grade level
Plan between collaborative teachers,
 other team members, and
 administrators
Evaluate outcomes

**Improving communication and
handling conflict**

Know and trust each other
Communicate accurately and
 unambiguously
Be sensitive to diverse cultures
Foster staff–family interaction
Process the team's well-being
Resolve conflicts constructively

Figure 1.7. Components of collaborative teaming.

about students during the school year, and repeatedly take team action (Component 4).
Some team members will teach collaboratively (Component 5). Most will work to improve interpersonal communication and address conflict within the team (Component 6).

When teams add new members at the beginning of each school year, the dynamics often
change; a reconfigured team should take
some time to review teamwork skills (Component 2) while getting used to its internal
changes.

Student Snapshot

Daniel's core team will change when he goes to second grade because Ms. James will no longer be a team member; however, many other members will remain the same. The members who remain (special education teachers, family members, related services staff) will plan team-building activities to prepare the newly reconstituted team for the beginning of the school year.

The ensuing chapters address the six components of collaborative teaming. Chapter 2 addresses building a team's structure: how to organize collaborative teams and the substantial roles that administrators play when schools prepare for, initiate, and maintain inclusion. Chapter 3, which discusses teamwork skills, delves into the basic elements of team members' work together. Chapter 4 describes the steps taken to problem-solve and sets forth various problem-solving methods. Chapter 5 addresses the major areas in which teams take action, such as writing IEPs and behavior support plans, making individualized adaptations in general education classwork, and evaluating student progress. Chapter 6 details collaborative teaching. Finally, Chapter 7 examines methods teams use to improve communication among members and to address areas of disagreement and conflict.

BENEFITS AND CHALLENGES OF COLLABORATIVE TEAMING

As inclusive education has gradually increased, researchers have reported the pivotal advantages of planning and creating solutions within collaborative teams and supportive administrative climates (e.g., Appl, Troha, & Rowell, 2001; Brownell et al., 1997; Foley & Lewis, 1999; Johnson, Zorn, Tam, Lamontagne, & Johnson, 2003; Rainforth & York-Barr, 1997; Salisbury & McGregor, 2002; Snell & Janney, 2000):

- Shared decision-making appears to yield better decisions and results.

- Both teachers and administrators appear to be motivated by the advantages of shared decision-making.

- Collaborative teaming is reported to enhance teachers' satisfaction with their jobs; they enjoy the regular exchange of resources and expertise, the sense of belonging, the freedom from isolation, and the intellectual stimulation.

- When team members have been instrumental in forming a plan, they report that they are more committed to the plan's implementation and success.

- Effective communication and the ability to work cooperatively with others are viewed as essential abilities for being effective in most jobs today.

The downside of collaboration, however, is the time, skill, and risk it takes for educators to work cooperatively and reach good outcomes (Brownell et al., 1997; Friend, 2000). Most educators have not received training to work collaboratively and, therefore, are learning to work as a team at the same time they must operate as teams. In inclusive programs, team members need to work cooperatively to provide educational supports using a variety of approaches: collaborative teaching, pull-in support, and, less often, pull-out support with teaming. Although each support approach entails time, skill, and risk, the outcomes reflect cooperative exchange and decision-making between team members and increase the likelihood that students with disabilities can be successful learners in general education classrooms alongside their peers.

Teams must face state and national standards for all students and the serious ramifications these standards hold for schools, staff, and students. Although these standards intend to raise student achievement, they do not always motivate positive improvement in students. Many teachers and parents object to single-shot, high-stakes tests imposed by state standards as being an inaccurate means for assessing achievement (Mabry, Poole, Redmond, & Schultz, 2003). Student learning has been shown to be difficult to determine, to remain unchanged from before testing was instituted, or to actually decline once testing begins (Amrein & Berliner, 2002; Amrein-Beardsley & Berliner, 2003).

The rising demand for statewide school testing and scoring of tests is reported to be threatening the limits of test accuracy (Henriques, 2003), yet students' futures will be greatly influenced by their performance on these tests. With changes in political party and state and national leadership will come more changes in philosophy, solutions, and federal and state requirements—an ever-swinging pendulum of "school improvements." In this climate, schools face many unanswered and looming questions about state assessments. As a result, collaborative teams must operate in a climate of uncertainly. Teams are focused not simply on stimulating student academic progress but also on enabling all students to meet state requirements and thereby graduate, while still being educated in general education settings. This book tackles many of the skills teams need to address this challenge.

Chapter 2

Building Team Structure

Student Snapshot

In one inclusive high school, the consulting special education teacher praised her principal's leadership: "Five years ago my principal really bought into inclusion. He let us bring in people to help the teachers understand it and prepare for it; many of us took trips to see model schools. Then, we spent lots of time just hashing it out. How would we decide what general education classes our students in special education would take? How could we pull off the scheduling so they would get these classes? Who would support the students who really needed support, and how could we make that work? When can teachers meet to plan? Our principal took an active part in these discussions, and we have a system today that works!"

In another high school, the consulting special education teacher expressed a very different view of her principal: "The only way I can get my special education students into general education classes is to beg teachers, and then the student must be perfectly behaved and able to do the work! A lot of teachers expect a paraprofessional even with these hand-picked students. No one seems to understand the importance of having all kids included and giving them the support they need. My principal missed his chance to get our school on the inclusion track. He just said that inclusion was a fad that would pass and that high school was not the place for inclusion."

Principals are pivotal in setting the tone for movement toward an inclusive school model (Villa, Thousand, Meyers, & Nevin, 1996). Thus, there seems to be a relationship between principals' beliefs about inclusion, their experiences, and the practices that are implemented in schools. For example, when elementary principals reported that they had an awareness of special education concepts and positive experiences with students with disabilities, they also were significantly more likely to have a positive attitude toward including students with disabilities in general education (Praisner, 2003).

Principals and their superintendents in local school systems are further influenced by the philosophical positions of their professional peers and the policies communicated from their state department of education. Duhaney noted that "policy/position statements on inclusion are considered significant because they often are intended to, and often do, guide school practices" (1999, p. 368). When the educational policies of all 50 states and the Virgin Islands were examined, Duhaney (1999) found that 17, or one third, had adopted specific policies on inclusion, while two thirds did not have such policies. An analysis of what these state policies said about the educational components of inclusion revealed several dominant themes (percentages indicate how widely the theme was reflected in the policies):

- Inclusion of students with severe disabilities into general education classrooms is appropriate (94%)
- Support services should be provided in the general education classroom (88%)
- Teaching is a shared responsibility of general and special educators (76%)
- Curriculum modifications are needed to accommodate students (71%)
- Collaboration is a goal (65%)
- Raised expectations for all students is a desired outcome (59%)

State policies on inclusion can have some bearing on school administrators and can guide them in adopting local inclusion policies, but there is no guarantee. In most states, where guiding policies are missing, the administrators' beliefs, experiences, and training are more likely to influence their practices.

When school districts do not have positions on inclusive education, they are advised to designate groups representing all stakeholders (e.g., teachers, administrators, related service professionals, parents) to guide them on the development of a position and a plan for implementation. Administrators are counseled not to move ahead of those who will implement inclusion (general and special educators), but rather to involve "direct service providers in a bottom-up method of generating and implementing policy, as well as providing the conditions, resources, and time to make successful inclusion . . . a feasible outcome that warrants the commitment of those charged with its implementation" (Cook, Semmel, & Gerber, 1999, p. 205).

ADMINISTRATIVE LEADERSHIP AND NEGATIVE STAFF ATTITUDES

In the early preparation phase, before inclusive programs and collaborative teams are implemented, the building administrator's leadership is crucial in getting staff to examine their values, understand inclusion, and learn how collaborative teaming aids inclusion of students with disabilities in general education. With the support of building administrators, teaching and professional support staff need to play a major role in developing the school's values regarding inclusion and collaboration, in addition to defining a structure that will support collaborative teaming (Salend & Duhaney, 1999; Salisbury & McGregor, 2002).

Negative attitudes toward the teaming process (Karge, McClure, & Patton, 1995) and resistance toward inclusion (Idol, 1997) are two of the major barriers that general education teachers report. Some possible reasons for teachers' negative views include their

- Lack of clarity about what inclusion is and why the school is advocating for it

- Fear resulting from limited experience with students with disabilities

- Fears about having in their class students with special needs who are not at grade level

- Focus on class size, teacher time, and the negative impact of inclusion on typically developing students

- Belief that students with more extensive support needs must always have an adult with them

- Lack of knowledge about what collaborative teaming entails or past bad experiences with teaming

- Anticipation that teaming will be time-consuming and concern about having adequate time.

Teachers' negative attitudes are also caused by the failure of the school community to examine its stance on inclusion or to work with staff to develop and implement a teaming structure for the school. Teachers should not be left out of the planning to implement inclusion and design a collaborative team structure.

When a solid teaming structure is put into place, it has the potential for counteracting these fears and some of the common sources of stress and burnout found among special education teachers. In their review of research on stress in special education teachers, Wisniewski and Gargiulo (1997) revealed some of the documented sources of stress. Figure 2.1 lists several of these stressors alongside the potential benefits others have credited to membership on collaborative teams. When teachers' work on collaborative teams is strongly supported by administrators, a peer support system is created that can help teachers manage their stress over work conditions, personal interactions, and teaching assignment. Providing teachers with scheduled times for collegial work and planning and giving them greater collective responsibility for student learning were two recommendations also supported in the National Commission on Teaching and America's Future to improve U.S. schools (Darling-Hammond, 1996).

Documented source of teacher stress (Wisniewski & Gargiulo, 1997)	Potential benefits resulting when schools build a collaborative team structure
Long hours and insufficient planning time to meet student needs	Time for teaming is created and preserved; responsibility for planning is shared
Loss of teacher control for design of programs	Active teacher role on teams and team influence on educational programs
Lack of participation and influence in decision-making	Active teacher role on team and team consensus on decisions
Professional isolation; limited interaction	Focus of team members on shared goals, problem solving, and working toward consensus
Stressful interactions to bring about inclusion	Participaton of general educators in school planning on inclusion and team planning for students with disabilities
Difficulty meeting needs of diverse special education population	Support from team members who instruct each other on teaching skills; shared responsibility
Dissatisfaction with lack of progress	Knowledge of problem solving and creation of action plans

Figure 2.1.   Teacher stress and potential related benefits of collaborative teaming.

PHASES OF POLICY DEVELOPMENT AND ADMINISTRATIVE SUPPORT FOR TEAMS

The process involved in adopting inclusive practices and implementing collaborative teams in a school can be broken down into three phases:

1. *Preparation phase*—schools organize for inclusion and teaming.

2. *Implementation phase*—students are included, and teams become adept at planning, problem-solving, and implementing student supports.

3. *Maintenance phase*—teams are in use and relied on by staff and building administrators; self-evaluation and improvement are ongoing.

Building administrators play a critical role in each phase. Figure 2.2 provides a checklist of some actions administrators may take to develop these three phases of inclusion.

Preparation

In many schools, principals and assistant principals initiate discussions with staff members in regard to potential school improvements and inclusion. These discussions often lead to recommendations by the staff, particularly special educators, for collaborative teaming. Sometimes, district policy changes have helped initiate inclusion and make teaming a recommended districtwide practice; however, before there can be schoolwide adoption of a structure and a procedure for team development, schools (and districts) need to examine their reasons for serving students inclusively and develop a mission statement or a shared purpose. Schools should not start forming collaborative teams without first taking some time to examine their values. Shared values provide a firm foundation for the creation of collaborative teams.

To define a common mission or shared school values, building administrators often schedule an in-service day and explore questions such as, "What are our beliefs regarding learning and the students we serve?" and

Phase			
P	**I**	**M**	**Actions that may be taken**
X			• Plan times for open dialogue at the district level and the school level about inclusive education and its benefits and challenges.
X	X		• Arrange for staff to view and learn more about inclusive school models (e.g., visits, videos, panels from schools). Participate in these workshop sessions with staff.
X	X	X	• Attend workshops on inclusion and related topics as collaborative teams; process in-service content as teams.
X	X		• Recognize that staff have varying levels of comfort, understanding, and values about inclusion; provide time for staff to learn and experience the new philosophy and gain comfort with the changes inclusion brings.
X	X		• With teachers, plan for a schoolwide program on ability awareness or "climate for learning" to emphasize themes of appreciation and understanding of diversity.
X	X		• Be alert to staff morale and use team-building activities during the school year to promote collegiality.
X			• Engage staff in creating a common definition of their school community—one that addresses what it is (or is becoming) and why. Expand this definition into a mission statement to guide school improvement.
X	X	X	• Involve all stakeholders in reaching mutual decisions.
X	X	X	• Identify school- and grade-level inclusion goals, and support taking small steps towards those goals.
X	X	X	• Make use of "round robin" brainstorming at meetings to hear all voices.
X	X	X	• Recognize that listening and being empathic may be more useful than solving a problem.
	X	X	• Recognize and celebrate successes.
	X	X	• Be alert and responsive to staff needs as they change over time.
	X	X	• Make consultative services available to general educators and collaborative teams.
	X	X	• Know that support takes different forms and functions for different classroom teachers; develop a school/district menu of support options.
	X	X	• Encourage staff/teams to share their ideas and resources with others.
	X	X	• Orient new staff to school philosophy and progress; link them with strong teams.
	X	X	• Find ways to record, share, and publicize student success stories.

P = Preparation: As schools are preparing for inclusion
I = Implementation: As teams are being planned and implemented
M = Maintenance: Once teams are in use

Figure 2.2. A building administrator's checklist for building collaborative teamimg during preparation, implementation, and maintenance phases. (*Sources:* Elliott & McKenney, 1998; Hennen, Hirschy, Opatz, Perlman, & Read, 1996; Idol, 1997; National Center for Children and Youth with Disabilities, 1995; Roach, 1995; Russ, Chiang, Rylance, & Bongers, 2001.)

"What is our purpose?" Sometimes, forums are held during which parents and other members of the school community who are interested in inclusion can voice their concerns and obtain answers to their questions. Information on inclusion is usually supplied in response to any concerns or questions that are raised and, consequently, a vision for a school begins to develop. Teachers and staff, along with representative parents and students, then work toward consensus on the school's vision for inclusion. Mission statements can guide the design of a school's major goals and its instructional program and activities and often clarify the need for collaborative teams (Idol, 1997; Janney, Snell, Beers, & Raynes, 1995;

Voices from the Classroom

The mission statement of one school system in Virginia identified five rules to follow in their integration of students with special education needs:

1. *"We accept the responsibility for the success of every student.*
2. *We believe in the inherent dignity and worth of each individual.*
3. *We believe every student can learn.*
4. *Projecting a segregated attitude within an integrated setting will not work.*
5. *What we are doing is consistent with what we want, believe, and know about children and educational best practice." (Roach, 1995, p. 8)*

Another statement was developed for a Texas school district by a representative but diverse team as a draft for district schools to consider and refine:

"The mission of the Nacogdoches Independent School District is to ensure that all children, regardless of disability, cultural background, or socioeconomic status, have available to them the resources, services, and support necessary to meet their unique individual and educational needs. The district will continually strive to provide the best educational services available. The school and community will function as a 'family,' to nurture and support the educational and social growth of everyone." (Idol, 1997, p. 387)

Mission statements can be written for entire states, as has been done in Michigan and New Mexico, for example. Michigan's broad mission statement for student outcomes applies to all school districts:

*   *"A person who values and is capable of learning over a lifetime*
*   *A person capable of applying knowledge in diverse situations*
*   *A competent and productive participant in society" (National Association of State Board of Education [NASBE], 1992, p. 9)*

The vision statement for the New Mexico State Department of Education reads in part: *". . . We believe education must challenge all students to reach their potential"* (NASBE, 1992, p. 20). Ultimately, the faculty and administrators of each school need to examine their school's philosophy and, then, establish consensus on the elements of their philosophy that define their unique mission.

Figure 2.3.   Examples of mission statements.

Roach, 1995). Figure 2.3 provides examples of several mission statements.

Having experience with educating heterogeneous groups of students seems to strengthen administrators' and educators' beliefs in inclusion over pull-out programs and self-contained classrooms (Villa et al., 1996). During the preparation phase, therefore, administrators are advised to provide positive, personal experiences that challenge existing beliefs and attitudes (Giangreco, Dennis, Cloninger, Edelman, & Schattman, 1993). In fact, what seems to have the strongest effect on negative attitudes about disability is information plus interaction with individuals with disabilities. Thus, schools may find it helpful to listen to teams from other schools who have been successful with inclusion and collaboration, to view illustrative videos on these topics, and to visit schools that practice inclusion and then evaluate these experiences as a group. Perhaps even more powerful than learning about methods of inclusion and collaboration are direct experiences with adults and students with disabilities. Giangreco and his colleagues tracked changes in the perspectives of 19 general education teachers who taught a student with extensive support needs (with the necessary individualized supports pulled in). They identified a positive "transformation" in 17 of the 19 teachers; the teachers gradually changed from being uninvolved and noninteractive with the student, to taking ownership, to increasing their involvement with the students, and, finally, to changing their language from cautious and negative to positive and optimistic. Teachers credited their transformations to several things: teamwork and shared goals, the efforts of the special education staff, recognition and validation of their contributions, and the presence of the child with disabilities (Giangreco et al., 1993).

The in-service training planned for schools during this phase needs to be tailored to match the staff's concerns in addition to their skills; therefore, administrators should work closely with teachers and inclusion specialists to plan each training session. (Inclusion specialists are individuals who have extensive firsthand experience with inclusive programs; they may be employed by the school district or hired as consultants to advise schools.) Giangreco and his colleagues (1993) found that traditional in-service training for teachers that addressed the inclusion of students with extensive support needs in general education classrooms was not as beneficial as expected. Some teachers thought that their initial fears about inclusion kept them from absorbing the information offered in these traditional preparatory workshops. These same teachers identified two beneficial methods for alleviating their fears:

- Direct experience working with a child with disabilities who comes to class with the essential supports

- Nontraditional ongoing training about inclusion and teaming (nontraditional meaning that both the content of training and the timing of its delivery were atypical)

The most influential of these nontraditional training practices identified by teachers included the following:

1. Hearing about the feelings and experiences of other teachers in inclusive classrooms

2. Learning about the elements of inclusion that were critical to starting the school year: teamwork, ways to interact with and what to expect from the included students, roles and schedules of the special education staff, and methods for involving class members in creative problem solving

3. Learning about successful approaches from experienced teachers: Cooperative groups and activity-based teaching, group strategies, ways to use and adapt typical materials, and class activities for students with disabilities

These valuable nontraditional training methods were implemented during the preparation phase once class placement decisions were made and before the school year started.

Student Snapshot

 Before Daniel's transition to first grade, his kindergarten teacher met with Ms. James to share her positive experiences of working with Daniel, despite her initial fears. The kindergarten teacher explained, "That first summer school session when we included children we never served in the regular classroom, we were just learning to be a team. We didn't know each other, and some of us didn't even know Daniel very well, but we all knew that if we could just get him communicating, it would help him so much. We knew there was no magical thing that would make him communicate overnight. We had to figure it out."

Following the development of a school mission statement and staff training, administrators, in cooperation with their school system and their faculty, must make several big decisions. These decisions concern 1) creating staffing arrangements that enable special educators to efficiently work with general educators, 2) improving the methods for delivering special education services to students, and

LARGE CASELOADS FOR SPECIAL EDUCATORS:
THE NUMBERS JUST DON'T ADD UP!

Figure 2.4. Balancing special educators' caseloads (From Giangreco, M.F. [1999]. *Flying by the seat of your pants: More absurdities and realities of special education* [p. 39]. Minnetonka: MN: Peytral Publications; reprinted by permission.)

3) considering reductions in the caseload of special education teachers and related services professionals. As jokingly portrayed in Figure 2.4, the outcomes of these decisions will affect how collaborative teams are able to function in a school. A research review on special education caseload (Russ, Chiang, Rylance, & Bongers, 2001) lends strong support to the connection that higher caseloads have with reductions in student attending, academic engagement, and achievement, and with increases in teacher attrition. Placing a realistic number of students on a special educator's caseload and limiting the number of general education classrooms that the same special educator must work with increases the probability for successful collaborative interactions. We know that teams are critical to the mechanics and success of inclusion, but for teams to succeed, some of the primary factors that "make or break" the success of inclusive programs must be addressed during this preparatory phase: staffing arrangements, service delivery model, and caseload.

Implementation

Because they exercise ultimate control over school schedules and space, school administrators play an important role during the team implementation phase. Basic questions need to be addressed, such as, "Why will we form teams (team purpose)?" "When will teams meet?" and "Where will we meet?" During the implementation phase, building administrators will continue to listen and respond to the obstacles teams face as they form and develop. With teachers' input, principals will arrange in-service training and consultation on teaming topics that refine teachers' emerging skills (e.g., problem solving, reaching consensus, teamwork skills) and that address implementation issues (e.g., ideas for teaching and assessing collaboratively, modifying schoolwork, improving family participation).

During both the implementation and maintenance phases, it is often valuable for building administrators to hold regular discussions with staff regarding their successes and concerns with inclusion. The meetings provide another collaborative forum for problem solving that involves the principal and extends to all staff. In one elementary school, for example, the principal holds monthly staff discussions on inclusion progress and begins these sessions by giving each staff member an opportunity to share a success story. The remainder of the time is then devoted to quick group problem-solving using an issue-action format:

- One person volunteers to take notes on large poster paper.
- Staff members take turns and share their successes.
- Staff members take turns and briefly describe a single concern they may have.
- The principal facilitates fast-paced brainstorming from the group.
- Needed actions are determined and given target completion dates, and responsible staff members are identified.
- The next meeting begins with quick updates regarding these actions.

Issue-Action Planning Form

Team/student/group: _Inclusion Support Meeting_   **Date:** _November 2, 2004_

Team members present: _Rob, Brenda, Ray, Kari, Sue, Maryanne, Norine, Alice, Jan, Kenna,_
Ruth, Kathy, Joslyn , Sarah, Flo, Bert, Miranda, Anna, Linda, and Joan

Issue	Planned action	Person(s) responsible
1. Novels on tape needed, esp. for students w/LD in third and fourth grades	check w/Recording for the Blind; student in building has these services & catalogs available	Kenna get catalogs to Maryanne
2. Self-esteem builders for class-rooms	Guidance counselor get info. for classroom teachers—get list of teachers—put in mailbox	Brenda
3. Absenteeism that is chronic—two students in fifth grade—at IEP meetings	Teacher share action plan w/asst. principal & he will write letter	Rob/Kari
4. Weed wacker during class times disturbs second grade, esp. child w/autism	Call maintenance dept. (principal) for before/after school weed wacking only!	Ray (principal)
5. Problems in many rooms w/underachievers; students without disabilities—"at-risk"	Need remediation ideas: • Contact spec. ed. office for ideas • Counseling groups w/guidance • Parent volunteers in classroom	Kenna Brenda Sue

Figure 2.5. Issue-action planning form.

As school staff members take turns sharing issues or asking for support with particular students or difficulties, the rest of the staff members gain a broader view of inclusion and teaming issues. A loose time structure of 6 minutes per teacher enables all kindergarten through fifth-grade teachers to share and obtain immediate feedback, in the form of four to five suggestions, from the other group members. Schoolwide inclusion meetings are over within an hour. The responsibility of taking notes rotates among the staff members. Once notes from the large paper are rewritten onto notebook paper and copied, each meeting has a record, and decisions can be reviewed. The principal actively provides suggestions and support. The outcomes of these collaborative group sessions include positive solutions and shared celebrations about progress. Sometimes, such a forum can give a team the boost it needs to move forward, either by assisting in the resolution of a concern or by giving staff members a feel for other teams' progress and issues. Figure 2.5 shows the notes from an actual issue-action meeting.

Maintenance

In the maintenance phase, some actions that administrators have taken during preparation or initiation (e.g., issue-action problem-solving at the school level, prescriptive in-service training) will continue, whereas other actions will be added or discontinued. The emphasis during this phase is on the refinement and evolution of the collaborative team's function and process. Team functions and outcomes need to be visibly integrated into the standard school procedure so staff members see the significance of their work. Improvement of team function will continue to be a priority during this phase, though in-service training might shift to more focused topics including communication, co-teaching, handling team conflict, and transitions between grades and schools.

DEFINE TEAM
PURPOSE AND FOCUS

The overall purpose of collaborative teams is to promote student learning and success in school. Teams may choose a narrow or wide focus in addressing these student-centered purposes. For students with numerous support needs, the team's focus is often on that particular student; other times, teams may work to address the needs of all students from a single classroom who require extra support to be successful.

- *Individual student teams*—Teams organized to address the needs of a single student. When a student is eligible for special education, this team also is involved in planning and reviewing the individualized education program (IEP).

- *Classroom/grade-level teams*—Teams formed to address support issues pertaining to individual students in a classroom or to an entire grade level (see Figure 2.6).

Student Snapshot

 Melanie, a fourth grader with autism, is a member of Ms. Ramirez's class. In addition to her classroom teacher, Melanie's core team includes her special education teacher (Ms. Pitonyak), her parents, and her speech-language pathologist. The core team meets once a month with frequent verbal exchange between meetings. Melanie's teachers meet weekly but interact daily as they work together to implement and adapt classroom instruction and school activities for Melanie. Also, on a monthly basis, Ms. Ramirez meets with the other fourth-grade teachers and Ms. Pitonyak to address student-focused, grade-level issues.

Although these two arrangements for collaborative teams (teams formed around a single student and those formed for entire classrooms or grade levels) are the primary focus of this book, teams can organize other ways to fulfill their purpose and focus on students:

Voices from the Classroom

 At Collingwood Elementary, a kindergarten through fifth grade school of about 475 children, most special education teachers are assigned to a combination of grade level teams, whereas special education teachers assigned to the fifth grade work with no other grade levels. One special education teacher who is trained across categories of special education works with the fifth-grade team. This teacher attends weekly fifth-grade team meetings during which many issues on students and inclusion are discussed among the teachers; she also attends weekly individual planning meetings (for the students with the most significant needs), during which she meets with a single fifth-grade teacher regarding a particular student. These meetings last about 15–20 minutes.

Figure 2.6. How special education teachers are assigned to grades in one elementary school. (Contributed by Kenna Colley.)

- *Multigrade teams*—When a school has only one to two classrooms per grade level, multigrade teams might be an option (e.g., kindergarten and first-grade team). The size of the team and the number of students on whom the team focuses may prevent adequate attention to students with significant needs. Thus, additional teams may be formed to focus on a single student.

- *Middle school grade-level teams*—Often, middle schools organize teams at single grade levels to share planning and instruction, problem-solve, and evaluate student performance. This approach allows a focus on the different concerns regarding students just entering or preparing to leave middle school.

- *Department teams*—Secondary school teachers often organize themselves into teams by academic department. When special education staff are active members (or regular drop-ins) on these teams, the learning and success of students with special needs who are enrolled in general education classes in that department can be promoted.

- *Teacher assistance teams, intervention assistance teams, ad hoc problem-solving, and "round table" teams*—These teams vary in their membership from just having teacher members to consisting of teachers plus professional support staff, the principal, and sometimes parents. They meet regularly to address specific students who are exhibiting difficulties and have been referred to them by a teacher in the school or district. The team provides assistance to the referring teacher. Both approaches—teachers only and teachers plus specialists—have been described as being effective over the years (Friend & Cook, 2003; Pugach & Johnson, 2002). A variation of this approach is the pre-referral team who helps teachers take preventative action before formal consideration for special education services and may, consequently, avoid referring a student to special educa-

tion (Friend & Cook, 2003; Porter, Wilson, Kelly, & Den Otter, 1991) (refer to Figure 2.7).

- *Related services teams*—These teams include teachers and therapists whose focus is on the students who receive the team's related services and the issues surrounding those services (e.g., scheduling, types of therapy support).

- *Building-level or system-level teams*—Teams also can form to address short- or long-term system-level and building-level goals. System-level goals may include writing a curriculum, planning textbook changes, or resolving a problem that affects some or all students in the school (e.g., drugs, bullying). Building-level teams address school-specific issues and make recommendations, such as designing plans to involve families, making site-based decisions, studying staff development needs, and designing a discipline plan.

The general principles for building teams, learning teamwork skills, problem-solving, taking team action, improving communication, and evaluating outcomes apply across all types of team arrangements. Figure 2.8 illustrates the variety of collaborative teams that can be implemented in inclusive schools in order to plan education programs for students and to collaborate on related changes within schools and at the systems level. The configuration of collaborative teams chosen by a particular school should relate to classroom, school, and system needs in addition to the phase of inclusion and team development that the school system or individual school is in.

ESTABLISH TEAM MEMBERSHIP

Teams should consist of those people who work closely with the student and know him or her well. For students who have IEPs, team members should be those service providers

What the Research Says

Studies of school-based intervention teams indicate that they have many names, are widely used, and conform to district or state practices, but they typically are not required (Bahr, Whitten, Dieker, Kocarek, & Manson, 1999). Prereferral teams are called by different names across states: *Teacher Assistance Teams, Teacher Intention Teams, Child Study Teams,* and *Support teams* (Buck, Polloway, Smith-Thomas, & Cook, 2003). Although their use is not mandated by the Individuals with Disabilities Education Act (IDEA) Amendments of 1997 (PL 105-17), 43% of states require their use, and 29% recommend it (Buck et al., 2003).

The concept is not new. In the 1980s, this non–special education problem-solving process was referred to as prereferral intervention and was directed toward preventing and reducing referrals to special education by having school staff meet to problem-solve students' learning or behavior problems, identify a plan of action, and implement and follow-up the outcomes of the plan (Buck et al., 2003). Buck et al. (2003) in their survey of states found that:

- General educators predominantly fill the team leader's role, while counselors, special educators, school psychologists, and administrators take this responsibility in decreasing order.

- Most states (63%) indicated that training was provided to participants.

- The resultant action plans included instructional modifications (96%), behavior management procedures (92%), curricular modifications (80%), counseling (51%), placement change or review (37%), and parent training (25%).

- States judged the school-based intervention team process as being usually successful (35%) or sometimes successful (45%).

These findings are encouraging in that they support the value most schools place on problem-solving by teams in order to prevent student failure and resolve student learning and behavior problems; however, some of the shortcomings of these teams also have been revealed (Bahr et al., 1999).

1. Team follow-up tends to be verbal rather than written (no team minutes or action plan), which means less accountability on the action plan and no permanent record of the intervention for the student.

2. Team effectiveness seems to primarily be judged by teachers' subjective opinion rather than objective data (e.g., graphing student performance, comparing baseline and post-intervention data, classroom observation).

3. Family members do not appear to be consistently involved. Because all of the principles of teaming addressed in this book may be applied to these teams, these short-comings can be easily improved on.

4. It is not known if the reauthorization of IDEA (in process) or No Child Left Behind Act will influence the use of prereferral teams.

Figure 2.7.   What the research says about teacher assistance teams or prereferral intervention teams.

listed on the plan who work with the student. Core team members play major roles in planning, implementing, and overseeing a student's daily education schedule; they include general educators, special educators, family members, and sometimes others. A student's whole team is often larger; in addition to the core team members, it includes other people who are needed in the educational process but whose involvement is required less frequently.

Three questions can be used to identify who should be on a single student's core and whole or extended teams (Thousand & Villa, 2000):

- Who has the talent and expertise that the team must have to make the best decisions for that student?

- Who is affected by the team's decisions?

- Who has an interest in participating?

	Examples in inclusive schools		
Collaborative team level	*Elementary school*	*Middle/junior high school*	*High school*
Student level	• Individual student teams • Classroom teams • Grade-level teams • K–1, 2–3, 4–5 teams	• Individual student teams • Grade-level teams	• Individual student teams • Department teams (math, English, social studies, vocational, health, science, phsycial education)
School level	• Site-based committee • Pre-referral or teacher assistance teams • Inclusion team • GIRDLE meeting[1] • Issue–action planning team	• Site-based committee • Pre-referral or teacher assistance teams • Inclusion Team	• Site-based committee • Pre-referral or teacher assistance teams • Departmental heads
Systems level	• District inclusion team • "Rocket scientists" team[2]	• Consulting teacher team[3] • Therapists team[4]	

[1] GIRDLE (Getting Into Really Discussing Learning and Experiences) meeting—A monthly meeting of all teachers aimed at problem-solving and voicing new ideas. Teachers submit issues; two are selected that seem to be the most pressing. Those whose issues have been selected have 5 minutes to present the issue, answer questions about the issue, and then listen as an invited guest while the other teachers brainstorm ideas to address the issue. The meeting is limited to 60 minutes. Snacks are served; the special education consulting teacher facilitates. Guests invited are from outside the school and are chosen to share new ideas or information on pressing problems. Another method involves one person describing an issue to the group, with whining allowed.

[2] A team whose members include special education teachers, representatives from related services (e.g., occupational therapy, physical therapy, speech-language therapy, adapted physical education), and general education teachers who meet at a district level to discuss and resolve concerns.

[3] A team whose members include all of the consulting special education teachers in a district; they meet, give and obtain information, discuss and resolve issues regarding inclusion, and take ideas back to their schools.

[4] A team whose members include all of the speech and communication therapists, or the combined occupational and phsycial therapist, with periodic meetings of all of the therapists together. Members meet at the district level to discuss and problem-solve issues that arise.

Figure 2.8. Examples of collaborative teams used at elementary, middle, and high school levels. (With contributions from Johnna Elliott and Cynthia Pitonyak.)

Several factors require careful consideration when deciding who will be a core or whole team member for a given student or for a set of students (Rainforth & York-Barr, 1997): 1) How many team members are needed? 2) How involved can members be? and 3) What skills do potential members have?

How Many Members Should Be on a Team?

Generally, smaller teams require less energy to gather together and fewer schedules to co-ordinate; consequently, they make communication easier. Members of smaller teams are more familiar with one another, which leads to more task involvement and a greater sense of responsibility (Johnson & Johnson, 2000). By contrast, larger teams often translate into more resources and greater expertise; however, coordination, accountability, and contribution by individual members may actually be reduced. Oftentimes, general education teachers are overwhelmed by too many team members serving the same student (Snell & Janney, 2000). A study of team membership for students with multiple disabilities found that team size ranged from 5 to 11 members (Giangreco, Dennis, Edelman, & Cloninger, 1994).

Student Snapshot

Sam is served by seven general education teachers (one from each of his subject areas), a number of teaching assistants who alternate across his day, and two special education teachers (one of whom oversees Sam's vocational training in the community). The guidance counselor and school psychologist are extended team members, and Sam's parents both work closely with the team as core members. Because 15 people provide support for Sam, about the only time everyone is in the room together for a meeting is when they are discussing Sam's IEP. A lot of communication is done in writing so that team members can provide input even if they can't be at the more frequent planning meetings. Ms. Elliott, Sam's lead special education teacher, knows that "whenever we have a planning meeting, almost everyone will have a conflicting meeting or two; therefore, we ask for everyone's input first and then give each team member information about the meeting's outcome. If it's an IEP meeting, the outcome is an issue-action plan or a program-at-a-glance. Once each team member is informed about the meeting outcome, I touch base with everyone and we work on-the-fly to make things happen."

Johnson and Johnson (2000) reported that effective teams had 2–25 members and the

IN AN EFFORT TO MAINTAIN A WORKABLE TEAM SIZE, MR. MOODY SUGGESTS LIMITING MEMBERSHIP TO THE NUMBER OF PEOPLE THAT CAN FIT IN A PHONE BOOTH.

Figure 2.9. Limiting team size can be challenging. (From Giangreco, M.F. [1999]. *Flying by the seat of your pants: More absurdities and realities of special education* [p. 34]. Minnetonka: MN: Peytral Publications; reprinted by permission.)

most effective teams had fewer than 10 members. When core team members meet frequently and there is good communication with whole team members, many of the advantages of both smaller (core) teams and larger (whole) teams can be realized (Giangreco, 1996). Although number of members is one way to limit the size of a team, an individual's time for involvement and his or her knowledge and skills are better selection criteria (see Figure 2.9).

How Involved Can a Team Member Be?

The degree to which a team member is involved on a student's team depends on the access he or she has to the student and the school, the distance that the member must travel to serve the student, and the "caseload" of students whom the member already serves. Sometimes, potential team members who do not have adequate access to the student or the environment will serve as consultants to the core team and visit "on demand," focusing on a specific issue.

Student Snapshot

 Ms. Baldino, a regional specialist on autism, participates periodically on Melanie's team. Because she serves several school districts, Ms. Baldino often is not available; however, when she is available, she contributes valuable information on autism to the core team members and adds new strategies to their plans. Ms. Pitonyak regularly e-mails Ms. Baldino with team meeting updates on Melanie.

What Skills and Knowledge Do Potential Team Members Have?

A third consideration for the selection of team members is their knowledge and skill level. Some experts suggest that team members should be selected based on their expertise, skills, and potential for learning new skills, not because of their position or personality (Johnson & Johnson, 2000). When there is overlap in ability and experience among the team members, though not in actual job title, it often is better to select a smaller team of members who have excellent access to the student than to have a larger team with redundant skills. Sometimes, team members will have training and experience that bridge different categories of disability (in special education, this is referred to as *cross-categorical training*). These individuals often are more versatile in the supports they provide, particularly on classroom or grade-level teams or with students with multiple disabilities.

The guiding principle for selecting team members is to balance these factors: teaming efficiency, team members' time available to work with students and other team members, and the match between members' abilities and students' needs (see Figure 2.10). When teams are selected to avoid role overlap, they are likely to be smaller, more efficient, and have less chance for territorial conflict. Over time, successful teams in inclusive schools seem to change as the roles and duties of members progress from rigidly distinct to being blurred, with more cooperation between members (Wood, 1998). These changes appear related to several things: 1) communication and trust, 2) the amount of role release teams engage in as members teach each other about their specialties, and 3) the success experienced by members as they broaden their role and duties with the student with disabilities.

Rule: Balance efficiency, time available, and diversity of knowledge and skill

1. When two or more potential members have similar competencies:
   - Select only one to be a member
   - Select the member who can address multiple challenges or student needs
   - Select the person with better access to the student
2. If none of the potential members have adequate knowledge/skills to address a priority area, identify a member with ongoing student involvement and provide technical assistance.
3. Let two members with similar but nonoverlapping skills work together and teach each other with the goal of a divided caseload (gives more time for involvement with individual students).
4. Focus on matching student challenges and needs with competencies of team members.

Note: The type/amount of services provided must match the IEP.

Figure 2.10. Guidelines for selecting support personnel as team members. (From Rainforth, B., & York-Barr, J. [1997]. *Collaborative teams for students with severe disabilities: Integrating therapy and educational services* [2nd ed., pp. 262–264]. Baltimore: Paul H. Brookes Publishing Co.; adapted by permission.)

TIME NEEDED
FOR TEAMS TO MEET

Several guidelines determine the amount of time teams need both for sit-down meetings and for on-the-fly communications:

1. Students with more complex disabilities, less supportive families, and/or atypical or disruptive social behavior usually need more support and require more involvement and time. The core team members of students with high support needs often meet weekly and communicate daily.

2. The core team members of students with fewer support needs may meet every 1–3 weeks but communicate at least weekly.

3. When paraprofessional staff are involved in the support, they should communicate daily with the special and general educators.

4. When related services staff are involved in the support, they should communicate with the classroom staff whenever they are scheduled with the student and should give verbal or written comments to the special educator on a preplanned basis.

5. Schools and teams decide on written approaches to preserve the decisions made in meetings (e.g., issue/action/person responsible notes, meeting minutes) and to share the decisions with team members.

6. Family members and teachers decide how they will communicate (e.g., in person before or after school, traveling notebook, telephone, voice mail, e-mail) and how often, as well as what meetings families will attend.

Communication among team members between meetings must also be planned and valued. The preceding guidelines for meeting frequency are only general rules, and most teams will adopt the general principle, "Meet when there is a reason to meet, and let the agenda drive the meeting."

FINDING THE TIME TO PLAN

Probably the biggest challenge for most teams is finding the time to meet (e.g., Idol, 1990; Kaczmarek, Pennington, & Goldstein, 2000; Karge et al., 1995). General and special education teachers may not have common planning times. Often, special education teachers in elementary schools have no planning time. Paraprofessionals, if part of the team, sometimes have contracts that do not pay after-school hours or paraprofessionals have after-school duties or other jobs. Related services staff frequently rotate across schools. Although public school teachers and school staff will always find scheduling difficult, there are some solutions.

First, building administrators and teachers need to confront the shortage of available time and schedule conflicts. Meeting times for teams will always be influenced by building-wide scheduling decisions (e.g., start and end of school, assemblies) as well as by the staffing assignment approach a school adopts for its special education teachers. Three common staffing approaches that facilitate collaboration include assigning special education teachers with the training to serve a broader range of students with disabilities to 1) grade-level or multi-grade teams in elementary schools; 2) interdepartmental, grade-level teams or families in middle schools; and 3) departmental teams in high schools. Teachers or therapists who are highly specialized (e.g., severe disabilities, mobility specialists) might rotate across all grades in a larger school or across several schools. When these assignment approaches are used, most special education teachers will have a defined caseload that matches the way general education teachers are organized, making common meeting times more likely and reducing the number of special educators a group of teachers must call on to collaborate. Furthermore, when principals understand the value of team meetings and have a logical staffing plan in place, they can work with teachers to explore ways to make time available and to coordinate staff schedules (Idol, 1997; Walther-Thomas, 1997).

Second, creative approaches make use of in-school planning time before tapping after-school or before-school time. Several common options are used for creating shared planning time (Friend & Cook, 2003; Rainforth & England, 1997):

- *Early school release or late arrival*—Adjust school schedules so that dismissing school early or starting late creates time for weekly or monthly planning with no reduction in student learning time. Get community support first and preserve the time for teaming.

- *Substitutes*—Hire a permanent substitute who is scheduled to teach across schools (e.g., one day on alternate weeks) or hire substitutes to rotate across classes, freeing up teachers to meet with special educators. Select substitutes who are able to rotate from class to class; save planning time by having substitutes review material rather than teach new material; and keep teachers accountable for their teaming interactions.

- *On-the-spot teaming strategies for co-teaching*—At the scheduled time for co-teaching, the classroom teacher tells students (and the co-teacher) what they will be working on and may stop instruction to let students review in an effort to check their understanding and to orient the special educator.

School staff can also brainstorm a list of options for creating or scheduling teaming time (see Figure 2.11) that is regularly reviewed.

Third, therapists or specialized teachers who regularly serve students with low incidence disabilities (e.g., severe disabilities, deaf-blindness, autism) can be scheduled for longer, blocked time periods in schools to increase the likelihood that they will be available to meet with core teams. Scheduling therapy becomes difficult for included students because they are not clustered in self-contained classrooms. Block scheduling of therapy (e.g., occupational, physical) refers to "allocating longer periods of time than usual (e.g., a half or full day instead of 30–45 minutes) to provide the time and flexibility needed to work in and move between the learning environments in which students with disabilities are integrated" (Rainforth & York-Barr, 1997, p. 267). By going to a particular school less often but staying longer, therapists reduce travel time between and within buildings and create teaming possibilities by being available before and/or after school or during planning periods.

Finally, efficiency is often the best antidote to a shortage of time. Several practices (discussed in more detail in Chapters 3 and 4) will increase the efficiency of even short periods of available time:

1. Teams should use and mutually enforce a regular schedule and process for meetings.

2. Team members must be respectful of each others' time by adhering to time limits: Start on time, stay on task, and end on time.

3. Teams should use an agenda, take notes, share notes with all members, and use notes from earlier meetings to review progress.

When these three practices are applied, a great deal can be accomplished in a 20- to 30-minute period.

SUPPORT TEAMS AND TEAMWORK

If changes are going to be meaningful and sustained in schools, building administrators need to do more than simply support them. They need to become directly involved with the change process; those who participate

Create time

- Adjust school schedules so that dismissing school early or starting late creates time for weekly or monthly planning without a reduction in student learning time.
- Hire a permanent substitute who is scheduled to sub across schools (e.g., one day on alternate weeks) or hire substitutes to rotate across classes, freeing up teachers to meet with special educators.
- Meet during independent work time, rest (in early grades), recess (while paraprofessionals or parents supervise the class), or planning periods.
- Free teachers by regularly scheduling parents, community volunteers, administrators, and retired teachers to teach.
- Use faculty meetings on alternate weeks for team meetings.
- Use part or all of some faculty meetings for sharing or for problem-solving; have the principal facilitate.
- Plan, schedule, and use collaboration days during the school year.
- Combine classes for a period to free up a teacher for teaming.
- Plan special events (by grade level or for the entire school) on a monthly basis that are operated by nonschool staff, freeing up staff members for team meetings. In middle schools, weekly or monthly time might be devoted community service requirements.

Coordinate schedules or staffing assignments

- Have principals and teachers design a school teaming schedule for the upcoming year at the end of the prior school year; preserve that time for the whole year.
- Schedule meeting times on a schoolwide basis so common prep time can be scheduled for all members of grade-level teams.
- Designate and coordinate planning times for grade/department planning meetings.
- Restructure school planning teams (grade level and department) so that special education teachers are members.
- Assign special education teachers to grade-level teams or departments so that their caseloads are defined and their participation in grade-level or department team meetings allows collaboration for students with support needs.
- Assign paraprofessionals to specific grade levels, and have them use their flex time to attend grade-level team meetings.
- For one day each week, schedule a common lunch period for teachers who work together; as possible, schedule this lunch period before or after a common prep period.
- Use parallel block scheduling (Snell, Lowman, & Canady, 1997) to create meeting times.
- Have principals arrange the master schedule so that art, physical education, and music are scheduled at a set time by grade level in order for teachers to collaborate by grade level.
- Advocate annually with the central office when the school calendar is planned to have professional time reserved for teaming.
- Include team collaboration time in students' individualized education programs (IEPs) as a related service.

Figure 2.11. Ideas for scheduling and creating team meeting time. (*Sources:* DeBoer & Fister, 1995–1996; Friend & Cook, 2003; Hennen, Hirschy, Opatz, Perlman, & Read, 1996; Idol, 1997; Rainforth & York-Barr, 1997.)

half-heartedly will find that little progress is made (Fullan, 1991). Administrators who exhibit initiator and managerial styles of leadership are the most effective at implementing change because they reflect both a willingness to collaborate with staff and an ability to delegate responsibilities among team members (Fullan, 1991). Typical actions of building administrators who manage with initiator and leadership styles often include the following:

1. They clarify and support the innovation (inclusion and teaming) through consul-

tation with teachers and reinforcement of their efforts.

2. They work in collaborative ways with others involved in the change (e.g., send support notes to staff, hold regular problem-solving sessions with staff).

3. They have their finger "on the pulse of the school" (e.g., are frequently seen in the hallways and classrooms, even teaching a class; are knowledgeable about significant innovations in the school).

4. They are actively involved in the school's work without being controlling of staff (e.g., monitor pupil progress by implementing a systematic policy of record keeping and review data, but have teachers keep the records; are involved in curriculum decisions and in influencing content, but do not take control).

5. They implement strategies to transform the school's culture (e.g., take action to improve the culture and reinforce change, share power and responsibility; Fullan, 1991).

Both the principal's "background" work and visible modeling make a difference in whether collaborative teaming continues in schools as a healthy, functional process or dies

an early death. Hargreaves described a high school principal who consistently supported a collaborative culture:

> The modest and unassuming principal . . . modeled what he most expected of his staff. He praised them, sent them notes to thank them, was always visible around the school to see and hear them, and often bought them corsages or other little gifts to show how much he valued them. When a teacher needed his advice, he willingly offered it. When he himself needed help, he unashamedly asked for it. And when teachers wanted to spend their preparation times planning together, he fixed the schedule to facilitate it. He promoted rituals and ceremonies . . . to bring the school and the community together. He encouraged experiments in cross-grade groupings of students and links between their teachers to bring teachers together. And he himself sometimes taught classes to show the importance of bringing the principal and students together. (1994, p. 194)

Perhaps the central role of administrators in supporting collaborative teaming is to recognize that collaboration is a "predictor for success in school reform" (Friend & Cook, 1990, p. 69). The extent to which schools can create conditions needed for successful collaboration will determine how meaningful inclusion becomes within a school community. Principals play a major role in creating and maintaining these conditions.

Chapter 3

Learning Teamwork Skills

Student Snapshot

Melanie's adapted physical education teacher arrived to the team meeting nearly in tears. "How did things get so crazy so fast?" she asked. "School has only been in session for 2½ weeks, and almost every day I come into this school, I have a new student. Initially, there were five, now there are eight, and I just learned there'll be two more next week! I need planning time with the PE teacher, but he's always busy. I have to talk to the physical therapist, but she's never here when I am. I know she is doing the same things with some of my kids, but when are we ever going to have time to figure out the overlap? I only have a few minutes with the classroom teachers, but then I'm usually preoccupied with keeping track of the students. There are just too many adults, too many kids, and not enough time."

Calling people a "team" is no guarantee that they will operate like a team (Villa & Thousand, 2000), which requires an array of collaborative skills and growth of positive relationships between team members (Appl et al., 2001). Some even suggest that a super anatomy is required (see Figure 3.1)! This chapter addresses the most basic of these teaming skills,

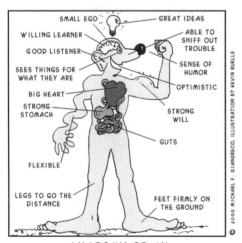

ANATOMY OF AN EFFECTIVE TEAM MEMBER

Figure 3.1. Anatomy of an effective team member (From Giangreco, M.F. [2000]. *Teaching old logs new tricks: More absurdities and realities of education* [p. 3]. Minnetonka: MN: Peytral Publications; reprinted by permission.)

from listening and interacting, to arranging and conducting team meetings. These skills are clustered together because they all are required to start a collaborative team. Subsequent chapters describe problem-solving methods, the actions teams take, co-teaching, and the interpersonal skills teams use to be effective.

LISTENING AND INTERACTING WELL

One of the best ways to understand effective interaction among team members is to spend time with experienced teams and watch them work together. Effective teams don't necessarily avoid conflict; instead, they minimize conflict, recognize it when it occurs, and establish strategies to address it. Smoothly functioning teams spend most of their time cooperatively engaged in "student-focused" discussion and working toward common goals. They typically use many strategies to communicate effectively, and they rely on one or several processes to identify and resolve problems.

Effective teams also regularly shift the focus to themselves as a team to address and build teaming skills, improve relationships among members, and resolve conflict (see Figure 3.2). Observation of teams who alternate their student focus with a team focus reveals the following predictable characteristics (Dinnebeil & Rule, 1994; Dunst, Johanson, Rounds, Trivette, & Hamby, 1992; Johnson & Johnson, 2000; Thousand & Villa, 2000):

1. Positive interdependence and mutual respect ("We are in this together, and we can all contribute.")

2. Frequent, focused, face-to-face exchanges

3. The use of processes to facilitate communication and shared decision-making (e.g., problem identification, consensus on decisions)

4. The use of methods for being responsible and accountable (e.g., setting an agenda, keeping written records of decisions)

5. Team trust derived from trusting one another and being trustworthy

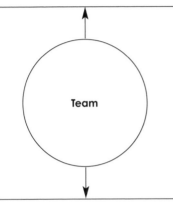

Team focus

1. Build team skills.
2. Improve relationships.
3. Address and resolve conflicts.

Team

Student focus

1. Identify common goal or problem.
2. Share information.
3. Brainstorm ideas.
4. Evaluate ideas against team criteria.
5. Select and develop solution.
6. Develop an action plan.
7. Implement and monitor plan.

Figure 3.2. Team and student focus.

Basic Communication Skills and Outward Behavior

Several basic strategies of effective interpersonal communication strongly influence whether teamwork skills will be successful (DeBoer & Fister, 1995–1996). Positive interaction starts with the outward behavior of team members and polite consideration of others. In most interactions, information is communicated most powerfully through one's facial expressions and body language. Voice (i.e., pitch, tone, and timing) is the second most powerful means for communicating information; actual words are the least effective means. The following guidelines reflect the power that nonverbal communication and facilitative listening have on interactions:

- *Attend to verbal and nonverbal behavior; look for your teammates' responses to your behavior*—includes body orientation, eye contact, facial expressions, gestures or touch, response time, interrupting others, and volume and tone of voice.

- *Listen first, then respond in ways that facilitate the exchange* (DeBoer, 1995)—encouraging ("Mm-hm"); paraphrasing without judgment ("What you are saying is . . ."); clarifying without judgment ("Are you saying that. . . ?"); reflecting on the person's feelings ("You are really frustrated with Sam"); and perception checking ("You sound like you've almost had it with Sam; have you?").

- *Avoid interrupting others when they are speaking.*

- *Contribute in ways that do not waste team time*—make points succinctly, steer clear of lengthy anecdotes.

- *Speak clearly and use a vocabulary that others can understand.*

- *Use team members' names.*

Although these six basic communication guidelines are simple, team members may not automatically practice them. These skills need to be habitual enough to withstand the disagreement and discussions of challenging issues that teams face.

Strategies for Leading Communication

Leading strategies can be used to keep an interaction going and to direct it in a particular way. Use leading strategies carefully, because they do not work if you have not first thoroughly listened to the team member or if you do not fully trust the person (DeBoer, 1995). Start by using an explaining strategy to state your position, such as

"Here is the picture I get, although I'm not sure it's fully accurate. Georgia feels we should not teach Melanie to use the photo book at lunch

time; however, Nora thinks she should teach at lunch and wants your support. As the teacher, you feel caught between them and want team agreement."

Next, encourage (e.g., "You certainly have been trying to use some new methods this semester") and assure (e.g., "I know that we can solve this problem as a team"). Present tentative ideas as one equal talking to another, such as, "Here is an idea I think may work with Sam's English assignment, but you may be in a better position to know if it will work." Use agreement or disagreement statements to indicate your opinion of whether another team member is right or wrong (e.g., "I can't really see how that approach will work with Walter at this point, but I appreciate the frustration you must be feeling"). Spontaneous humor can relieve tension and create a connection between you and your teammates (e.g., "They say that making mistakes is part of the process—and if that's right, we should be getting the prize!")

Questioning Strategies to Facilitate Communication

Questions can be used to to keep a discussion going by encouraging responses. Questioning methods include open- and close-ended questions, as well as direct and indirect questions (DeBoer, 1995). Both open-ended and indirect questions are "inviting" strategies that have been developed by counselors and consultants to 1) summon others to listen, and 2) move through the difficult times of stalled interaction and disagreement (DeBoer, 1995). By contrast, close-ended and direct questions do not invite others to freely respond, unless the speaker is simply seeking information.

- Use open-ended questions to encourage people to describe their perspective (De-Boer, 1995). They are broad and invite people to share their views, feelings, and ideas. Open-ended questions usually begin with "how" or "what" and allow team members to explain their ideas or explore further (e.g., "How does this math adaptation for Daniel seem to you?"

"What kinds of things does Vanessa do when she doesn't understand the science material?")

- Close-ended questions need to be used carefully, as they can leave colleagues with the feeling that they must agree or be rejected (DeBoer, 1995). They tend to seek a yes or no response or specific information and usually begin with "are," "do/don't," "have," "should," "will," "can," "when," and "where" (e.g., "How many students do you have in each of your reading groups?" "It's clear that Vanessa is not really disruptive, don't you agree?")

- Use indirect questions to create a cooperative climate (DeBoer, 1995). They are statements that ask without appearing to ask; listeners understand that their response is being sought (e.g., "I guess that this approach will be difficult to use." "I really don't understand what Asperger syndrome is, and I'd like to know more.")

- Be aware that direct questions may create a nonequitable climate (DeBoer, 1995). The listener may feel put on the spot or spoken down to. Direct questions are clear questions with a rising intonation and a question mark at the end. They may be open (e.g., "How hard would it be to use this adaptation in your class?") or closed (e.g., "Yes, it is hard to plan for three reading groups, isn't it?").

Signs of Difficulty

Many signs indicate that teams are challenged by their shortcomings with communication (Briggs, 1993; Johnson et al., 2003; Senge, Roberts, Ross, Smith, & Kleiner, 1994).

- Nonverbal behaviors suggest that attending and listening skills are missing or trust is lacking (e.g., members have poor eye contact with each other; members appear tense, rushed, or preoccupied).

- Speaking skills are poor (e.g., rambling, speaking too quietly), and there is little evidence of verbal skills (e.g., using encouraging words/phrases, clarifying ideas through restatement, checking for agreement).

- Team members are overly cautious and make many conditional statements.

- Words are mismatched with speaking tone and mannerisms.

- Team members rarely acknowledge one another.

- Viewpoints are stated as facts or formed into questions.

When these behaviors occur during team exchanges, the team must evaluate its communication. Recognizing, verbalizing, and agreeing that a difficulty exists are important first steps. An outside observer can give unbiased comments and honest feedback on team dynamics. Viewing videotapes of both model and problem teams at work can also be an excellent method of isolating, observing, discussing, and practicing collaborative communication skills (e.g., see Garner, Uhl, & Cox, 1992a, 1992b, and Chapter 6).

Improving interpersonal skills does not happen quickly. Team members must pay attention to the ways in which they interact with each other in order to reach their goals without becoming sidetracked by unnecessary hurt feelings, incompatible communication styles, misunderstandings, or disputes.

ESTABLISHING SHARED VALUES

In addition to positive, flexible communication that involves all team members, a second essential characteristic of teams, according to parents and teachers, is having a set of common philosophical beliefs and shared values (see Figure 3.3). These principles and beliefs may pertain to teaching and learning, student motivation, disability, inclusion, interpersonal communication, and working together (Rainforth & England, 1997). Examples of important shared values include the following:

- We all have equal status and something to contribute to our teamwork.

- We share the same goals and work together to achieve them.

- The student's needs drive the services.

- All students can learn skills of value.

- Family members must be our partners because they are the constants in our students' lives.

- We respect and trust each other and show it in a variety of ways.

- When we work together, we make better decisions and we accomplish what we cannot accomplish independently.

Allowing individual members to describe their values and work toward the identifica-

---

What the Research Says

When 226 teacher team members and 397 parent team members were asked by several researchers to respond to the question "What things enhance the ability of your team to collaborate?," two team traits were closely agreed on and frequently referenced (Dinnebeil, Hale, & Rule, 1996, pp. 334–335):

1. *The team's ways of working together* (half of the team members' comments fell into this category): Team members have effective communication that is conducted in flexible ways; is characterized by honesty, positive tone, and tactfulness; and enables the exchange of information that is both relevant to the child and contributed by all members.
2. *The team's shared philosophical beliefs and values* (a quarter of team members' comments fell into this category): Shared principles guide the relationship, such as value of parent perception and knowledge, optimism about the child's potential, mutual respect and trust, and sensitivity to each others' feelings.

Figure 3.3. Effective team characteristics. (Source: Dinnebeil, Hale, & Rule, 1996.)

tion of a small set of shared values is useful. Shared values help identify the bonds that make a team cohesive. (Chapter 4 describes team criteria for selecting solutions to identified problems; these criteria will link back to a team's shared values.)

Setting Ground Rules

Ground rules are informal directives set by the team that reflect each member's view of conditions that enable comfortable and honest communication. They help team members strike a balance between 1) completing the work or tasks of the group and 2) keeping the relationships among team members positive and rewarding (Rainforth & York-Barr, 1997). Some of the more critical rules of conduct cited by Johnson and Johnson (2000) include

- Attendance: starting on time and ending on time; no interruptions to make or take telephone calls (except in emergencies)

- Discussion: everyone participates, no exceptions

- Confidentiality: nothing discussed leaves the room without team permission

- Analytic approach: facts are essential for reaching informed decisions

- End-product orientation: all members have tasks and all complete them

- Constructive confrontation: finger pointing should be avoided

- Contributions: all members perform real work

One way for a team to compile ground rules involves each team member writing down his or her answer to the question, "What would it take for me to feel safe communicating openly and honestly in this group?" Responses to the question can be anonymously compiled into a single list by a nonteam member; the resulting list can become the group's ground rules for teamwork. No group member is asked to identify or defend the

rule(s) he or she contributed; however, team members may need to explain or restate a particular rule if other members do not seem to understand it. Some teams use a more informal approach, openly discussing their own suggested rules and rewording them until agreement is reached. The following are some examples of ground rules:

1. Begin and end team meetings on time.
2. Start every meeting with celebrations (i.e., recognition of recent accomplishments).
3. Share responsibiity for staying focused and following the agenda.
4. Use person-first and jargon-free language.
5. Appreciate feedback, and provide feedback and recognition for others.
6. Be kind and respectful, and refrain from complaining.
7. End every meeting with a summary of accomplishments and a list of agenda items for the upcoming meeting.
8. Laugh some; enjoy and be supportive of each other.

Another stimulus question that can be used to identify ground rules is, "What does it take for our team to get its work done?" Basic operating rules about time and participation include

- Everyone's participation is important.
- Meeting times are a priority; we begin on time and end on time.
- Share the load: take turns volunteering for responsibilities, taking notes, contacting other teachers or administrators, and so forth.
- Actions taken by team members are team-generated.

Both the values a team shares and the ground rules by which the team decides to operate are specific to that team. Once identified, written out, and shared with team members, team values and rules should be used. Teams should also revisit their ground rules or shared values periodically to reaffirm them and revise any that have changed. As the comfort level of a team grows, these rules could also be examined openly and revised as a group as well as used to self-assess team performance.

Student Snapshot

 In order for Daniel's mom to meet face-to-face with her son's whole team every 6 weeks, she had to balance her work and child care schedules. Her input in weekly core team meetings has been primarily through telephone calls, on-the-fly conversations, and a daily log book. At the first whole team meeting of the year, everyone but Daniel's mom was late, which meant the meeting started late, finished late, and Daniel's mom was late picking up her kids at child care. Ms. James apologized to Daniel's mom as she hurried out the door, but it was clear that one of the primary ground rules that the team had established several weeks before had been broken. The team stayed on and spent the next 15 minutes brainstorming ways they could guarantee to start and end on time. That evening, Ms. James called Daniel's mom to apologize and share the team's plans for being as prompt as she had been.

Signs of Difficulty

When teams have problems using their ground rules, their members exhibit the following behaviors (Senge et al., 1994):

- Team members slip up on priority ground rules.

- Very few people follow the ground rules.

- No one can state the ground rules.

- Too many topics are taboo, or important topics are routinely avoided.

- Disagreement exists about what the team designates as acceptable and unacceptable team member behavior.

- Irritating behaviors occur (e.g., members miss meetings, arrive late, leave early, or don't participate).

Team members should review their ground rules, independently rate their preformance on them, or even start with a clean slate and write new rules. Asking an impartial observer to attend the team meeting and tune into the behavior of members is often effective. Without relevant ground rules, teaming becomes inefficient and noncollaborative, and members' motivation for teaming erodes.

DEFINING ROLES AND RESPONSIBILITIES

Staff roles change frequently in inclusive schools where collaboration is practiced (West & Idol, 1990; Wood, 1998). Collaborative teachers are more likely to seek help from other teachers and from support staff than are teachers who work alone. They are also apt to plan instruction together, to draw on related services professionals, and to solicit help from family members. General education teachers usually have command of the content and primary responsibility for the class. In contrast, special educators bring their complementary skills of designing teaching programs suited to students with special needs. One special education teacher, Chris Burton, put it this way: "General educators are the content specialists who know the curriculum; special educators are the access specialists who make instruction accessible to everybody in the classroom" (personal communication, September, 1997).

Collaborative teaming requires that team members learn how to communicate, plan, and deliver coordinated services jointly. Several years ago, team members in an inclusive elementary school were asked about the duties they and their teammates had to fill during inclusion, as compared to the days when students with disabilities were "pulled out" for services (Snell et al., 1995). Different team members were asked about their own roles and responsibilities and each others' roles (e.g., general and special educators, related services staff, the building administrator, paraprofessionals). Several things became evident:

- Their roles had changed because of inclusion.
- They felt positive about these changes.
- Staff agreed about what their roles were.

Finally, each team member included him- or herself in sharing the responsibility of promoting peer involvement with the included students. The specific themes these staff members described in their role changes are listed in Figure 3.4.

Because role changes and turf protection can cause considerable concern among staff, team members should be actively involved in defining the changes. Conceptual barriers can also hinder special educators lending support to classroom teachers. For example, general and special educators may not know or agree with each others' teaching strategies, they might be divided by a feeling of hierarchy if special educators take on consultant or expert roles, and classroom teachers may view the increase in support staff traffic for students with IEPs as intrusive (Wood, 1998). Therefore, an early step in building teamwork is to think about, discuss, define, and clarify team members' roles and responsibilities concerning the student with disabilities and other students in a classroom or activity. Once defined, teams can identify and problem-solve issues that arise and make needed revisions in their roles and responsibilities.

Self-Perception of Strengths and Weaknesses

Personal style, professional training, and perception of strengths and weaknesses influence how team members envision their jobs and professional duties. The duties that teachers elect to fulfill will change 1) when they gain

experience with a broader diversity of students in inclusive programs, 2) as the team to which they belong works to support various students, and 3) as the team's composition changes. In a study of three collaborative teams in inclusive elementary schools, Wood (1998) found that the role boundaries between general and special educators were initially rigid, with a clear division of duties. These roles softened when the team became more cooperative over the course of the school year. Special educators initially developed all of the academic and behavior programs for the included students and supervised the instructional aides in an effort to "protect" classroom teachers from extra duties. This initial division of labor meant that classroom teachers 1) were less a part of the core team, 2) had less influence on how services were pulled into the classroom, 3) focused mainly on the child's social goals, and 4) were unable to express their dislike of disruptive pull-in schedules and special teaching. But as the year and the children progressed both socially and academically, classroom teachers "became more accountable to curricular strengths and needs of the children included in their classrooms," and there was less ambiguity between the roles and duties of general and special educators (Wood, 1998, p. 190). When there was no clarification of the role overlap and redundancy of effort between the teachers, it was viewed as being detrimental to teachers' self-concept:

> The problem isn't with the kids, the problem is with us . . . Our problem is the fact that we're both feeling responsible and proud of what's going on, and we probably both want to take the credit for it. And we both want to do something to help it. But the direction we want to help in doesn't always go in the same direction. (Wood, 1998, p. 192)

Role clarification can be facilitated in several ways (DeBoer & Fister, 1995–1996):

1. In-service training is provided for grade-level teams or for entire schools on topics

Responsibilities of general educators

- Treat the child like other students.
- Model for peers.
- Develop and use adaptations.
- Function as a team member.
- Serve as the child's primary teacher.
- Be flexible.

Responsibilities of special educators

- Serve as the inclusion facilitator and case manager.
- Work with general education teachers.
- Collaborate.
- Make curricular adaptations.
- Teach and supervise the teaching assistant.
- Provide information on the child.
- Develop, assist in implementing, and supervise behavior programs.
- Work with peers.

Responsibilities of the principal

- Initiate and be active in a school integration committee.
- Prepare teaching staff for the change to inclusion.
- Provide teacher support when needed.
- Address the concerns of parents and others about inclusion.
- Participate in problem-solving around specific children.
- Handle the logistics that affect inclusion.

Responsibilities of teaching assistants

- Implement team-generated plans.
- Work with other students.
- Be part of the team.
- Know and work well with the target child.
- Help the child fit into the class.

Responsibilities of related services providers

- Reduce pull-out services and use opportunities to work in the context of the class activities.
- Provide equipment that helps the child participate in class activities.
- Have flexible schedules that allow therapy to be provided during the most relevant times (e.g., physical therapy during physical education).
- Based on the teacher's unit topics or lesson plans, weave therapy into the planned class activities.
- Come prepared with adaptations and "be able to jump in and do whatever the class is doing."
- Be sensitive enough to know when to stay and when to leave.

Responsibilities for all team members in promoting peer involvement

- Answer questions.
- Model appropriate interactions.
- Monitor interactions unobtrusively.
- Include students in peer planning groups.
- Help peers problem-solve.
- Assign buddies.
- Use cooperative learning groups.

Figure 3.4. Changing roles in inclusive schools. (From Snell, M.E., et al. [1995]. Changing roles in inclusive schools: Staff perspectives at Gilbert Linkous Elementary. *Kappa Delta Pi Record, 31,* 104–109; adapted by permission of Kappa Delta Pi, an International Honor Society in Education.)

such as effective teaming, collaborative problem solving, and methods of pulling in special education services and co-teaching. Training helps teachers and other team members define the skills that are needed to include students and presents teachers with different models for planning and delivering coordinated special education supports.

2. Special education teachers meet individually with general education teachers to determine the general education teachers' preferences for teaming roles and responsibilities.

3. Team members identify and share their responses to questions about their strengths/resources and needs/fears regarding inclusion and teaming: What skills, talents, knowledge, and experiences do I bring to the team? What are my emerging skills? What supports and resources do I need? What supports can

I provide? What situations do I find stressful? What fears do I have about inclusion and teamwork?

4. Team members identify and discuss their styles of working in a group (e.g., achiever, persuader, risk-taker, supporter, analyst, optimist, worrier).

Student Snapshot

Melanie reads fairly well, but not on grade level; writes some words and phrases using a computer; and communicates through a combination of words, gestures, and symbols. Her curricular adaptations involve a combination of simplified objectives in math and language arts as well as functional objectives in school routines, self-help, and communication (see Figure 3.5). At some times during the day, Melanie works on the same objectives as her classmates, except at a different level. For instance, when her classmates are using the writing process to compose book reports, Melanie might write a brief book report on the computer by completing a form developed by her special education teacher. Melanie also takes several preventative movement "breaks" and has opportunities to use self-calming strategies when necessary to lower her frustration level and to help her stay focused.

Melanie's core team includes her mom and dad, Ms. Ramirez, Ms. Pitonyak, and Melanie's instructional assistant (Ms. Johnson). Before the school year started, Ms. Pitonyak discusssed her preferences for teaming roles and responsibilities with Ms. Ramirez. Ms. Ramirez thought she'd feel comfortable carrying out team ideas when Melanie was in the classroom for whole- or small-group instruction, but she wanted Ms. Johnson to implement the plan to teach relaxation and self-calming and any one-to-one instruction. At the same time, Ms. Ramirez was concerned that Ms. Johnson would need some supervision; therefore, the team decided that Ms. Pitonyak would observe every other Friday, and they would touch base weekly in their Friday lunchtime meeting. Both teachers wanted to share the assessment of Melanie's progress, so they decided to take turns on alternate weeks.

Role and Responsibility Worksheet

Discussions about roles and responsibilities can be further facilitated by using a matrix that lists team members across the top and typical responsibilities for delivering coordinated programs on the left-hand side. Figure 3.6 provides an example of such a worksheet that Melanie's team used in planning their roles to support her. Notice that the responsibilities are truly shared among Melanie's team members but that the people with the primary responsibility for a task are identified.

For teams for secondary students, the worksheet will need to be expanded to include other general education teachers who are team members and who share responsibilities. Focus should be redirected to the assignment of roles and responsibilities whenever a new member joins the team or the team reforms at the beginning of a new school year. When students move from one school to another, a student's team may need to be completely reformed. Teams can smooth these major transitions by meeting with new team members well before the change.

Teams have shared ownership of the students on whom they focus, although special education teachers ultimately are responsible for knowing and implementing special education procedures consistent with school policy and state law. In classrooms that are truly inclusive, however, the special education teacher does not have primary responsibility for every item on the team role and responsibility checklist, and the general education teacher is not left to figure things out alone.

ESTABLISHING A TEAM MEETING PROCESS AND SCHEDULE

It is helpful for team members to answer several questions to establish the team process they will use:

Program-at-a-Glance

Student: *Melanie*   Date: *September 2004*   Grade: *4*

IEP goals

Social/communication
- Use devices/systems to express needs, feel-ings, ask questions, make choices, yes/no, greetings
- Use gestures consistently
- Relate recent events in two- or three-word sentences

Functional skills
- Follow task directions from cues
- School arrival, departure, lunch routines
- School/classroom jobs

Math
- Identify numbers 0–1,000
- Number line for less than, more than
- Time to minute (face, digit)

Language arts
- Comprehension questions, novels
- Computer journal writing
- Read/write/spell functional words
- Inventive spelling for class assignments

Content areas
- Key words/concepts for each unit

Academic/social management needs
- Peer planning at beginning of year and as needed
- Reduced information per page
- Checklists & graphic organizers for time limits & beginnings/endings

IEP accommodations
- Receive special education assistance/instruction with academics, daily routines, transitions, support for communication techniques, peer interactions
- Weekly curricular adaptations by special and general educators
- Designated location in school for breaks
- Home/school communication log
- Educational team familiar with and uses all augmentative communication methods
- Behavior intervention plan to teach relaxation & self-calming

Comments/special needs
- Anecdotal records for IEP progress
- Core team meetings weekly; whole team monthly
- Share autism information with all team members/relevant staff

Figure 3.5. Melanie's program-at-a-glance.

- What do we want to accomplish in our team meetings?
- How will we proceed during our meetings?
- When and how often/long will we meet?
- Where will we meet?
- How will our process be suited to the student's family members?

What Do We Want to Accomplish in Our Team Meetings?

What occurs during meetings is closely related to team roles and responsibilities and students' status as class/school members and their progress as learners. For example, if and when teams have concerns about students' academic

Team Roles and Responsibilities

Classroom: _Ms. Ramirez's fourth-grade classroom_   Date: _10/24/2004_

School: _Roundhill Elementary_

Teaching and support team members:

Classroom teacher: _Ms. Ramirez_   Instructional assistant: _Ms. Johnson_

Special educator: _Ms. Pitonyak_   (Other):

Key: x = Primary responsibility
          Input = Input into decision-making and/or implementation

Roles and responsibilities	Who is responsible?			
	Classroom teacher	Special educator	Instructional assistant	Other
Developing lessons, units	x	x		
Adapting curriculum	input	x		
Adapting teaching methods	x	x	input	
Adapting materials	input	x	input	
Monitoring daily/weekly student progress	x (daily, weekly)	x (reports IEP)	x (data log)	
Assigning grades	x	x		
Assigning duties to/ supervising assistants	x (daily)	x (training)		
Scheduling team meetings:				
• IEP teams	x	input		
• Core planning teams for specific students	input	x		
Daily or weekly communication with parents	x	input	input	
Communication and collaboration with related services		x (service coordinator)	input (notes, logs)	
Facilitating peer supports	x	x (peer planning)	input	

Figure 3.6. Team roles and responsibilities checklist. (From Ford, A., et al. [1995, July]. *A team planning packet for inclusive education.* Milwaukee: The Wisconsin School Inclusion Project; adapted by permission.)

progress or social acceptance, these concerns can be aired during team meetings, and teams can determine whether to take action to address them. Most student-centered teams direct their energies toward facilitating student learning and membership within classes, school ac-

tivities, and peer groups. For example, they develop lessons; adapt curriculum, teaching methods, and materials; assess student progress; assign grades; and address interaction issues. Teams use agendas as their primary strategy for defining the tasks they need to accomplish:

- An agenda, even if just verbal, is established prior to a team meeting (or in the minutes of the prior meeting) and provides the reasons for meeting.

- The agenda is reviewed at the beginning of the meeting; revisions are made until the team agrees on the content, number and order of items, and time needed for each item.

- Once reviewed and agreed on, the agenda is used to guide the meeting.

- Agendas include student-focused items and team-focused items (e.g., team celebrations, processing).

- At the end of the meeting, any important agenda items that have not been addressed in addition to other items that have cropped up during the meeting are placed on the agenda for the next meeting.

How Will We Proceed During Our Meetings?

Teams use several general procedures to address agenda items:

- At the beginning of the meetings, team members volunteer to fill roles that will help the group accomplish their tasks and allow leadership to be distributed among team members. These roles should rotate each meeting (see Figure 3.7).

- Teams proceed through their agenda as determined at the beginning of the meeting.

- Team members apply a variety of procedures to each agenda item as needed. They may define the issue or concern, share and discuss information relevant to an issue or concern, brainstorm potential solutions, evaluate ideas and select acceptable options, make decisions through group consensus, and/or translate these decisions into action plans.

- As a record of the meeting, teams develop or adapt a meeting form that reflects their procedures and facilitates note-taking. Meeting note forms may be simple (such as the issue-action planning form in Figure 2.5) or more complex, such as the Collaborative team meeting worksheet (see Figure 3.8). Complex forms provide a place for noting who is present and recording

Team role	Role description
Note: All team members participate in the meeting while also filling one of the following roles.	
Facilitator	Leads the meeting, keeps members focused on the agenda, encourages all members to participate, and suggests other options for reaching agreement.
Timekeeper	Watches the time and warns fellow members when the designated time for each agenda item is almost over and is finished.
Recorder	Writes down team meeting details (e.g., people present, agenda items, roles) and takes brief notes on relevant information and team decisions. Quickly captures the essence of group ideas without evaluation. May read noted back to group for clarification. The team may use two recorders: one to take notes that are visible on wall-hanging paper and the other to record notes on a laptop computer or paper for later distribution.
Jargon buster	Is alert to terms used by members that may not be understood by other members and signals the user to explain or define the terminology in simpler or more complete terms.
Processor or observer	Pays attention to the teaming process and whether members work together collaboratively. Reminds the team to process, and priases good team communication. Alerts the team when group tension requires discussion or problem solving.

Figure 3.7. Roles team members take to accomplish team tasks and distribute leadership.

Collaborative Team Meeting Worksheet

Date: _____

Members present	Members absent	Others who need to know
_____	_____	_____
_____	_____	_____
_____	_____	_____
_____	_____	_____
_____	_____	_____

Roles:	**This meeting**	**Next meeting**
Timekeeper	_____	_____
Recorder	_____	_____
Facilitator	_____	_____
Jargon buster	_____	_____
Processor or observer	_____	_____
Other: _____	_____	_____

Agenda

Items   **Time limit**

1. Celebrations _____

2. _____

3. _____

4. _____

5. Process: How are we doing? _____

6. _____

7. _____

8. _____

9. Process: How did we do? _____

Action plan

Action items   **Person responsible**   **By when?**

1. Telling others who need to know _____

2. _____

3. _____

4. _____

5. _____

Agenda building for the next meeting

Date: _____   Expected agenda items

Time: _____   1. _____   3. _____

Location: _____   2. _____   4. _____

Figure 3.8. A collaborative team meeting worksheet. (From Thousand, J.S., & Villa, R.A. [2000]. Collaborative teaming: A powerful tool in school restructuring. In R.A. Villa & J.S. Thousand [Eds.], *Restructuring for caring and effective education: Piecing the puzzle together* [2nd ed., p. 273]. Baltimore: Paul H. Brookes Publishing Co.; adapted by permission.)

agenda items and expected times, team decisions and action plan, and information about the next meeting.

When and How Often/Long Will We Meet?

Teams need to determine a meeting frequency and duration that suits team members and allows enough time to address team goals. Once frequency and duration have been established, teams should identify a regular time to meet. Whole team meetings should be scheduled less often and be less flexible; core team meetings should be scheduled more often, and their times may need to be more flexible. The following guidelines may assist teams in planning this part of their process:

- Meet only when there is a clear purpose.

- Promptly address current and serious student or staff issues.

- Meet when necessary material and information is available and key members can attend.

- When a team meeting is held to discuss new information, consider distributing printed information before the meeting or instead of holding the meeting.

- Regularly held meetings (e.g., 4 o'clock on Tuesdays) are predictable and easier to schedule.

- Schedule meeting times early in the year for the whole school year or at least an entire semester (Rainforth & York-Barr, 1997); unnecessary meetings can simply be canceled.

- Meetings must be long enough for team members to address the essentials (e.g., build relationships, celebrate, organize, discuss, problem-solve, plan, process the discussion). Skilled core teams can accomplish these essentials in meetings as short as 20–30 minutes.

- Teaming procedures require high-energy thinking and interaction and can be exhausting, especially after a long school day. Twenty- or thirty-minute meetings often allow many issues to be adequately addressed (Thousand & Villa, 2000).

Teams initially may construct long agendas, thinking they can accomplish more than they actually can; over time, as team members learn to use the process and procedures and to work with each other, teams increase their productivity without increasing their meeting time (Thousand & Villa, 2000).

Where Will We Meet?

Choose a pleasant location that is quiet and has comfortable chairs, a seating arrangement that facilitates face-to-face communication, a table surface to ease notetaking and examination of materials, and refreshments to provide needed energy and create a collegial atmosphere. Classrooms that are free of students and nonparticipating staff sometimes are suitable, but other staff members or students should not be able to hear or observe the meeting. Staff members may need to post signs on meeting room doors to prevent unwelcome interruptions, turn off cell phones, and explore how to lower or eliminate the school intercom volume in the meeting room. Some teams prefer to use two team recorders: one to take notes on a worksheet or a laptop and another to take notes on a blackboard or on large newsprint that can be taped to the wall for all members to see. It is particularly advantageous to display the meeting notes on the wall or blackboard when the team is large; remarks are easily referred back to, memory need be relied on less, and progress made on action plans can be easily reviewed. A blackboard and chalk or an easel, markers, tape, and newsprint will need to be available in the meeting location.

How Will Our Process Be Suited to Family Members?

Teams that include family members need to ensure that their team meeting process works

Daniel's core team meets weekly, at 3:30 on Mondays, for 30 minutes. Team members "touch base" at least once daily and problem-solve issues that arise between meetings. Daniel's mom is sometimes part of the scheduled meetings, but usually her concerns/advice are expressed in the daily log that moves between Daniel's home and school. The two teaching assistants who work with Daniel (one in the morning and one in the afternoon) do not usually attend team meetings due to their schedules; however, they are asked about issues beforehand and are kept updated.

For meetings, the classroom and special education teachers target potential discussion topics, such as ways to build peer support, how to teach Daniel to use a daily schedule (with objectives for each activity), and ideas to improve team communication with and between the two assistants who work with Daniel. Daniel's related services specialists (i.e., occupational therapist, physical therapist, speech therapist, and vision teacher) give updates to the special education teacher twice a month during individual 15-minute meetings; this information is shared with Daniel's second-grade teacher, and the teacher's concerns that need the specialists' expertise are shared with the specialists.

The team sets an agenda for each meeting, uses an informal problem-solving approach, aims for consensus on all decisions, writes action plans for team members to implement, and makes and shares meeting minutes.

Figure 3.9.   How Daniel's team works.

not only for staff but also for students' families. Teachers may need to individualize their approach to suit family members' level of sophistication, comfort, and preferences. For example, parents may or may not want to fill a role during the meeting and other family members will participate initially by listening and only later by talking. Many barriers can hinder parents from being active participants in their child's education, such as economic constraints on their time, cultural discomfort, and negative school experiences as a child or as a parent. When team members communicate respect to parents for their knowledge about their child, parents can gain new confidence about their interactions with teams.

If parents are able to meet regularly with the core team, communication prior to each meeting allows a check on the time and place and a review of the agenda. When family members cannot meet regularly, pre-meeting communication is still valuable because it allows current family input to be considered; communicating with family members following the meeting helps keep the student's family linked to the team process (Figure 3.9).

During meetings, team members will find that the following practices communicate sensitivity to the concerns and perspectives of family members:

1. Treat team minutes as confidential and don't list specific details about students in the team minutes.

2. Teach and prompt teaming procedures by using simple guidelines for problem-solving methods. Hand out a printed list of team roles and their definitions, or post a large listing on the wall where you meet.

3. Strive to generate an action plan for implementing solutions.

4. Attend to interpersonal apects: Be aware of how your outward behavior in meetings communicates interest and disinterest. Avoid professional jargon, be a good listener, and monitor dominance by staff members. Seek the input of family members by posing open-ended questions one at a time and listening to their comments.

5. End meetings on time, but also be sure to review major outcomes and plans, thank team members, and establish a time for a follow-up meeting or contact.

6. When parents cannot attend meetings, include their input and then share the meeting decisions with them.

If there are cultural and/or language differences between the team's staff members and family members, staff should take steps to prevent those differences from becoming barriers:

- The composition of the student's team could be reconfigured to include a staff member of the same culture, one who speaks the family's native language, or one who is well-informed and can heighten the awareness of other staff members.

- Staff members could ask a family member to share information regularly on the student's home and culture to enlighten staff and assist them in relating to the family and student more meaningfully.

- Staff could seek in-service training on multicultural sensitivity, family-centered programs, and ways to provide services that are culturally responsive (Harry, Kalyanpur, & Day, 1999; Parett & Petch-Hogan, 2000; Turnbull, Rothstein-Fisch, Greenfield, & Quiroz, 2001).

PREPARING FOR AND CONDUCTING TEAM MEETINGS

A team's initial meetings make important impressions on members; therefore, the initial team leaders, organizers, and supporting administrators should strive to make the team's first meeting successful (Katzenbach & Smith, 1993). Initial meetings should focus on team-building activities such as redefining the school's mission into goals that are specific to the team, defining shared values, identifying ground rules, determining members' roles and responsibilities, and clarifying the teaming process members will use. Once teams have established these fundamentals, they are ready to tackle specific issues concerning students. Initial meetings and group interactions often determine team members' impressions of how successful a team will be. Whether all members attend (particularly anyone seen as being in charge or an organizer), show up on time, play by the estab-

lished rules of conduct, participate, and stay the entire session are good indicators of whether team members will view initial sessions as successes. Team members tend to focus on the person perceived as being in charge, observing their behavior more closely than their words and making predictions about the future of the team based on these impressions (Johnson & Johnson, 2000).

Conducting Meetings

Although meetings are conducted according to the team process members have designed, this design will be fairly similar for all collaborative teams that focus on students:

1. Team members take a few minutes to socialize with each other.
2. Someone (perhaps a predesignated facilitator) opens the meeting.
3. Team members assign roles, unless previously done.
4. The facilitator leads a discussion about agenda items (i.e., clarity, priority, and team time required to address each item).
5. The facilitator leads a review of action plan progress; the team celebrates successes.
6. Using the team process, the facilitator provides structure and helps members focus on each agenda item as time allows.
7. The timekeeper reminds the team of the meeting's schedule.
8. Members filling other roles play their part (e.g., jargon buster, notetaker, process observer, encourager).
9. Members work to process the functioning of the team.
10. For each agenda item that requires action and as time allows, team members discuss and identify the concern, share information, brainstorm ideas, problem-

solve and select potential solutions, and create an action plan.

11.   The facilitator brings the meeting to a close and summarizes outcomes.

12.   Notes taken by the recorder are disseminated to team members.

Preparation for the Next Meeting

At the conclusion of a team meeting, most members leave with a defined part in one or several action plans.

Student Snapshot

When Daniel's team members left the previous meeting, each had a copy of the meeting minutes, which listed "new issues and responsibilities." All had a part in implementing or assisting with Daniel's use of his communication switch, adjusting the wheelchair foot rests, using the slant board, or getting Daniel to participate in the "coat off and hung" routine. Each member came to the October 15th meeting prepared to report the status of these "old issues." Likewise, when they left that meeting, members had signed on for new responsibilities to carry out before the next meeting. (Review the team minutes from Daniel's meeting in Figure 3.10.)

When team members come to a meeting unprepared, team morale is low and team effectiveness suffers. A consistent lack of preparation by one or more team members is a clear indication of team trouble and requires team processing. Some questions to explore when determining the reasons why team members are unprepared include

•   Are team members overloaded with too many competing commitments?

•   Are team responsibilities distributed unevenly in their action plans?

•   Do action plans set forth workable and defined responsibilities?

•   Are those responsible for action plans in agreement with the plans (was consensus reached)?

•   Are team members in agreement on their team's general goals and purpose?

•   Do team members share and operate by a common set of values?

Clarifying Team Goals

Team goals can be either

•   Broad, overall goals (reflected in shared values and roles and responsibilities)

•   Immediate goals (reflected in ongoing action plans and current meeting agendas)

Awareness of and attention to both levels of team goals is evident in almost every step of conducting a team meeting. Teams need to be aware of their purpose and reasons for gathering. When overall and immediate goals are vague or undefined, several indicators of potential trouble will arise (Senge et al., 1994):

•   Repeated changes in direction during a meeting

•   Recurrent disagreement about team action

•   Concerns about the size or appropriateness of the goals or team's focus

•   Inaction and frustration

•   Extreme lack of confidence regarding team decisions and actions

When these problems arise, forging ahead with the agenda often simply results in more frustration. Instead, it helps to refocus on the team goals by asking, "What are we about in this school (e.g., team mission, shared values, or roles)?" or, "What are we doing now to move things forward for this student (e.g., clarify the boundaries of our immediate goals, reach consensus on their priority for the student and team, simplify or combine goals to workable size and complexity)?"

Student: _Daniel_   **Date:** _10/15/04_

Members present: _Nina James (classroom teacher), Cyndi Pitonyak (special educator), Nora Johnson (morning assistant), Sue Evans (occupational therapist), Danielle Seale (Daniel's mother), Georgia Allen (speech-language therapist)_

Members absent: _Jim Harris (afternoon assistant), Pita Thomas (physical therapist)_

Old issues and "to-do" list reviewed

1. *Communication switch works, and Daniel is using it (Georgia & Sue).*
2. *Wheelchair footrests have been adjusted (Danielle & Pita).*
3. *Slant board helps Daniel's visual attention to materials (Sue & Nina).*
4. *Daniel is making progress on coat on/off and hanging it up (partial participation) (Danielle, Sue, Nina, Cyndi, Nora).*

New issues and responsibilities (person)

1. *Regular recordings need to be made by peers for the CheapTalk communication device (Nina, Georgia).*
2. *Teach staff/peers how to offer choices: give meaningful options, position choices close, know what to say and how long to wait (Cyndi, Georgia).*
3. *Monitor peer assistance with equipment placement; peers should help only when Daniel is out of equipment (Pita, Sue, Nina).*
4. *Weekly peer support group will start next week (Cyndi with Joan Washington, counselor).*

Next meeting date: _11/19/04_   **Place:** _Nina's classroom_   **Time:** _2:45–3:45_

Figure 3.10. Team meeting minutes. (Contributed by Kenna Colley.)

GIVING AND RECEIVING INFORMATION

Team plans for action and those actions that are ultimately put into place are an integrated meld of known practices, ideas, "best guesses," and revisions from various members. The process for developing team plans requires team members to frequently turn to each other for information. Consistent with the concept of role release, defined in Chapter 1, team members (from the core team or the whole team) take turns stepping into the role of teacher when their knowledge and skills are required by other team members. Therapists (occupational, physical, and speech-language) often function as teachers or consultants to other team members.

Sometimes, the student may be put in the role of teaching team members. Less often, individuals from outside the team teach the team methods or information to address student or team concerns.

The occupational therapist has frequently provided demonstrations to staff members and to Daniel's mom on lifting and positioning in ways that encourage Daniel's active movement.

Melissa's team called on the regional autism specialist twice last year as a team consultant.

The following six guidelines strengthen the teaching role of team members (Rainforth & York-Barr, 1997, p. 287):

1. *Work as an equal, not an authority*—Remembering the cardinal rule of parity among

team members will make it easier for team members to learn from their fellow team members' instruction.

2. *Participate in school routines*—The information taught to team members must be integrated into school routines in order to benefit the students. The more familiar team member "teachers" are with students' routines, the more likely their knowledge will be applicable.

3. *Nurture relationships with fellow team members*—Learners who feel comfortable have increased motivation to learn and are more at ease asking for assistance or clarification.

4. *Expect to learn from others and acknowledge when you do*—When team members who teach are also willing to learn, all team members will gain.

5. *Use an experiential learning approach that allows learners to be successful*—Presenting general information or holding in-service sessions are generally less helpful to adult learners than providing actual demonstrations, opportunities to practice, and feedback.

6. *Ask for feedback about your consultation or teaching of others*—Team members can usually improve their teaching by asking for feedback from learners.

MAKING DECISIONS BY CONSENSUS

Making decisions by consensus means that team members agree on a solution; the group's collective opinion is determined after sharing and hearing each team member's respective viewpoints during an open discussion (Rainforth & York-Barr, 1997). Although it is best to reach consensus on important decisions, it is not always possible. Decisions can also be made in ways other than by consensus:

- Poll the group, or take a majority vote.

- Average the opinions of team members.

- A minority subset of the group makes the decision (e.g., the therapists combine to decide a therapy issue).

- A person who has authority over the group makes the decision (building administrator).

- A person viewed as an expert in a discipline of central concern (who may or may not be a member of the team) makes the decision.

None of these nonconsensus options for reaching a decision are without problems, especially lack of commitment to implementation (Rainforth & York-Barr, 1997) and the erosion of team values (e.g., all opinions are valued, we have equity with each other). If combined with open discussion, some of the previous methods can lead to consensus. For example, listening to an expert or a minority composition of the team and then batting around team reactions and viewpoints will often lead to agreement on an issue. Most experts on teaming agree that making decisions through consensus has more benefits than other decision-making approaches because 1) team members share a commitment to resolve the issue and implement a solution and 2) decisions made by consensus usually reflect a broader set of perspectives and talents.

Deciding How Consensus Is Reached

Teams need to determine how they will make decisions, when they should reach a decision by consensus, and when they should rely on one of the other methods of decision making. For example, team position on important issues can be explored by taking a vote verbally or in writing, but important issues should be decided by consensus (Senge et al., 1994). There are several ways that teams can test for consensus. First, they can use data as the basis for decisions. Second, the meeting facilitator can ask whether the entire team consents when several members appear to be in agreement. ("Millie and Johnna have made a case for involving Sam in the Activity Club; does anyone feel uncertain about this decision?"). Third, the facilitator can let the meeting time determine whether discussion should be shifted to consensus building. During team building sessions, discussion should be directed to these options for collaborative decision-making, and teams should identify their preference. If teams reflect on the pros and cons of using noncollaborative decision-making options, they are more likely to decide in favor of using one or more of the collaborative approaches.

Signs of Trouble

Senge et al. (1994) listed several indicators of potential trouble in reaching decisions:

- Team members cave in to others' opinions when no supporting data exist or are presented.

- Decisions are made by default, members don't respond, and silence is interpreted as agreement.

- One or several team members strong-arm the others into agreeing.

- One or several team members make the decision despite a lack of team agreement.

- Hasty reversion to "the majority rules" in order to avoid open disagreement.

When any of these indicators are present, a team discussion on decision-making is necessary. Some team facilitators might preface an open discussion with data on the team's behavior; an outsider would be asked to observe how the group makes decisions and give the team feedback.

TEAMING EFFECTIVELY ON-THE-FLY

Remember that teaming interactions occur within two basic formats: planned, sit-down meetings and on-the-fly interactions between team members. Figure 3.11 compares and contrasts the characteristics of each of these two formats. Because productive communication is the desired outcome during both

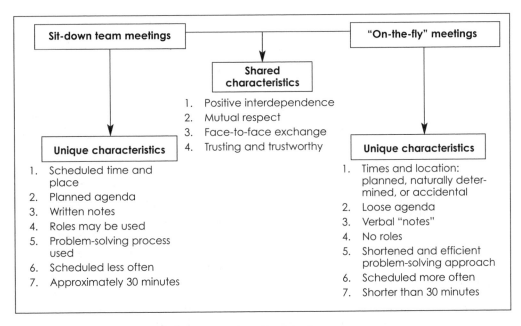

Figure 3.11. Shared and unique characteristics of teaming formats.

planned meetings and hurried, on-the-fly exchanges, person-to-person sensitivity must occur regardless of the format. Sensitivity encompasses mutual respect, positive interdependence, face-to-face exchange, and trust.

Planning Team Communication Between Meetings

Team members should plan how they will communicate with one another and with the student's family members between meetings. Strategies for communicating with family members often differ from those strategies used by team members and usually require input on what approaches would best suit that particular family. Parents should be given the opportunity to determine how they want to be involved with their son or daughter's program and to what degree (Salisbury & Dunst, 1997). The type and amount of involvement is likely to change over time in response to family and child circumstances.

Two general methods of communication exist: 1) written (including e-mail), which is delayed, and 2) person to person (including telephone), which is "live." Types of written communication from which team members can select include

- Informal notes in mailboxes
- Rotating notebook (notebook between home and school)
- Stationary notebook (notebook that remains in a safe, designated place in the classroom in which team members who come and go may leave comments if conversation is difficult)
- Team consultation logs (related services staff record their presence and general activity)
- Individual student progress notebooks or specific forms to record student progress (see Janney & Snell, 2004)
- Specific forms that reflect/preserve team decisions or describe team plans for mod-

ifying school work or supporting students' problem behavior (see Janney & Snell, 2000, 2004).

Beyond scheduled "sit-down" meeting times, team members need to find time to talk in person and check on student progress or team efforts to implement team plans. Options for on-the-fly interactions include obvious or creative times that may be 1) prearranged before or after school, 2) highly probable because work schedules place team members in the same location during school (e.g., lunchroom, planning time), or 3) spontaneous during or after school (Doyle, York-Barr, & Kronberg, 1996). Obviously, team members need to devise their own plans for keeping communication current in between meetings; although these communication plans must be taken seriously, they also need to be kept flexible and revised if they are inadequate.

Implementing Team Recommendations and Meeting on the Fly

On-the-fly teaming between team members in inclusive schools takes place frequently throughout the school day; the focus of these interactions typically relates to implementation of team decisions. These meetings

1. Are described by teachers as "checking back," "comparing notes," or "touching base" and entail ongoing communication about students' progress with (or without) an adaptation or accommodation (Snell & Janney, 2000, p. 483)

2. Involve validating the intermittent view of the special education teacher who comes and goes with the ongoing view of the general education teacher who stays with the class

3. Are meant to adapt or refine solutions emanating from meetings, not to design new solutions

4. Have a dynamic focus: "You just keep trying until you hit on something that looks right" (Snell & Janney, 2000, p. 483).

Regardless of the intensity of a student's needs, team members will communicate between team sit-down meetings during the school day regarding the implementation of their plans. For students who need extensive support, such as Sam, regular informal interchange between teachers (and Sam) is an essential supplement to weekly team meetings. These exchanges allow teachers to refine their plans by reducing, strengthening, or changing instructional and behavioral supports depending on Sam, the day's conditions, and team goals. For students whose instructional support program, once in place, is easily maintained and successful, meeting on-the-fly may become the primary collaboration strategy to keep the student's instruction working well.

If teaching assistants are part of the support plan for a student, they usually confer with classroom teachers about the student's progress during the day. They need to have regular, planned opportunities to interact with the special education teacher to whom they report. If predictable exchanges or trust between them are lacking, this link will be weak; however, when teams trust and consensus exist, this arrangement is very beneficial. Teaching assistants' views of a student's progress or problems may lack the sophistication of those of the professional team members; however, the views of the assistant are usually rich in valuable detail. Paraprofessionals may be asked to supplement their verbal descriptions of a student's progress or problems with clarifying demonstrations, ("Show me what Melanie did when you had her add") or may be directly observed ("Just continue, and I'll watch").

The paraprofessional should not be the sole link of communication between the classroom teacher and the special educaiton teacher. Sometimes this communication gap occurs when special educators are heavily booked in resource teaching, have too many

classroom teachers to link to, or choose to rely primarily on the paraprofessionals' perspective. When this happens the special education teacher 1) does not know what is happening in the general education classroom and cannot provide resource support that is relevant; 2) does not know if students transfer their skills back to the classroom; 3) lacks a picture of student behavior in the classroom; and 4) is not present to support students in the classroom or monitor the paraprofessional. The special educator must have both an ongoing direct line of communication with the classroom teachers and a predictable presence in the classroom (Snell, 2002; Snell & Macfarland, 2001).

REFLECTING ON THE TEAM PROCESS

When teams are in full motion, members should be involved in discussing and resolving agenda items and tuned into group process (teamwork). Sometimes, teams resist devoting a few minutes to team processing; many team members have found, however, that this time is critical to the maintenance of collaborative interactions (Johnson & Johnson, 2000; Rainforth & York-Barr, 1997; Thousand & Villa, 2000).

Processing often consists of posing simple questions about team functioning and progress:

1. Questions about prior team achievements and student progress should be asked at the beginning of meetings: What have we accomplished since our last meeting? Let's celebrate the successes! Let's reconsider the areas of little progress.

2. Questions regarding individual team member accountability may be asked when team members give and receive information and report back to each other: Is each team member held accountable for completing his or her work? Would more assistance or encouragement help?

3. Questions about ongoing interpersonal relationships and their effect on teamwork may be asked at any time during or near the end of a meeting: How are the relationships among us as team members? What can we do to reduce the tension? Let's discuss our teamwork skills.

4. Questions regarding progress being made in the current meeting may be asked anytime during or near the end of a meeting: Are we making progress on our tasks for this meeting? Do we need to make agenda adjustments? Is each team member held accountable for his or her participation?

5. Questions about accomplishments made in the current meeting should be asked at the end of the meeting: How well did we do as a team? As problem-solvers? In pulling together an action plan?

The processor plays a key role in helping the team members reflect on their interpersonal interactions and their actual work progress. When problems are identified in either area, the team should determine their course of action (e.g., set aside, discuss, collect observation data on group, problem-solve, develop an action plan). Chapter 7 describes team processing in more depth.

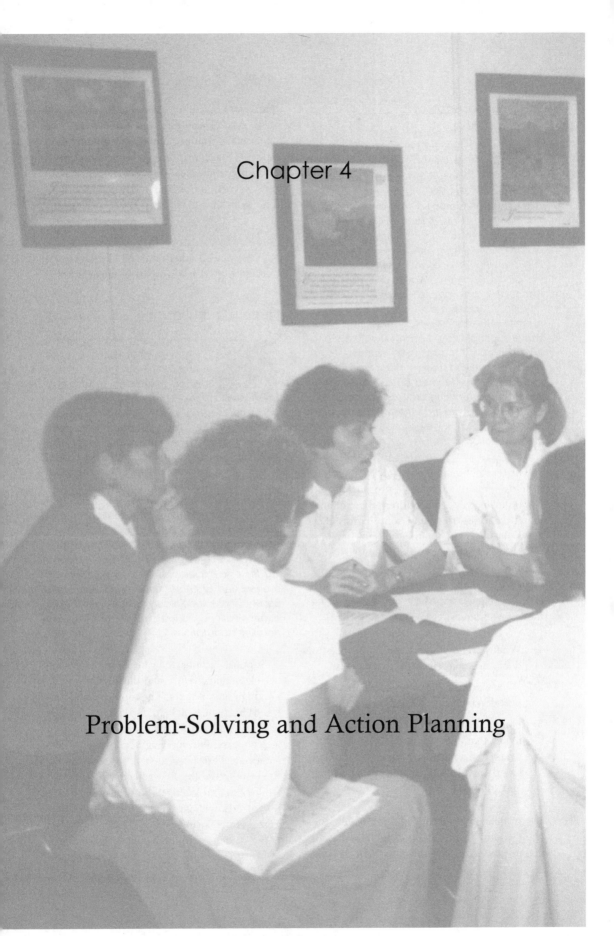

Chapter 4

Problem-Solving and Action Planning

Student Snapshot

Walter, an eleventh grader with mild mental retardation, attends general education classes. He is doing well in his English and geometry classes and understands much of the vocabulary and geometry concepts. In fact, Walter's teachers no longer have to adapt his guided practice or homework assignments. They can wait until they see what he does with them before making any adjustments. Walter also has many friends at school and blends in well socially.

Walter's success is due in part to the effectiveness of his team. Several years earlier, when Walter's school was preparing structurally and philosophically for a move to inclusion, team members received strong support from the administration. They learned basic teaming skills, developed a teaming process for interacting with each other around students, and learned how to problem solve—all skills essential for creating action plans.

The overall function of team meetings is to develop students' school programs and schedules in ways that address their educational priorities, to ensure some consistency in program implementation, and to problem-solve any relevant issues that arise. In the beginning of year, core teams should focus on the student's daily schedule and how the student participates across the day by answering the following questions:

1. What parts of the schedule can the student participate in with no supports?

2. What parts of the day will require supports? Which supports?

3. Do we need to plan routines or other activities that must be completed apart from peers (e.g., personal care, community-based instruction)? If so, when, where, and with what support?

For students with fewer support needs, the team would begin by sharing information about the student and the classroom. Special education teachers must learn the typical classroom procedures that the student will experience: routine activities, frequently used student tasks/responses, homework, texts and other materials, classroom teacher assistance, evaluation, rules, norms, and routines. The team then asks:

- Do we need to make any adaptations?

- Do we need other kinds of supports to increase academic and social participation?

Student Snapshot

Vanessa, a 13-year-old with a learning disability in reading and written language, is enrolled in a typical schedule of seventh-grade courses. She and other classmates have a study hall/tutorial session each day, which Vanessa uses to complete tests and assignments and to receive instruction and assistance in doing written assignments. Vanessa participates fully in a regular academic curriculum with supplementary curriculum adaptations in writing processes and study skills. Modifications to her instruction provide her with extra time, copies of teachers' notes or note-taking assistance, a laptop computer for taking notes, books on tape, oral testing for essay questions, and no penalties for spelling and grammar errors on in-class work. Beyond these special services and her IEP accommodations, Vanessa requires virtually no ongoing adaptations.

Support options may be different during the elementary years than during the middle and high school years. The support categories listed in Figure 4.1 have defined support options available to high school students in a school system in Virginia. Students like Vanessa, who have lower support needs, might only use the first category of support, while Sam and Walter, who have greater support needs, will experience most of the support options during their high school career.

For students with high support needs, such as Melanie and Daniel, the team could begin

1. **General education instruction with consultation and accommodation**—The student is enrolled only in general education classes. The special education teacher informs other teachers of the student's needs and monitors the student's progress in all classes. When accommodations are required (having tests read aloud) or instruction is needed (assistance with organizing a paper), the class teacher or the student makes arrangements with the special educator to provide these services. The special education teacher regularly communicates in person with the classroom teacher.

2. **Support from a teaching assistant in one or more general education classes**—The student may need a teaching assistant for help with accommodations (e.g., reading or note taking, completing projects in vocational or elective classes). The classroom teacher and the assistant consult with the special education teacher to monitor the student's progress.

3. **Special education instruction in the content of one or more general education classes (pull-in support) and/or a general education tutorial**—General and special education teachers collaborate within the regular classroom to ensure that the student is successful in content classes. The nature of these collaborative relationships vary depending on the staff involved but are more intense than the first two levels. These students may be working on adapted curricula (e.g., different goals, materials) or on an unmodified class curricula with accommodations as needed.

4. **Special education instruction in a pull-out setting**—A few students request or require instruction in a small class or in a one-to-one setting for one or more periods during the school day. This support also may be provided as needed throughout the day. One or more places in the building are designated for this category of support including the study hall, library, or another quiet, private area. Students who have emotional or behavioral problems often use this setting as a "safe zone." This category of instruction can be used to provide individualized reading instruction, math tutorials, functional academics, consumer math, or instructional settings for students whose behavior precludes participation in general education classes.

5. **Special education instruction in the community**—Students with more significant disabilities receive community-based and vocational instruction in the local community for part or all of their school day. This category of instruction should increase as the student reaches his or her senior year. Typically, these students receive an additional 2–3 years of postgraduate schooling that is conducted primarily in the community.

Figure 4.1. Levels of support provided in secondary school settings. (Contributed by Johnna Elliott.)

with these same steps (understand the student, assess the classroom procedures) and then develop the student's program by creating a matrix of IEP objectives plotted against the classroom schedule of activities, times, and locations (see Figure 4.2). Objectives that can be addressed during each time block are checked; any needed support may also be indicated in each block.

Student Snapshot

Melanie's learning needs are clustered in communication, independence building, math, and language arts. By constructing a matrix of Melanie's class schedule with her IEP objectives, her team planned ways to integrate her objectives into her daily schedule. For example, at lunchtime, Melanie goes with her class and works on communication and functional objectives: using pointing and yes/no to answer questions and indicate food choices, using a picture schedule to make the transition to and from lunch, following the cafeteria routine, and watching for cues from peers.

For students with high support needs, a detailed matrix plus observations of the student across the day allow team members to plan when and how that student's priority objectives can be embedded within ongoing class activities and routines. For students who require more supports, team discussions will center on four questions, whereas for stu-

Program Planning Matrix

Student: _Melanie_   Class: _Ms. Ramirez_   Date: _September 2004_

IEP objective	Morning class schedule								
	Arrival	Journal	Reading	Language arts	Break	Spelling	Math	Shared reading	Lunch
Communication									
1. Use pictures/devices to express needs, ask questions, initiate, make choices, and indicate yes or no	x	x	x	x	x	x	x		x
2. Relate recent events in two- or three-word sentences		x	x	x					
Functional skills									
1. Use picture schedule to make transitions	x	x	x	x	x	x	x	x	x
2. Participate in arrival/ departure and lunch- room routines	x				x				x
3. Follow task directions from cues				x	x	x			
4. Participate in school/ classroom jobs	x								
Math									
1. Identify numbers 0–1,000							x		
2. Use a number line for greater than, less than							x		
3. Tell time to the minute (with face and digital clocks)	x						x		
Language arts									
1. Answer comprehension questions about novels			x	x					
2. Participate in computer journal writing		x							
3. Read, write, and spell functional vocabulary words		x		x	x				
4. Use inventive spelling for class assignments		x		x	x				

Figure 4.2. Matrix of IEP objectives plotted against the morning classroom schedule.

dents with fewer support needs, the team problem-solving will center primarily on the last two questions:

1. How do we mesh instruction of these functional goals with the classroom schedule and curriculum?

2. Do we need an extra pair of hands to increase academic and social participation?

3. Do we need to make adaptations (e.g., curricular, instructional, alternative)?

4. Do we need other kinds of supports to increase academic and social participation?

The team then works to problem-solve any needed adaptations and to schedule support to match the student's needs. The adaptation planning process is addressed in detail in another book in this series, *Modifying Schoolwork* (Janney & Snell, 2004).

PROBLEM-SOLVING METHODS

Observations of collaborative teams in elementary schools revealed that teachers' thinking processes follow a cycle of steps sim-

ilar to those of the problem-solving process in Figure 4.3; however, the teachers cycled repeatedly through the steps as they fashioned, tried out, and refined solutions to each student concern over time (Snell & Janney, 2000). The basic process involved repeating a multiple-step cycle to reach and refine a solution:

- Identify concerns (define the problem).
- Watch and talk (gather and share information pertinent to the problem).
- Throw out ideas (brainstorm).

Interpersonal considerations	Step	Procedural considerations
• Establish a climate of trust. • Share relevant information.	**Step 1. Identify the problem**	• Focus on the problem, not the solution. • Reach agreement on the problem.
• Encourage input from all parties. • Defer judgment about the solutions. • Be supportive rather than attacking.	**Step 2. Brainstorm possible solutions**	• Generate as many alternative solutions as possible.
• Evaluate the solutions, not people. • Elicit input from all parties. • Be accepting of differences.	**Step 3. Evaluate the possible solutions**	• Identify criteria by which the solutions are judged.
• Ascertain that all participants feel some ownership of the trial solution.	**Step 4. Choose a solution**	• Modify and combine the solutions as needed. • Select a trial solution.
• Reach a decision by consensus.	**Step 5. Write an action plan**	• Determine what materials (if any) will be needed. • Assign responsibility for the specific steps. • Set a timeline. • Establish measurement procedures. • Schedule a follow-up meeting.

Figure 4.3. Elements of problem solving: Interpersonal and procedural considerations. (From Beck, R. [Ed.]. [1997]. *PROJECT RIDE: Responding to individualized differences in education.* Longmont, CO: Sopris West; adapted by permission.)

- Say whether each idea sounds good or won't work (evaluating the ideas and finding the best).

- Give the best idea a shot (trying out the solution).

- Watch and talk more (evaluating the solution, refining it, and beginning the cycle again).

To problem-solve a solution, teachers would focus on a problem, observe, talk, brainstorm, decide what to try, and try it out. To reach "real" solutions, they repeated this process, restating the problem as the solution was refined or as the problem changed. The process was not "cut and dried."

Problem solving methods range from simple to complex. The five steps in Figure 4.3 are simple, but the Osborn-Parnes Creative Problem-Solving Process (CPS; see Figure 4.4) is a six-step method with divergent/convergent thinking at each step (Giangeco, Cloninger, Dennis, & Edelman, 1994). Using the generic steps of problem solving as a framework, the following sections provide guidelines for solving concerns teams have about students.

Step 1
Identify the Problem

 Before teams search for solutions, they need to take time to explore, define, and reach agreement on the problem. In inclusive elementary schools, students' concerns were found to fall into one of three categories (Snell & Janney, 2000):

1. *Student goals and abilities:* "What is this student capable of learning?" "What is reasonable, functional, and important to teach this student?" and, "Where shall we begin instruction?"

2. *Participation in instructional activities and routines:* "How will this student take part in class activities and school routines with classmates?" "How will this student learn his or her IEP objectives in this class?"

3. *Classroom community and belonging:* "How can we improve this student's membership in the class?" "How can we give him or her unobtrusive support to interact with peers?" "How can we reduce 'special treatment'?"

These same categories of problems may exist at middle- and high-school levels; however, more research is needed to determine whether additional categories arise with older students or with students who have fewer support needs than those in the study. Problem categories can be used to help identify the problems that need attention first.

Student Snapshot

 Every spring, Walter's whole team meets to address his IEP, class schedule for the following year, and transition plans. At this time, the team also confronts its concerns regarding Walter's goals and abilities. In addition, the team establishes directions that will be followed by the core team in the coming year. Clearing up these issues beforehand allows the core team to focus on Walter's meaningful participation in classes. For example, during a lunch meeting, Walter's math and special education teachers can identify and problem-solve three participation issues: adapting an upcoming assignment, simplifying next week's instructional worksheets, and keeping Walter's attention focused.

To identify a problem to be resolved, a team needs to agree on what issues are problems; on what problems need attention immediately; and on a specific statement describing the problems. Reaching agreement in these areas can be accomplished in several ways:

- *Take a divergent/convergent approach*—List all of the visible problems and activities of concern. Then, converge on one problem or a combination of problems. Define or

Stage 1: Objective-finding ("mess" finding)
Divergent:
- List broad objectives or goals of a program; imagine potential challenges (without judgment, explanation, or discussion).

Convergent
- Converge on the best way to state the objective; select the best way to state the challenge.

Stage 2: Fact finding
Divergent:
- List as many facts as possible regarding the objective/challenge: facts might concern the student's needs or the class or activity.
- Present facts without explanation, judgment, or discussion in 5–8 minutes:
  Facts can include team members' feelings.
  Facts include what people believe to be true about the challenge situation.
  Facts are recorded and saved for later use (during idea finding).

Convergent:
- Select a subset of relevant facts to assist problem-finding in the next stage.

Stage 3: Problem finding
Divergent:
- Clarify the challenge or problem by considering different ways of viewing it.
- "In what ways might we...?" Repeat the question until the team feels confident that it has teased out the real issue.

Convergent
- Select one of the new challenge statements that the team agrees it most wants to solve.
- Prompt consensus by asking team members questions such as
  Which of these challenges do we most desperately want to accomplish or solve?
  If we could could resolve one problem for the student, what would it be?

Stage 4: Idea finding
Divergent:
- Ideas are potential solutions to the challenge statements from Stage 3.
- Ideas emerge through brainstorming (i.e., a divergent process to stretch beyond the obvious): short time periods; people speak quickly in short phrases, not sentences; ideas are recorded quickly; aim for quantity; use free-wheeling or round robin.
- Use techniques and "idea joggers" to jar ideas loose:
  Forced relationships/rearrange: Combine two ideas/objects with little apparent relationship in some way to generate a new idea to solve a problem.
  Synectics: Make the strange familiar and the familiar strange so things can be seen in new ways (facts about student and challenges).
  Make some fact about the situation smaller or bigger, rearrange it, eliminate it, reverse or turn it upside down or inside out.
  Hitch-hiking effect: Build new ideas on ideas of another.

Convergent
- Separate out the ideas with the most promise and appeal.

Stage 5: Solution finding
Divergent
- List criteria or ways to evaluate the ideas generated.

Convergent
- Focus on each idea and evaluate it by each criterion; asking whether it meets or fails the criterion. Eliminate all but those judged as acceptable to the team. Combine those ideas to create the solution(s).

Stage 6: Acceptance finding
Divergent
- Find ways to implement the ideas by asking the following questions: who, what, where, when, why, and how?

Convergent
- Develop a plan of action that delineates actions to be taken, by whom, and when.

Figure 4.4. Stages of the Osborn-Parnes Creative Problem-Solving Process. (From Giangreco, M.F., Cloninger, C.J., Dennis, R.E., & Edelman, S.W. [1994]. Problem-solving methods to facilitate inclusive education. In J.S. Thousand, R.A. Villa, & A.I. Nevin [Eds.], *Creativity and collaborative learning: A practical guide to empowering students and teachers* [pp. 321–346]. Baltimore: Paul H. Brookes Publishing Co.; adapted by permission.)

restate the problems to reflect the team's view.

- *Prioritizing*—List an array of concerns and rank them from high to moderate to low in an effort to identify the top one or two to resolve.

- *Re-write the problem in observable language*— Write down team members' views of the problem; without discussing solutions, identify and redefine imprecise terms, and seek to condense and identify the problem focus the group agrees on.

- *Categorizing*—Determine the type or category of problem (e.g., goal/ability, participation, membership) and decide whether other types of problems exist in the same category. Add these to the problem statement to fully define the concern.

- *Apply consensus-reaching methods*—Compare the identified problems with actual student data; when there seems to be some agreement, ask the team if everyone feels comfortable addressing the problem. Or, set a time limit for discussion, then ask for consensus.

The step of clarifying the problem on which to focus was referred to as "problem-finding" by Giangreco (1993) and Isaksen and Parnes (1992). Most agree that this step must not be skipped or hurried or the resultant problem-solving efforts might be misguided. While many start problem-solving by identifying the problem, problem-finding is the third step in the Osborne-Parnes CPS Process that teachers have used on collaborative teams in inclusive programs (see Figure 4.4). Giangreco and Isaksen and Parnes view problem-finding as a two-phase, divergent/convergent process that involves expanding the problem list prior to defining or limiting it. The expanded list can serve as a worksheet for the team and may help shift the focus from the original problem to one that is more relevant to the student or situation, is of higher priority, is more comprehensive or encompasses earlier problems, or needs to be resolved first.

Student Snapshot

 At the beginning of fourth grade, Melanie's behavior was at its worst. Her team figured that it was due to the big transition of returning to school after summer break. They had a team-generated IEP and good plans for involving her in class activities, but they did not have plans to help Melanie with the tantrums she had whenever she was asked to work with others in a group. After last year's success, the team had thought that Melanie's tantrums were gone forever. The team met after 3 days of school to address the new concerns. Ms. Ramirez was concerned that Melanie was not staying with the group for more than a few minutes. Melanie's instructional assistant, Ms. Johnson, was distressed that Melanie didn't interact with her peers and refused to do the math problems she'd enjoyed last spring. Ms. Pitonyak and Melanie's speech-language pathologist noticed that Melanie was communicating (using words, pictures, or gestures) when she got upset. Beneath the first concern of disruptive tantrums at group time, Ms. Pitonyak wrote a list of specific problems. When the team prioritized the problems in terms of what to address first, it became clear that communication was the most needed and would allow them to address the rest.

Step 2
Brainstorm Possible Solutions

 Brainstorming involves generating as many alternative or potential solutions as possible regarding the challenge or problem on which a team is focusing. The three most commonly used approaches tend to operate best when team members follow the basic rules of brainstorming (Johnson & Johnson, 2000; see Figure 4.5). As illustrated in Figure 4.6, the most frequent mistake people make during brainstorming—evaluating ideas while generating ideas—is the biggest hindrance to creativity.

Brainstorming approaches that are not difficult to use include the following:

---

1. No negative reactions or comments are allowed.
2. Freewheeling is welcomed; save criticism for later.
3. Withhold discussion and judgment.
4. Focus on quantity, not quality.
5. Set a short time limit; generate ideas quickly.
6. Assign a recorder who writes fast and translates ideas into phrases or key words.

Figure 4.5. Rules for brainstorming. (From David W. Johnson & Frank P. Johnson, Joining Together: Group Theory And Group Skills, 6/e. Published by Allyn and Bacon, MA. Copyright © 2003 by Pearson Education. Adapted by permission of the publisher.)

• *Freewheeling*—Team members state their ideas as quickly as possible without taking turns. Ideas stimulate other ideas (i.e., chaining, piggy-backing, or springboarding). This method promotes the most spontaneity and enthusiasm and is the easiest to use; however, it may become too lively for the recorder to write down all of the ideas, and less assertive members may be hesitant to contribute.

• *Round robin*—Team members take turns stating their ideas in an around-the-circle fashion. If a team member cannot contribute an idea within a few seconds, that member passes, and the next person in the circle takes a turn. Brainstorming concludes once each consecutive participant has passed. This method is most useful when some team members dominate and others are hesitant to participate.

• *Slip method*—Team members write out each of their ideas on separate slips of paper and pass them to the recorder. The ideas are then mixed and written on newsprint for the entire team to see. Although this method is useful when the problem is controversial, the process is slower than the other two methods.

• *Brainwriting*—Similar to slip method, team members write several ideas on a page; place it in a pile in the middle of the team table; select another member's list, read it, and add their own ideas; and then repeat the process until no new ideas result (Friend & Cook, 2003). This approach promotes creative spring-boarding but is slower than the first two methods.

Giangreco, Cloninger, Dennis, and Edelman (1994) described additional approaches for generating ideas during brainstorming. These approaches are used within the structure provided by freewheeling, round robin, or the slip method to help teams lengthen their list of ideas (diverge) and separate out those that are most promising (converge).

INSPIRED BY ALEX OSBORN

© 1999 MICHAEL F. GIANGRECO. ILLUSTRATION BY KEVIN RUELLE

GENERATING AND EVALUATING IDEAS SIMULTANEOUSLY IS LIKE TRYING TO RIDE A BIKE BY PEDALING WITH THE BRAKES ON.

Figure 4.6. The biggest hindrance to successful brainstorming. (From Giangreco, M.F. (1999). *Flying by the seat of your pants: More absurdities and realities of special education* [p. 76]. Minnetonka, MN: Peytral Publications.

1. *Diverge to generate direct ideas*—Direct ideas result from comparing the two lists generated earlier regarding a given problem

Facts about Walter and his needs (partial list)	Facts about the class/activity (partial list)
• He is talented in art. • His English objective is to compose brief journal entries and essays. • He needs practice locating information in reference sources.	• Assignment is to learn and tell about a famous mathematician. • Assignment is due in 2 weeks. • Assignment should be on paper.

Question: What about Walter's art skills and his English needs (from the list of facts about Walter) relate to the assignment on a mathematician biography?

Answer: Walter could complete drawings for his report about the selected mathematician and supplement the drawings with shorter written remarks.

Figure 4.7. Idea finding through a divergent/convergent process: Comparison of facts about the student with facts about the class or activity.

(e.g., facts about the student and the student's need and facts about the class/activity). Team members can seek connections between the two lists through a comparison of facts (see Figure 4.7), revealing "naturally occurring opportunities for meaningful inclusion" that can be taken advantage of without making major changes in routine (Giangreco, Cloninger, et al., 1994).

2. *Diverge to generate indirect ideas*—Indirect ideas result from the team's use of "idea-stimulators." The team's creativity facilitates the discovery of additional solutions by "jogging ideas loose," seeing things differently, building on ideas, and combining ideas (Giangreco, Cloninger, et al., 1994; Parnes, 1992). Sometimes the wildest ideas lead to the discovery of another unique but practical idea that would have otherwise not been found.

3. *Converge to find the most promising ideas*—Teams follow their idea-finding session by converging on the most interesting, promising, or intriguing ideas (Isaksen & Parnes, 1992). The recorder might move the group through each generated idea and ask, "Keep for now (circle) or toss (cross out)?" This activity is not the same as comparing ideas against team criteria; it simply helps narrow the list. Team

members may need to offer brief explanations of ideas that were not fully explained during the divergent brainstorming and reword them for clarity. Some ideas may be combined. All ideas that are circled for further exploration are considered during the evaluation of possible solutions.

Brainstorming takes time and cannot be combined with selecting a solution. Logistical barriers—not enough time, key team members missing, pressure to act—have been shown to interfere with this step. When these barriers occur, teams select simple, quick, satisfactory "solutions," rather than work to seek optimal solutions that come from Steps 2 (brainstorming) and 3 (evaluate possible solutions) or the careful weighing of alternative solutions (Snell & Janney, 2000).

Step 3
Evaluate the
Possible Solutions

Evaluating the possible solutions helps teams narrow their ideas down to those that will make the best solution. A study of teachers' problem solving in inclusive classrooms found that teams naturally evaluated solutions when they allowed time for it. A special educator described it this way:

> You just keep talking about it until you arrive at the next idea. I think that [what] we've experienced in our little round table discussions [is that] one person will say, "I don't think that will work, but if you take that idea and do a little something different to it, it might work." (Snell & Janney, 2000, p. 485)

When you think back on how you have decided what solution has the best chance of working, you can recall some common sense criteria most of us automatically apply:

- *Feasibility*—"That's sounds possible" versus "That's not feasible in my class!"

- *Team consensus*—"I think his parents would really approve" versus "That won't work for his parents."

- *Peer approval, nonstigmatizing*—"That's something that the kids would help with" versus "The kids will laugh."

- *Cost*—"We have all the materials we need to use that idea" versus "Where will we get the money to pay for the materials, the staff time, and so forth?"

As with most of the problem-solving steps, evaluation involves a divergent and a convergent phase. In the divergent phase, team members generate the criteria they will use to evaluate their ideas. In the convergent phase, team members systematically compare each idea against the criteria and judge its acceptability; then, they pull the "winning" ideas together into a solution. Teams who work together for a while often develop some standard criteria that match their shared values and the students they support (see Figure 4.8). However, even these teams can benefit from reviewing their criteria list for possible omissions before evaluating potential solutions. Using a criteria worksheet can help teams be more systematic at this stage of problem solving. Figure 4.9 shows a form teams have found useful for evaluating their ideas according to their criteria (Giangreco, Cloninger, et al. 1994).

Applying criteria to potential solutions:
Judging if an idea or potential accommodation is a good one

____ 1 Is it "doable" and reasonable?
____ 2. Is it time-effective?
____ 3. Does it promote school/community access?
____ 4. Does it provide opportunities to interact with peers?
____ 5. Does it provide opportunities to communicate?
____ 6. Is it cost effective?
____ 7. Is it safe?
____ 8. Is it team generated?
____ 9. Is it related to specific classroom demands?
____ 10. Does it empower, rather than humiliate, the student?
____ 11. Is it student-validated or generated?
____ 12. Does it meet class requirements?
____ 13. Does it incorporate best practices?
____ 14. Other: _____
____ 15. Other: _____

Figure 4.8. Criteria for deciding if an idea is a good one. (From Giangreco, M.F., Cloninger, C.J., Dennis, R.E., & Edelman, S.W. [1994]. Problem-solving methods to facilitate inclusive education. In J.S. Thousand, R.A. Villa, & A.I. Nevin [Eds.], *Creativity and collaborative learning: A practical guide to empowering students and teachers* [pp. 321–346]. Baltimore: Paul H. Brookes Publishing Co.; adapted by permission.)

Solution finding	Criteria				
Potential solutions	Addresses student need	Neutral or positive for students without disabilities	Likely to support valued life outcomes	Perceived as usable by users (e.g., teacher, student, parent)	Other
1.					
2.					
3.					
4.					
5.					
6.					
7.					
8.					
9.					
10.					
11.					
12.					

Figure 4.9. Solution-finding worksheet: Evaluating ideas and finding solutions. (From Giangreco, M.F., Cloninger, C.J., Dennis, R.E., & Edelman, S.W. [1994]. Problem-solving methods to facilitate inclusive education. In J.S. Thousand, R.A. Villa, & A.I. Nevin [Eds.], *Creativity and collaborative learning: A practical guide to empowering students and teachers* [pp. 321–346]. Baltimore: Paul H. Brookes Publishing Co.; adapted by permission.)

Step 4
Choose a Solution

Although team members select the "best bet" when they choose a solution, the solution should be viewed as only a tentative one until it proves workable. Also, teams may find several "winning" solutions that can be combined into a more comprehensive answer to the problem. When teams have time to address several problems in a session, multiple solutions will be chosen. The agenda needs to allot enough time for team members to examine the solutions to each problem and reach agreements by consensus (e.g., a quick check by the group facilitator, "Is everyone okay with this?"). Attaining team consensus must not be sacrificed due to a lack of time, particularly if the team members not in agreement with the solution are those who will be the primary implementers of it. Sometimes, it may be better for teams to move forward with some solutions and delay others until agreement can be reached.

Student Snapshot

Once Melanie's team decided to focus on Melanie's communication, they agreed to gather one day of antecedent-behavior-consequence (ABC) observations, noting each tantrum instance and the antecedent (e.g., teacher calls for

small group time) and what happens following the tantrum (e.g., Melanie left the group and worked alone at her desk). They knew that these observations would help refine the solution by confirming what triggered and what maintained Melanie's tantrums. The next day when they shared their examples and recalled examples from earlier days, it became clear that getting out of disliked activities was the primary function of tantrums. This allowed the team to confidently agree and refine their solutions even further, and everyone was convinced of the importance of promoting Melanie's communication.

Step 5
Write an Action Plan

Teams need to build enough time into their agendas to complete action plans. The primary elements of an action plan are

- *Issue*—What is the issue on which we need to take action?

- *Action*—What action do we agree to take to resolve this issue?

- *Who is responsible*—Who will help develop or implement this action?

- *By when*—When will the planned action be implemented?

Teams are usually motivated by their results at this point in a session, and, if everyone has been participating, it usually is easy to reach consensus on each element planned for the issues addressed. Consensus at this point of problem-solving is just as important as at any other point because team members are deciding how their ideas or solutions will be implemented.

Sometimes, teams will identify preparatory steps that need to be undertaken before an action plan can be fully developed or implemented (e.g., checking with student, peers, or parents; assessment; preparation of materials). This step includes checking with team members or outsiders who were absent when the plan was discussed—but are nonetheless critical participants—so the plan reflects team consensus.

Step 6
Evaluate the Plan and Make Needed Changes

Once an action plan is made, the team will schedule a follow-up meeting to evaluate its implementation, unless regular core team meetings are already in place. Often, team members repeatedly "touch base" with each other as they implement the plan and observe its effects, sometimes even making quick refinements without drawing the team back together again (Snell & Janney, 2000). These on-the-fly interactions help the plan get going more smoothly and allow staff to coordinate their efforts during initial implementation. Face-to-face discussion at team meetings allows teams to develop excellent plans, but it is usually through actual "field-tests" and conversations on location that planned solutions can be refined through use.

PROBLEM-SOLVING APPROACHES USED BY ADULT TEAMS

This section and the following one present brief overviews of problem-solving approaches used either primarily by adult teams or by student teams with adult facilitation. Several of these approaches have evidence supporting their positive effect on student progress.

Osborn-Parnes Creative Problem-Solving Approach

The Osborn-Parnes CPS Process, introduced in Figure 4.4, is designed to take 30 minutes when used by a highly experienced team. Initial team exchange considers what the "mess" is and what problems constitute the mess (e.g., the famous mathematicians assignment requires many skills that Walter has not demonstrated on his own; Stage 1). Next, the team lists and describes relevant information about the student, the task, and the class and then circles the facts that relate most to Walter and the mess (e.g., Walter's IEP objectives in writing or language arts, due date, assignment requirements, Walter's interests, available support; Stage 2). Third, the team returns to the mess and generates a listing of the many related challenges or problems that are relevant (e.g., the assignment needs be adapted so that Walter can actively participate in all steps and learn some things that are relevant to his IEP). This problem is then rephrased as a question to be answered (e.g., In what ways might we modify the geometry assignment so Walter can actively participate in all steps and learn some things relevant to his IEP? Stage 3).

Once a concern has been identified and information has been shared that is pertinent to the concern, teams shift to the task of creating a solution (Stage 4). Next, team members create, review, or revise a list of criteria against which they judge each generated idea (Stage 5). Teams that have time limitations might shorten this step by using previously set criteria. Teams will use both sit-down meetings and on-the-fly meetings to problem-solve and may need to truncate the on-the-fly process due to time limitations and the pressure to "do something" (Snell & Janney, 2000, p. 487). During sit-down meetings, teams may spend additional time fashioning the solution as they discuss strategies for gaining team consensus (from absent team members and the student) on the solution and plan the actions that need to be taken, by whom, and when.

A specific form is only used during the last stage. For the other stages, teams use large pieces of paper with the step number and title at the top in large letters. These pieces of paper are taped to the wall, or the blackboard is used instead of the paper. One recorder writes the team contributions on these large pieces of paper for all team members to see (teams often need to refer back to their comments as they move through the steps), while a second recorder documents the details of the action plan on the issue-action planning form.

Get Some Help from SAM

The Get Some Help from SAM approach is a shorter version of the six-stage CPS method previously described, with SAM (not an acronym) simply symbolizing a friend who might help (Giangreco, Cloninger, et al. 1994). Very experienced teams can apply this method in 15 minutes, but it is easier to use when a team has 20–30 minutes. This approach is easy to learn and helpful to adult teams first applying problem-solving steps (particularly when accompanied by guiding worksheets). SAM frames the problem-solving around the target student's IEP objectives (Giangreco, Cloninger, et al. 1994). This approach has been used both by teams of staff and parents and by teams of students. When peers are very familiar with the target student, this approach can work well. The teacher directs peers to a cluster of relevant goals for the target student and then asks them to consider these goals while seeking solutions to a problem.

Teams begin with a problem stated as follows: "In what ways might we address the educational needs of (student) in (class/activity)?" Next, they move through the four steps in the SAM process:

- *Fact finding*—List facts about the student and the student's needs; list facts about the class or activity.

- *Idea finding*—Generate direct and indirect ideas through brainstorming.

- *Solution finding*—Evaluate each idea against the team's criteria.

- *Acceptance finding*—Write actions plans that address the what, who, where, how, and when.

When teams use the SAM approach to problem-solve, it is particularly helpful to write notes on large newsprint organized to match

Issue-Action Planning Form

Student/team/group: _Walter_   Date: _11/16/04_

Team members present: _Chris Burton, Arlene Brown_

Issue	Planned action	Person(s) responsible	By when
Assignment on famous mathematicians	1. Walter will listen to Joan (teacher assistant) read biographical information about the mathematician. 2. He will tell aloud what he has gotten out of the information while Joan writes it down. 3. He'll type it into the computer and print it. 4. He'll use his art skills to illustrate the one-paragraph report.	Chris will write out, review with Joan, and monitor. Joan will implement.	11/18
Next week's lessons	Chris will prepare his worksheets by eliminating all the algebraic equation problems.	Chris	11/17
Behavior checklist to self-monitor	No change; Walter will use his checklist to monitor his attending and talkouts. Teachers will examine the checklist at the end of each class and comment to Walter.	All	11/17 to 11/23

Figure 4.10. Issue-action planning form for Walter in geometry.

the form originated by Giangreco, Clonginger, et al. (1994, pp. 336–337; see Figures 4.9 and 4.10) in addition to recording written notes on a smaller form to preserve meeting deliberation and results.

Issue/Action Planning

The success of the issue/action planning approach (see Figure 4.10) rests on the participants being skilled collaborators and knowing the classroom situation and student well. The approach involves the key steps of identifying the problem, brainstorming, reaching agreement on the solution, and translating the solution into a format of 1) issue (problem), 2) action (solution), 3) completed by whom (team members involved), and 4) by when (proposed date for implementation).

Unified Plans of Support

Several studies have documented the effectiveness of teachers using individualized Unified Plans of Support (UPS) to guide the team planning and ongoing support of elementary children either at risk for disability or with severe disabilities enrolled in general education classrooms (Hunt, Doering, Hirose-Hatae, Maier, & Goetz, 2001; Hunt, Soto, Maier, & Doering, 2003). The procedure has been applied in a number of urban elementary schools where students with disabilities were included with peers in general education classrooms. Hunt and her colleagues (2003) examined the impact of a collaborative teaming process on six students included in two fourth-grade classrooms. Two teams in different schools developed and implemented individualized UPS for several students, some of

Student	Participation and interaction	Reading	Writing	Math
Francisco *fourth grade*	Adults will prompt Francisco to ask a peer for assistance by signing ASK A FRIEND. The inclusion support teacher will make a photograph conversation book for Francisco that will assist him to initiate and maintain interactions with peers. Francisco and his lunch buddies, who will be chosen on a weekly basis, will walk from class to the cafeteria and will eat together (without instructional assistant support).	Francisco's parents will find a reading tutor to work with him two times a week after school. Francisco will be given ability-level books to read with a peer during reading time and to read with his family at home.	Francisco will be given a Polaroid camera to photograph things of interest and use the pictures as writing prompts with peer support during writing centers.	With a peer and with adult support, Francisco will practice money recognition, time telling, and simple addition during math time. Francisco will use computer math programs with a peer to practice simple math skills.
Alina *fourth grade*	Alina will be encouraged to ask a friend for help whenever she needs it. Alina will be encouraged to tell the teacher when she does not understand something during a large group lesson.	Alina will work with a trained peer partner using Hooked on Phonics to practice reading skills on a regular basis. Alina will frequently take a book home to read with her sisters.	Alina will be taught to use both *spell check* and *grammar check* when using word processing programs.	Alina will use multiplication flash cards with a classmate to practice the multiplication tables. A classmate will go over written math directions when Alina needs help on math worksheets.

Figure 4.11. A sample of items for the United Plans of Support for Francisco (a child with severe disabilities) and Alina (a child at risk for a disability). (From: "Collaborative Teaming to support students at risk and students with severe disabilities in general education classrooms" by P. Hoto, G. Soto, J. Maier, and K. Doering. Exceptional Children Vol. 69 #3 spring 2003, page 319, 220–221. The Council for Exceptional Children, Copyright 1986, 2002. Adapted with permission.)

whom were considered at risk for disabilities and others who had severe disabilities. The team-generated plan for each student identified academic adaptations in reading, writing, and math, as well as ideas to promote student general participation in classroom activities, communication with others, and social interaction (Figure 4.11). Four primary elements were involved in this process:

1. *Regularly scheduled meeting of the student's team*—Teams including the classroom teacher, special educator, teaching assistant, inclusion support teacher, parents, and sometimes the speech-language pathologist and assistive technology person met monthly for 1.5 hours.

2. *Planning and development of supports to increase the student's academic and social participation in*

the classroom—Teams first reviewed information on the student's academic status, extent and quality of class participation, and interactions with others. Second, the team brainstormed ideas for support strategies and reached team consensus on the best ideas. Finally, the team identified who would be responsible for implementing each support. (See examples for two students in Figure 4.11.)

3. *A system of accountability*—On a monthly basis, team members rated each support on the extent to which it was being implemented, from fully to not at all (see Figure 4.12).

4. *Flexibility to change and improve supports that the team found ineffective*—As a result of team discussions, supports that were poorly implemented might be refined or improved, while those that were not implemented were eliminated. Also other supports might be added to the UPS plan.

Results of both studies showed that when this four-step process and the UPS plans were consistently used by teams for each student, students made gains in academic skills, classroom engagement, interactions with peers, and self-initiated interactions. Consistent with the problem-solving approaches described in this chapter are the uses of brainstorming, consensus reaching, and the development and evaluation of action plans in the context of regular team meetings.

SIMPLER PROBLEM-SOLVING APPROACHES USED BY PEERS

Peer problem-solving is a valuable tool; however, teaching and monitoring is required. Problem-solving skills can be applied during class meetings to resolve problems presented by any student (not just students with disabilities), to work through class conflicts (provided that the methods are used in a respectful manner), and to resolve issues that develop in the school community (Giangreco, Cloninger,

et al., 1994; Nelson, 1987). When peers are the problem-solvers, the student with disabilities is often included in the problem-solving sessions; however, teachers—along with the student and his or her parents and friends—should make that decision. Peers will typically apply peer norms to the problem and often are more sensitive than adults to the student's chronological age and to what is not "cool." Classmates are typically aware of natural supports that students will find agreeable and that may lead to positive peer connections. In addition, peers often think on a different plane than adults. Just when adults are ready to give up, peers offer ideas of which adults never dreamed.

Although including peers in the problem-solving process can prove quite beneficial, opening team issues to peers requires certain precautions to maintain the dignity of target students and to protect their rights. The student should be asked in private whether he or she objects to peer involvement in lending support and in seeking solutions. These plans, if not developed along with the student's parents, are then shared with them. Most parents like the idea of involving their child's peers, but they want the involvement of their child's classmates to be "empowering" and not patronizing or stigmatizing. Information regarding the student's disability is private and confidential and should only be shared with permission and with sensitivity.

Elementary and middle school students are less likely to be involved in team meetings with professionals and more likely to contribute ideas during small-group or class problem-solving activities. The processes for involving peers are as varied as the teacher's imagination. The three presented next have been field-tested with peers in inclusive schools.

1-Minute Idea Finding

The 1-minute idea-finding process (which can last longer than 1 minute) consists of on-the-spot brainstorming by students regarding a situation that needs immediate resolution.

Unified Plan of Support (UPS)

Student: _____   School: _____   Date: _____

Team members present:

_____   _____

_____   _____

_____   _____

Educational support
(e.g., adaptations, circular modifications, instructional modifications, peer supports)

Supports	Person responsible	Implementation rating
		☐ Fully ☐ Moderately well ☐ Somewhat ☐ Not at all
		☐ Fully ☐ Moderately well ☐ Somewhat ☐ Not at all
		☐ Fully ☐ Moderately well ☐ Somewhat ☐ Not at all
		☐ Fully ☐ Moderately well ☐ Somewhat ☐ Not at all

Social support
(e.g., buddy system, circles of support, interactive media, social faciliation)

Supports	Person responsible	Implementation rating
		☐ Fully ☐ Moderately well ☐ Somewhat ☐ Not at all
		☐ Fully ☐ Moderately well ☐ Somewhat ☐ Not at all
		☐ Fully ☐ Moderately well ☐ Somewhat ☐ Not at all
		☐ Fully ☐ Moderately well ☐ Somewhat ☐ Not at all

Figure 4.12. Unified Plans of Support form. (From: "Collaborative Teaming to support students at risk and students with severe disabilities in general education classrooms" by P. Hoto, G. Soto, J. Maier, and K. Doering. Exceptional Children Vol. 69 #3 spring 2003, page 319, 220–221. The Council for Exceptional Children, Copyright 1986, 2002. Adapted with permission.)

The focus student may be present or absent depending on the situation and the student. For example, a kindergarten teacher might ask her students, "How can we get Nate to play more with us?" An eighth-grade homeroom teacher might say, "Erica needs to get things out of her backpack and put things into it every class period, but the pack hangs on her chair behind her and is difficult for her to reach and move. How can we help Erica with this?" Time may not allow enough creativity beyond "standard" answers, and students may need additional information in order to provide higher quality ideas, but this simple approach allows peers to be a part of the solution and gives them an opportunity to develop the life skills of solving problems.

1-Minute Idea Finding with a Fact-Finding Back-Up

The 1-minute idea finding with a fact-finding back-up approach begins with a problem statement and brainstorming as in the prior method. With this approach, however, the teacher assesses whether additional information is needed to focus or to stimulate more effective brainstorming. The teacher might ask idea-jogging questions ("What would happen if Erica was tired of asking you guys for help every time?") or provide needed information ("It takes longer for Erica to pick things up because she has cerebral palsy, and that means that the muscles in her arms and hands don't always do what she tells them to do; most times they work slower than she wants them to"). This approach often helps students get "unstuck" from ideas that will not work.

Problem-Solvers Club

Salisbury and her colleagues (Salisbury, Evans, & Palombaro, 1997; Salisbury & Palombaro, 1993) described the Problem-Solvers Club approach, which was developed in an elementary school. The second, third, and fourth graders in the club learned to use

collaborative problem-solving steps, which they applied in cooperative groups to problems that arose in their inclusive school. The five steps were not unlike those that teachers use to identify solutions (Salisbury & Palombaro, 1993):

1. *What's happening here?*—Deciding on what the problem is when you know something is not right

2. *What can we do?*—Brainstorming solutions and figuring out what should be tried first

3. *What would really work?*—Asking questions for every possible solution (e.g., Will it be good for all kids? Will you or your group really be able to do this? Do you have the materials and the time?")

4. *Take action!*—Getting everyone to agree on the best solution, then trying it out

5. *How did we do? (Did we change things?)*—Figuring out if the solution worked as desired or if further action is necessary

The team tackled problems such as 1) getting people with injuries or disabilities out of the school safely during fires or fire drills, 2) name calling in school, and 3) kids in class who are bullies or bothersome. The club's solutions often worked partially, and the evaluation step allowed them to revisit their ideas and improve them. The Problem-Solvers Club proved that students often simply need a little structure and guidance and the permission to apply their creativity to problems they are interested in resolving. Adults do not control these groups; rather, they facilitate them, listen to students, and show respect for the students' voices and ideas (even if they may not always agree).

COMMON PROBLEM-SOLVING ISSUES

Common problem-solving issues involve required special education procedures (deter-

mining supplementary aids and services, behavior support plan) and general education
issues (general planning of supports needed
by students for successful participation in
general education, evaluation and grading
of students, addressing problem behavior).
When students do not have IEPs or have
IEPs with fewer support needs, these lat-
ter issues will be resolved in the context of
teacher assistance teams or prereferral teams
or simply as a part of grade-level or multi-
grade teams that address all students in need.
When students have higher support needs,
these problem-solving issues are addressed in
student-focused teams that meet more often.
Regardless of the team context, good teaming practices and rules for problem-solving
still apply.

Determining Supplementary Aids and Services

After writing the IEP goals and objectives for
a given student, the team turns its attention to
the services and aids that are needed in order
to accomplish each goal. Placement is addressed only after these supports are specified
and agreed on by the team (Bateman & Linden, 1998). The problem-solving process
teams follow for identifying needed supports
is set forth in Individuals with Disabilities
Education Act (IDEA) of 1990 (PL 101-476)
and has been clarified in court decisions.
Schools must take meaningful steps to include
students with disabilities in general education
with supplemental aids and services, including—but not limited to—behavioral support
consultation and planning, resource room
assistance, teacher and staff training, modifications to curriculum, computer-assisted devices, and note takers (Etscheidt & Bartlett,
1999). As specified in the IDEA Amendments
of 1997 (PL 105-17), this process applies when
identifying supports that allow the student:
"(I) to advance appropriately toward attaining
the annual goals . . . (II) to be involved and
progress in the regular curriculum . . . and
(III) to be educated and participate with other

children with disabilities and nondisabled
children" [§1414(d)(1)(A)(iii)].

Etscheidt and Bartlett (1999) described a
four-step process that involves team problem-
solving and consensus at each step and ends
with action planning and evaluation:

1. *Write the student's IEP goals and objectives*—
   Examine the student's present level of
   educational performance and discuss
   how the student's disability affects his or
   her participation and progress in general
   education. Identify goals and short-term
   objectives that pertain to the student's
   disability and difficulty being successful
   in general education and that will enable
   the student to participate and progress in
   general education.

2. *Discuss supplemental aids and services*—Identify what special education, related services, and supplementary aids and services are needed so the student can
   benefit from the general education setting. Discuss the 1) physical dimension
   (e.g., accessibility, classroom arrangement, proximity to teacher or work);
   2) instructional dimension (e.g., lesson
   planning and delivery, assessment practices, assistive technology); 3) social-
   behavioral dimension (e.g., social skill or
   self-management training, peer support,
   using classwide or schoolwide procedures for improving behavior); 4) collaborative dimension (e.g., teacher training,
   team consultation on needed topics, assistance in the resource room); and 5)
   "other" dimension (e.g., brainstorming
   "what else?" might be appropriate for a
   given student).

3. *Document the decision-making process and
   product*—Write an action plan that sets
   forth for each supplementary aid and
   service 1) who is responsible for providing the support, 2) by when, and 3) its jus-
   tification (e.g., the academic and nonaca-
   demic benefits that are anticipated, any
   potential disruptive effects it might have
   in the classroom).

4. *Determine the evaluation process and schedule*— Evaluation can be viewed as another action plan which specifies 1) how student progress on each goal will be monitored (e.g., direct observation, evaluation of permanent products), 2) who will gather these data, and 3) how often (e.g., weekly, monthly).

Success for students with IEPs is often as dependent on the team's ability to set meaningful goals and identify relevant supports as it is on the school's ability to carry out these plans. These guidelines and the dimensions of support (Etscheidt & Barlett, 1999) suggest that IEP teams should broaden their range of thinking when they problem-solve.

Addressing Problem Behavior and Providing Positive Behavior Supports

Probably the most stressful problem-solving issue teams face is challenging student behavior. Often, before they can lend students support, teams will need some support for themselves (e.g., maintaining a positive, person-centered approach) (Bambara, Gomez, Koger, Lohrmann-O'Rourke, & Xin, 2001). Teams also need fairly comprehensive skills to effectively understand problem behavior and replace it with appropriate behavior. Janney and Snell (2000) described steps that teams should take to identify, define, and assess problem behavior and to create behavior support plans that build and maintain appropriate behavior.

Evaluating Student Progress

Periodically, student progress needs to be assessed to determine if team-generated teaching or support plans to address IEP objectives are working. Under current federal special education requirements, teachers are required to report student progress to parents as least as often as they do for typical peers; they also must report whether the student's rate of progress is sufficient to achieve the annual goal (Bateman & Linden, 1998). Testing and grading constitute two sides of the evaluation process that applies to every student in school.

Tests

Some students with disabilities require accommodations during learning and evaluation (i.e., changes made by others to assist the student) such as extra time, instructions in Spanish and English, sitting close to the chalkboard, having a quiet place to study, or using a calculator to perform math calculations. When this is true, accommodations are written on the student's IEP, and both classroom tests and state standards tests will also reflects the same accommodations. Accommodations can address presentation of the material (e.g., large print, directions/ questions read aloud), response (e.g., someone to write the student's response given orally), setting (e.g., separate location, small group), timing or schedule (e.g., extra time or breaks) (Washburn-Moses, 2003).

Vanessa, Sam, and Walter have testing accommodations spelled out in their IEPs. All three are allowed extended time to take their tests; Sam may take them in another location.

In addition to accommodations, test content and testing method may need to be individualized as recommended by the student's team. The methods team members use to assess progress will vary depending on the student and the skill. For many students receiving special education supports, the same general assessment methods used with other students are also applied to the focus student but with adaptations made in the content, the form, or the response modality.

Curriculum-based measurement (CBM) procedures have been used by an increasing number of special and general education teachers to measure ongoing progress on IEP objectives in reading, writing, and math. This approach enables continuous and precise assessment and has resulted in increased student achievement. CBM also has been coupled with easy-to-use computer graphing methods to facilitate reporting to students and team members (Gunter, Miller, Venn, Thomas, & House, 2002; Pemberton, 2003).

Student Snapshot

Miranda and her classmates regularly take a mad minute test of math facts and keep track of their own progress on a personalized chart. This year Ms. Ramirez is using 1-minute reading samples with all her students to keep track of their growth in reading aloud accurately.

Adapted testing methods (like adapted teaching methods) are needed when students have sensory, motor, communication, or behavioral limitations around which teachers need to work. These methods must be individualized by the team and often require some on-the-spot problem-solving to refine them so the student's learning progress can be assessed without interference from the sensory or motor limitation (Rainforth & York-Barr, 1997).

Student Snapshot

To assess Daniel's progress on taking turns with peers during interesting games (e.g., computer games, electronic toys), his team members are careful to check his positioning and his hand or head switch and to allow enough time for him to initiate his switch response following the peer's signal: "It's your turn, Daniel," while touching his left hand.

Grading

Most students with IEPs who are included in general education also get school report cards about six times a year. Research indicates poorer outcomes for students with IEPs in comparison to peers without disabilities (Munk & Bursuck, 2001). For example, stu-

dents with learning disabilities had high-school grade point averages of 2.3, with ninth and tenth graders averaging 1.9 (U.S. Department of Education, 1994).

Grading of students with IEPs often poses problems for students and for teams. Students may not understand how they are graded and, with unclear grading criteria, may feel unmotivated to complete homework or to study because of low grades (see Figure 4.13). General and special educators may be confused about whose role it is to establish grading criteria and assign grades (Wood, 1998). Parent or student input typically is not sought on the grading process, and most school districts do not have guidelines for adapting grades, even though it is a legitimate strategy for students with disabilities (Munk & Bursuck, 2001).

The criteria used to grade many students who receive special education supports may be different from their peers and, like assessment and teaching methods, should be team-generated. Salend and Duhaney suggested a set of eight guidelines whereby districtwide grading policies for all students are examined and improved in order to "balance the need for a common set of standards and the individual needs of students" (2002, p. 9). There are many legitimate options for adapting grades that teams can consider: 1) adapting grading criteria by changing the weight of certain assignments or giving grades both for the completed products and for the effort taken; 2) proving written or portfolio information to supplement a letter grade; and 3) using pass-fail grades and competency checklists instead of letter grades (Munk & Bursuck, 2001).

Personalized Grading Plans (PGP) (Munk & Bursuck, 2001) are another way to address the problem of meaningfully grading students with IEPs in general education. The approach consists of five steps:

1. The student, parents, and teachers each identify what purposes the grade should meet (e.g., motivate student, communicate work habits, communicate progress on goals and mastery, help teachers plan instruction).

Voices from the Classroom

Probably all students could benefit from a process Jackson and Larkin (2002) reported that has been used to teach younger students with learning disabilities about grading. Many students do not understand why they are given certain grades. They may think that getting a good or bad grade means that the teacher likes or dislikes them.

Rubrics are scoring tools that show clearly what is expected and "what counts". Teaching students to use a simple grading rubric can provide them with an objective means for assessing their own work and understanding how teachers will determine their grade for a class project.

First, students are introduced to simple grading rubrics and taught to use them. Then, they are instructed to use the rubric strategy with a learning buddy (p. 42):

Read the rubric and the material to be graded.

Use the rubric to give an initial score.

Bring a buddy to help you rate again.

Review the material together.

Identify and award the scores together.

Check the scores again.

Once students learn to use rubrics, they can use them to guide their effort toward reaching the criteria set up for a school project.

Figure 4.13. Teaching students to use grading rubrics (From: "Rubrics: Teaching students to use grading rubrics," by C.W. Johnson and M.J. Lakin. Teaching Exceptional Children vol. 35:1, Sept–Oct. 2002, page 42. The Council for Exceptional Children, Copyright 2002. Adapted with permission.)

2. The student, parents, and teachers meet to review the school's grading policy and a menu of grading adaptation options.

3. The group then reviews its purposes for grades and reaches agreement on one or more purposes that will guide their selection of a grading adaptation. Grading adaptations that all agree on are chosen.

4. The school team works to implement the PGP.

5. Effects of the PGP are evaluated (student's grade, satisfaction, perception of accuracy).

Using this approach with five middle school students with learning disabilities, individualized grading adaptations were designed by parents and teachers with input from the student (Munk & Bursuck, 2001). These researchers found that parents and staff were generally satisfied with the outcomes even though teachers found them slightly more time-consuming. Students reported that they were happier with their grades and understood more clearly how they had been graded (Munk & Bursuck, 2001).

Student Snapshot

After getting a C and a D in science, Vanessa worked with her team and parents to create a PGP for that class. The plan included two changes: 1) the weights of her assignments were modified (i.e., tests and quizzes were reduced from 40% of her grade to 30%, while participation and portfolio management was increased to 10%) and 2) extra credit points were given for showing her updated portfolio to her teacher every Friday and for completing homework independently after reading and reviewing directions with the teacher.

REVISING TEAM ACTION PLANS

Teams are under more pressure than ever before to regularly assess and report on student progress and to make predictions about the rate of progress made toward IEP goals (Bateman & Linden, 1998). Although this is often a demanding task, it is crucial that teams know the effects of their recommendations on students. Assessment data, teaching observations, peer and family comments, and observations from the student all constitute useful information as teams work to make improvements in their programs and action plans for students. Making changes and improving a student's instructional program require exactly the same team methods as we have already described: identify the problem, brainstorm possible solutions, evaluate possi-

ble solutions, choose a solution, write an action plan, collaborate to design the teaching program and needed services, deliver the program in a team-coordinated manner, assess student progress, and review and revise team action plans. Revisions made in a team's action plans are assessment-based and team-generated. The process, which is ongoing and dynamic, depends on the cooperative capability of the collaborative team.

Chapter 5

Coordinating Team Action

Student Snapshot

Before Daniel entered kinder-garten, his parents visited the school with him and met the principal, the physical thera-pist, and the special educa-tion teacher. While touring the school, they ex-perienced several stairs with no ramps, a bath-room that was difficult to maneuver, and drinking fountains that were too high. Soon, Daniel's parents returned to discuss building accessibility changes that they thought were needed. The problems were clear, so the meeting focused on finding solutions. When they reached a consensus with the school divi-sion architect, the changes were made the summer before Daniel started school.

Teams are composed of people in different professional and nonprofessional roles. Al-though individual personalities and experi-ences add enormous variance, team mem-bers' roles and preparation for those roles predict in part their ways of working and thinking. For example, family members tend to be highly invested emotionally in their chil-dren's welfare but less knowledgeable about the school setting and curriculum. Teachers have responsibility for accomplishing an agenda of learning in a group of students but must operate within the rules and culture of a given school. Related services professionals take a specialized role in teaching students a prescribed set of skills as well as in improving the learning setting to support these new skills. Typically, paraprofessionals spend most of their time working with students and are assigned to students with the highest support needs, even though they have the least amount of training to fill these responsibili-ties. When team members are sensitive to these role differences, taking steps to improve communication and coordinate their actions results in working together with less friction and more efficiency. This chapter focuses on the ways teams can coordinate to improve their effectiveness by 1) organizing support options with staff schedules and training,

2) organizing paperwork, and 3) coordinating across different team members.

ORGANIZING SUPPORT OPTIONS WITH STAFF SCHEDULES AND TRAINING

Inclusive schools often organize the support for included students according to the needs of the students (Giangreco, Broer, & Edelman, 1999; McLaughlin & Warren, 1992; Roach, 1995). The intensity of support given to a student should rest primarily on the extent of the student's needs and the recommendations of the student's team, not on the resources a school has available. In many inclusive schools, IEP committees define support in part by matching the type of collaborative re-lationship with the amount or intensity of sup-port needed by a target student. Student and staffing schedules are then coordinated so the supports can be delivered. Although not regu-lated by law in most states, Teacher Assistance Teams or pre-referral teams (discussed in Chapter 2, Figure 2.7) work in the same way to informally coordinate schedules so the needed supports identified in an action plan can be provided to target students.

Other practices within school districts (or within particular states) might dictate or in-fluence how special education teachers are assigned to students, which, in turn, may in-fluence how collaborative teams design edu-cation programs. For example, experienced special education teachers might be desig-nated as consulting teachers in middle and high schools or across several elementary schools. Consulting teachers coordinate the efforts of other special education teachers, oversee procedures (e.g., eligibility and IEP meetings), troubleshoot, and serve as the liai-son between administration and students. Though consulting teachers often have a slightly smaller caseload of students, the school district's support structure allows them the flexibility to handle any crises that arise.

In other schools, the principal and teachers use their experience and shared decision-making authority to devise their own procedures for organizing special education support for different grades and students. School districts also may seek waivers from state guidelines when regulations conflict with a district's innovative organization. Waiver options, with some safeguards for abuse, can positively influence change in school districts and improvement in state policy. Thus, school organization and local and state policy may influence team formation and the ways in which special education teachers are assigned to support students; this in turn affects how collaborative teams design support for the students they serve.

ORGANIZING PAPERWORK

Consistent with what planning teams do and with the programs and support schedules they design, teams will need to develop ways to organize information about students and to keep records of the students' schedules and staff schedules.

Student Information

Consulting special educators who oversee special education at the middle and high school level and special education teachers who work with more than a few classrooms find that it is essential to keep a large notebook containing student information and support schedules in a safe place but readily available to team members. In one section of the notebook, materials are arranged by student; the information is kept current and tells at a glance where each student who requires special services is during each period of the day (i.e., student schedule), students' grades and personal information, and a listing of their objectives and accommodations (refer to Melanie's program at-a-glance in Chapter

3, Figure 3.5). A Program Planning Matrix is another piece of useful planning information that may be kept in the student section of the notebook (refer to Chapter 4, Figure 4.2). *Modifying Schoolwork, Second Edition* (Janney & Snell, 2004) and *Behavioral Support* (Janney & Snell, 2000) describe several other student documents. Teams might design additional forms for particular students to be kept in a team or grade-level notebook Often, standard forms are more useful to a team when they are adapted to correspond to the team's own style and organization.

Teacher and Class Paperwork

This section describes several forms that pertain to class support and teacher support. The Classroom Support Plan summarizes each student's general support needs, when the classroom teacher meets with the special education teacher, any peer supports used, type(s) of support from special education staff, and a plan to follow if difficulties arise. Whenever a student is scheduled to be included in a class, a Support Plan is completed for that class period.

Student Snapshot

Sam has several classroom teachers, so his team members must communicate effectively to ensure consistency. In the beginning of the year, Sam's core team completed a Support Plan for Inclusion for English 9 (see Figure 5.1) and Teacher Assistance Guides (see Figure 5.2) for each inclusive classroom. The Guides describe class tasks and test characteristics and detail the ways in which special education staff will assist.

Information on school schedules of special education support is confidential and should not be openly displayed or discussed; use of student initials or codes rather than actual names is preferable.

Support Plan for Inclusion

General education teacher: _Ms. Wilson_

Special education teacher: _Ms. Elliott_

Class: _English 9_   **Period:** _5_   **Room:** _V-1_   **Date:** _10-2-04_

---

1. Students who require special support in this class (attach Program-at-a-Glance for each student):

   Sam: Social and behavioral support

   Ted: ADHD—attention/focus difficulties

   Ed: Learning disabilities—written Language

2. Schedule for consultation with special education teacher:

   Fridays—6th period

3. Plan for adapting materials:

   Sam has study hall during which he will try to complete some homework.

   Ms. Elliott will modify assignments if necessary.

4. Peer support plan within this class:

   Most students know Sam and support him.

   If problems arise, Ms. Elliott will talk to students individually—may do a whole class or peer planning.

5. Amount and type of assistance needed from special education staff:

   Ongoing daily support, co-teach when possible

6. Intervention plan if difficulties arise:

   Ms. Elliott will deal with Sam and pull him out if he becomes too disruptive.

Figure 5.1.   Support plan for inclusion for Sam and others in English class. (Contributed by Johnna Elliott.)

COORDINATING ACROSS TEAM MEMBERS

Team members who implement and those who support must communicate. The primary work of implementing action plans is done by the classroom and special education teachers; however, for some students, paraprofessionals may play a critical part in putting action plans into place. When students require services from related services staff (e.g., occupational and physical therapists, speech-language pathologists, vision and mobility specialists, nurses), the program design should reflect the input of these staff members. Coordinating the efforts of team members to ensure smooth delivery of students' programs is challenging.

Coordinating Between General and Special Educators

Team meetings between general and special educators are not enough to coordinate team action. Special educators need to plan their schedules with classroom teachers so that they regularly spend time in *all* of the general education classrooms of students on their caseloads. This allows them to learn the class schedule, dynamics, and instructional content;

Teacher Assistance Guide

Teacher: *Ms. Wilson*   Class: *English 9*   Semester/year: *9-04*

Typical classroom tasks:	Homework tasks:
Take notes from overhead	*Write book reports*
Participate in discussion	*Write paragraphs on assigned topics*
Turn in grammar worksheets	*Write research paper*
Use reference material in library	

Testing:

Format: multiple choice and short answer

Test types:

- *Literature: short answer*
- *Grammar: proof and correct sentences for mechanics and usage*

Sources of information:

- *Class notes (most of literature test taken from notes), literature selections, grammar book*

Recommended study guide format:

- *Literature: flashcard method; make cards from class notes*
- *Grammar: none recommended; class practices on grammar worksheets daily*

General teacher assistance requested:

Ms. Wilson would like help with the following tasks as time permits:

- *Duplicate grammar worksheets a few days in advance*
- *Take small group to library to help using reference materials (may include non-identified students as indicated by teacher)*
- *Check off those turning in homework as they come into class*

Additional notes:

- *During grammar lesson on Fridays, pull specified students to study for tests or help them in library with their research*

Figure 5.2. Teacher assistance guide. (Contributed by Christine Burton and Johnna Elliott.)

monitor the students' social and academic performance; and assist with instruction. When special education teachers' caseloads are so large that they cannot have quality time in these classrooms, caseloads need to be re-examined and adjusted with building administrators (Downing, Ryndak, & Clark, 2000).

Without meaningful classroom contact, special educators are less relevant to the general educator, and their contributions to team decisions about specific students are greatly compromised. For example, in a study of inclusive classrooms (Snell & Macfarland,

2001), one special educator who could not meet with teachers because she was busy with resource all day said, "I have to rely on them [students] to let me know . . . how it's going. I would need to count on them to say 'well we tried this review sheet and it didn't work. Let's try something else.'" Special educators and others who consult with students across classrooms or even schools must have enough contact with the students on their caseload that they are current with student performance and class context or they lose credibility with the team.

Coordinating with Paraprofessionals

Student Snapshot

 Ms. Johnson was in her first year as a teaching assistant for Melanie. She had worked with a range of students with IEPs in her prior 2 years in this role. In October, she expressed her frustration to Ms. Pitonyak, saying that she had a hard time with Melanie's tantrums. Ms. Ramirez noticed Ms. Johnson's frustration and worried when she observed Ms. Johnson speaking harshly to Melanie and using a timeout procedure that was not in the behavior support plan. Unfortunately, Ms. Ramirez was too busy at the time to do anything. At the weekly meeting between Ms. Ramirez and Ms. Pitonyak, both professionals felt that Ms. Johnson should be the topic for discussion. They both knew that Ms. Johnson needed and deserved more supervision and feedback than she got from them. They admitted to feeling a conflict between treating Ms. Johnson as a colleague and teammate and supervising her as a subordinate. After 20 minutes, the teachers had drawn up a plan to meet with Ms. Johnson, get her view of the challenges of teaching Melanie, set up regular supervision and feedback sessions, and review the behavior support plan.

Ms. Johnson is like most paraprofessionals in that 1) her major job responsibility is teaching (Marks, Schrader, & Levine, 1999; Wadsworth & Knight, 1996), but she rarely has written plans from a teacher (French, 2001); 2) the school district requires no specific training for the job and the training she received was on-the-job and crisis driven; 3) she takes primary responsibility for giving personal care to students and for lunchroom and playground supervision (French, 2001); and 4) even though IDEA requires that paraprofessionals be supervised (Educational Resources Information Center, 2003), she has little planning time with teachers and is not regularly supervised or given feedback (French, 2001; French & Chopra, 1999; Giangreco, Edelman, Luiselli, & MacFarland,

1997). All too often, schools hire paraprofessionals based mainly on the recommendations of IEP teams as a "pair of extra hands" and then give them responsibilities that exceed their training. At the same time, school districts typically have failed to create requirements for in-service training, competencies, supervision and feedback, meeting times with teachers, and the use of teaching guidelines prepared by teachers. Most teachers have no training in the tasks of supervising paraprofessionals (Wallace, Shin, Bartholomay, & Stahl, 2001).

Several researchers have documented the phenomenon of well-intentioned teaching assistants who are "too close for comfort" and create dependencies with the children they are assigned to or get in the way of peer interaction (see Figure 5.3) (Giangreco et al., 1997). Assigning paraprofessionals to teachers and whole classrooms rather than to individual students is a practice to reduce this problem and to avoid the over-hiring of teaching assistants (Downing et al., 2000). Finally, while many believe that paraprofessionals make a difference in student achievement, no literature supports this belief (Giangreco, Edelman, Broer, & Doyle, 2001).

Schools must think more broadly about supports for students with IEPs who are included and move beyond the routine hiring of paraprofessionals as a requirement for their inclusion. Several authors have suggested guidelines for determining whether paraprofessional supports are really needed (see Figure 5.4). When it is clear that paraprofessionals are needed schools must:

- Develop clear job descriptions and an in-service training agenda with input from the team

- Create a schedule and guidelines for supervision and link supervision to in-service training

- Provide daily work schedules and written guidelines and link to supervision and in-service

GUARDIAN ANGEL SUPER-MAGNET

STUCK LIKE GLUE HOVERCRAFT

HELPING OR HOVERING?

Figure 5.3. Paraprofessionals can be too close for too long. (From Giangreco, M. [1998]. *Ants in his pants: Absurdities and realities of special education* [p. 74]. Minnetonka, MN: Peyton Publications; reprinted by permission.)

• Support the active involvement of paraprofessionals on the collaborative teams of the students they serve.

Although most school districts are weak on providing paraprofessionals with job descriptions, teaching guidelines, and in-service training (French, 2001; Giangreco et al., 2001), these practices will need to change. Taking these steps will help schools meet the federal requirements of "highly qualified" paraprofessionals in No Child Left Behind legislation by 2006 (http://www.ed.gov/offices/OESE/esea/).

Develop Clear Job Descriptions

Job descriptions provide a framework for hiring, performance evaluation, and in-service training. A study of paraprofessionals in inclusive classrooms indicated five dominant roles that can be used as a guide for skill assessment and in-service training as well as a means for individualizing the responsibilities for a particular paraprofessional job (Minondo, Meyer, & Xin, 2001):

• *Instructional role*—team membership, emotional support for students, monitoring student performance and staff development

• *School support role*—general school duties, basic classroom support tasks, community-based instruction

• *Liaison role*—adapting materials, peer facilitator, linkage with family

• *Personal support role*—personal care, therapy objectives, assist student with work, assist with entire class

• *One-to-one role*—provision of in-class support to individual students

The team or teams a paraprofessional is hired to work with should collaborate with school administrators in both the development of a job description and the process of hiring or assigning people for positions (French, 2001; Riggs, 2004). Writing a job description first will help focus the selection on the needed skills and responsibilities a team designates for the position.

Create Guidelines for Supervision

Supervision must not be viewed as annual written evaluations by administrators (Riggs & Mueller, 2001). Paraprofessionals need 1) face-to-face contact with their immediate professional supervisors (typically, general and special educators), 2) regular observation as they engage in the activities they do most often, and 3) constructive feedback on their performance. Feedback should include comments on what they are doing well and modeling on what they can do better. When disagreements and problems arise, supervising teachers must take the initiative to clarify the problem and resolve it with the teaching assistant, using problem-solving and communication strategies that are a part of teamwork.

1. *Rely on collaborative teamwork*—An effective team often makes better decisions than an individual and may prevent the need for an additional person.

2. *Build capacity in the school to support all students*—Shift the thinking to support for the classroom rather than simply support for the student.

3. Consider paraprofessional supports individually and judiciously and avoid assignment paraprofessionals as a "simple solution."

4. Clarify the reasons why paraprofessional supports are being considered and address those reasons.

5. Seek a match between identified support needs and the skills of the person to provide the support.

6. *Explore opportunities for natural supports*—Use people who are present anyway (e.g., teachers, classmates, office, staff, school nurse, librarian).

7. *Consider school and classroom characteristics*—Rearranging the environment can reduce the need for supervision and increase access to peers and staff; reduce class size.

8. Consider special educator and related services caseloads.

9. *Explore administrative and organizational changes*—Schedule paraprofessionals with the school's master schedule for better use of their time; re-allocate paraprofessional positions for special educator positions.

10. Consider if paraprofessional support is a temporary measure to a problem, and identify with administrators the steps needed to resolve the actual problem.

Figure 5.4. Guidelines for deciding whether paraprofessional supports are needed. (From Giangreco, M.F., Broer, S.M., & Edelman, S.W. [1999]. The tip of the iceberg: Determining whether paraprofessional support is needed for students with disabilities in general education settings. *Journal of The Association for Persons with Severe Handicaps, 24,* 285–289; adapted by permission.)

A paraprofessional's immediate supervisors should actively model teaching and data collection methods with students, ensure that paraprofessionals understand and follow school policies (e.g., health, safety, behavioral guidelines, documentation of accidents and student performance); allow time for daily exchange of information; answer questions about students, classroom practices, and legal topics; and develop daily work schedules with written guidelines for teaching (French, 2001; Friend & Cook, 2003; Riggs & Mueller, 2001).

In one of the few studies where paraprofessional training was tested, researchers built several characteristics into their teaching program (Parsons & Reid, 1999; Parsons, Reid, & Green, 1996). First, they focused on specific skills needed to teach students (e.g., task analysis, prompting methods). Second, they used an efficient 1-day program of instruction that was planned to be acceptable to staff. Finally, they built in measures to demonstrate training effectiveness (assessed staff mastery of skills and subsequent student learning). It is important that other team members also use and value the skills targeted for paraprofessionals, that they involve paraprofessionals in the planning of the teaching sessions, and that there is a nonthreatening way to assess outcomes and motivate skill use.

Student Snapshot

 Just before school started, Sam's team decided that he would benefit from learning to self-monitor his ability to make the transition between classes without disruptive behavior. They devised a simple rehearsal and self-checking procedure for staff to teach him to use before and after every change of class. Mr. Lilly, the paraprofessional who assisted during hall transitions in Sam's high school, agreed to learn the procedure. Together with Ms. Elliott, she planned a 2-hour teaching session in August with role playing; when school started, they involved Sam and practiced the routine. Data from Sam's use of the procedure agreed with Mr. Lilly's observations. Not only had Mr. Lilly learned to teach the *skill, but also Sam's performance by the end of September showed consistently appropriate movement between classes.*

Provide Daily Work Schedules and Written Teaching Guidelines

Work schedules should be developed collaboratively. Most schedules will need reexamination and revision on a regular basis as class activities and student supports change. Instructional guides should be written in simple language with steps spelled out and then demonstrated for paraprofessionals. It is crucial that teachers instruct paraprofessionals about the intended outcomes of a lesson or activity, rather than assume them to be obvious.

To teach the actual instructional procedures, some suggest using role play first (teacher models, paraprofessional takes a turn), followed by opportunities to apply the procedure in class with students (teacher models, paraprofessional takes a turn). The same approach would be followed when related services staff teach paraprofessionals (and others on the team) to apply their recommendations (e.g., the physical therapist teaches team members how to lift and move Daniel from his chair to his prone stander for art). Team-generated plans for addressing problem behavior also must be directly discussed and taught so that paraprofessionals use the same approaches to prevent, redirect, and replace problem behavior.

Paraprofessional competencies identified in job descriptions and evident from their ongoing supervision should be linked to the inservice training agenda. For example, before school starts, all paraprofessionals might benefit from learning school policies and frequently used teaching tactics (e.g., using an instructional guide format and basic prompting methods, observing and recording student performance). Teams will want to identify a location for paraprofessionals' daily schedules, along with a notebook where teaching procedures for specific students and IEP goals and data collection forms are kept when not in use. Doyle (2002) gives some clear guidelines for establishing the roles and responsibilities of paraprofessionals and their daily schedules in inclusive schools.

Support Active Involvement of Paraprofessionals as Team Members

Several benefits result when teaching assistants are actively involved in team planning: 1) their addition of information and ideas adds to the quality of team decisions, 2) their participation enhances their knowledge and skill development, and 3) being active team members contributes to their positive relationship within the school community (French & Chopra, 1999; Riggs & Mueller, 2001). The biggest barrier to team participation (as well as to regular supervision, feedback, and planning) is time and money. Paraprofessionals often are employed for school hours and cannot come early or stay late for meetings with professional team members unless they are compensated and their job descriptions include these meeting responsibilities. Teams need to work with administrators to create the needed time both during school hours and periodically before and after school hours.

Coordinating with Related Services Professionals

Student Snapshot

When Ms. James first observed Daniel at the end of kindergarten, she became concerned about his inability to walk, sit without support, grasp and release, and talk. How could she possibly teach him? The day she visited, Daniel's physical therapist was assisting with adjustments to Daniel's computer. The kindergarten teacher noticed Ms. James's facial expression and whispered to her later in the hall, "Don't worry; you are never alone when teaching Daniel—you get all of the help you need, and he is learning because of it!"

When therapy is provided in the context of classroom activities, teachers and specialists confer with each other four times more often than when therapy is on a pull-out basis (McWilliam, 1996). The increased teaming should lead to more consistent use of therapy by more staff, better connections between students' classroom needs and therapeutic interventions (e.g., seating, mobility, communication), and more rapid problem-solving when therapy issues arise (Dole, 2004; McWilliam, 1996). Therapists and other specialists (e.g., behavior consultants, mobility instructors, adapted physical educators) should work with the team to clarify their roles and responsibilities in the classroom, their schedules, the direct services (instruction and assessment of the student) and indirect services (staff planning and consultation) they provide, and the class activities with which they are involved.

If related services personnel are not active team members, professional turf can dominate decision-making in place of collaborative principles. For example, a survey of professionals and parents regarding team practices (Giangreco, Edelman, & Dennis, 1991) illustrated the following:

- Many related services personnel make independent decisions regarding the amount and types of services a student needs prior to fully understanding the student's IEP objectives; thus, related services may not be integrated with IEP objectives.

- Having separate pages of IEP objectives written by therapists is not unusual and often means that the program is fragmented. Related services may not be educationally relevant to the student.

- Often, professionals from related disciplines prefer having control over decisions relating to their own services (e.g., amount, delivery model) rather than sharing these decisions with the team.

When any of the previous practices are operating, teamwork becomes a "tug-of-war."

Teams, not individuals, should make decisions regarding the amount and types of related services and equipment needed by students and the ways in which these services will be delivered within the student's daily routine.

Therapy should be integrated instructionally and contextually into daily, class, school, and home activities and routines (Rainforth & York-Barr, 1997). An integrated approach to therapy requires team members to share their priorities and explain their rationale as well as express their different viewpoints. Ideally, this process leads to "opportunities for reaching agreement."

During times such as these, team members need to remind each other that their unifying goal is to help the student and then refocus the meeting on the current student concerns. To help teams maintain a student-centered focus, one special educator suggested placing a photo of the student on the meeting table.

Related services team members tend to participate periodically at team meetings and are more likely to attend the team meetings when the meetings are based in the same building as the target student. Sometimes, special education teachers will address the unavoidable absences of related services staff at team meetings by simply meeting separately with them when they have time. Although this solution is time consuming for the special education teacher, it enables related services professionals to provide input, keeping both them and the team informed of the student's progress and team deliberations. Rainforth and York-Barr (1997) described another alternative: block scheduling of related services. Staff schedule themselves to be present in particular schools for longer blocks of time, either weekly or bi-weekly; when in the building, the professional has the flexibility to work with multiple classrooms, staff members, and students providing consultation, collaborating with team members, or providing direct services to students.

When elementary teachers were asked to describe the roles of related services providers in delivering coordinated programs in inclusive classrooms (Snell et al., 1995), they provided the following guidelines:

1. Reduce pull-out services, and use opportunities to work in the context of the class activities.

   Melanie needed to gain fluency with turn-taking during conversations with her peers. Melanie's speech therapist prompted her participation during the many back-and-forth exchanges that occurred during structured partner activities in science.

2. Provide equipment that helps the child participate in class and school activities.

   Daniel's physical therapist helped resolve the team-identified problem of proximity to peers during art activities by suggesting he be moved from his wheelchair to a new chair that scooted under the table surface in the art room.

3. Have flexible schedules that allow therapy to be provided during the most relevant times.

   Daniel has his physical therapy on a daily basis during physical education. His speech-language therapist observed the first-grade physical education routine and, with team members, devised ways to involve Daniel during scheduled games and activities. Daniel now uses his switch-operated communication device to announce which team gets the point (e.g., "Spartan's point" "Cavalier's point") during games.

4. Based on the teacher's unit topics or lesson plans, weave therapy into planned class activities.

   Daniel's physical education teacher gives his physical therapist a monthly schedule of target sports, games, and fitness goals; Ms. James shares the weekly unit plans with the physical therapist and the speech-language therapist.

5. Come prepared with adaptations, and be able to facilitate the student's active participation in the class.

   The speech-language therapist continues the use of Daniel's talking switch during free choice time. Daniel selects one activ-

ity from several picture options and uses pictures (e.g., a smiling face to stand for the message "I like that"; a boy pointing to himself to stand for "Can I have a turn?") during a marble rolling game.

6. Be sensitive enough to know when to stay in the classroom and when to leave.

   Melanie's occupational therapist worked with her in the tutoring room to teach her some simple relaxation exercises. Later, Melanie invited her peers to learn the exercises so that they would understand what she was doing.

Coordinating with School Administrators

During the implementation and maintenance phase of inclusion, building administrators must lend meaningful support to teams and teamwork:

- *Assigning caseloads*—The caseload responsibilities of special education teachers and related services professionals are planned to facilitate collaborative teaming.

- *Sharing decision-making*—The administrator relinquishes some control and involves teachers in making decisions.

- *Demonstrating school leadership*—The building administrator is willing to be part of the team-generated educational or behavioral support plans for some students.

- *Using problem-solving*—The principal resolves issues by sharing success stories and using the issue/action/person responsible planning process to tackle issues.

- *Being a spokesperson for the school*—The principal reports meaningful and positive examples of inclusion and collaborative teaming to parents and members of the school board and community and appeals to the district level for assistance when innovative supports are needed.

- *Planning ways to monitor team functioning*—Building administrators have regular sessions with special educators, read the team's minutes to keep track of team decisions, respond appropriately to teams regarding administrative concerns, attend meetings periodically, and review the decisions being implemented with the teams.

Coordinating with Family Members

Student Snapshot

Vanessa's parents both work long hours and share a home with the their other four children and Vanessa's maternal grandparents. Life is fast-paced and allows little time for school meetings; usually the grandmother attends.

Teams cannot function meaningfully without including parents and other family members. Although school teams change, family members typically remain connected to the student. The relationship that is built between teachers and their students' families is dependent on school, teacher, student, and family factors:

• *School and team factors*—Is the approach welcoming? Are interactions respectful? Are events planned to attract and involve families?

• *Teacher factors*—What level of experience and skill is shown when communicating with a range of families? Are interactions individualized to suit families with different resources, attitudes, and cultures? Do teachers build family confidence in being critical team members?

• *Student*—What are the student's social and academic needs and abilities? Does the student have a history of success or failure in special education? Are there problem behaviors at school?

• *Family*—What are the family's time constraints and financial frustrations, and how do these impact on their involvement with schools? Do family members speak English or does the school have interpreters readily available? What are the parents' own experiences with school?

Teachers often complain that the families "who need to be involved" are not involved in their children's education. Teachers want parents to show up for meetings at the school, talk openly about their children's abilities and challenges, and follow school requests concerning their children's school work (e.g., complete forms, read with them at home, enforce homework time). When parents do not meet these expectations, schools usually focus on family limitations and aim to get families more "involved" ; however, evidence does not support a cause-and-effect relationship between improvements in parent involvement and improvements in student learning (Mattingly, Prislin, McKenzie, Rodrigues, & Kayzar, 2002).

Most families do not anticipate the need to participate on an educational team and feel that it is unexpectedly thrust on them (Friend & Cook, 2003). Family time, resources, attitude, and prior experience figure into every family's ability and desire to "be involved" with their child's education.

Student Snapshot

Walter comes from a single-parent family; he lives with his mother, who has been on unemployment for the past 5 years. She left school in her early teens. She considers Walter's completion of high school as important for getting a good job and does not agree with the school label of "mental retardation." Instead, she says, "He just doesn't like books and numbers, but he's not stupid."

When involvement is viewed as information sharing rather than simply attending school meetings, schools can improve the relationships between families and teams.

Sharing Written Information with Families

Schools share a lot of written information with families (e.g., parent rights handouts, grades and progress reports, school announcements). Examining what is sent home and eliminating, condensing, or combining announcements is imperative. When specialized terms are unavoidable (e.g., eligibility, IEP), providing a short glossary of definitions can be helpful. Schools should supplement written information about child progress, development, program options, and special education procedures with relevant visits to programs or videos about the content and informal face-to-face exchanges so that questions can be addressed. Teachers should not rely solely on written information and may need to work with families to determine how they prefer to communicate. If an interpreter is needed, avoid using the student, but when hiring an interpreter, be cautious about confidentiality and the parents' comfort (Friend & Cook, 2003).

Learning About Students from Their Families

Student Snapshot

Daniel has two younger siblings, and his parents are both teachers in the same school system. They work hard to balance work and family time but always come up short, particularly with all of the extra demands of Daniel's disability.

Teams should use good communication practices when trying to learn about students from their families. A home–school journal or a backpack sharing notebook can be put through a trial run with the family at the beginning of the school year (see Figure 5.5). Determine with the parent which teachers will see the notebook, what will and will not be written, who will write in it, and how often (Davern, 2004; Hall, Wolfe, & Bollig, 2003). Notebooks can be used to tell parents what happened at school; to tell teachers what happened at home; to give families assurance about participation, behavior, and health issues; to inform families about school events, meetings, homework, and school projects; and to report progress. Teams should periodically discuss notebooks to see how they can be more useful or whether there is consensus on their use. Do not let notebooks become the teachers' ways to communicate trivial or bad news or a substitute for direct communication. Instead, notebooks should be a vehicle for sharing positive and relevant information about students between home and school.

Facilitating Parent Participation in Team Interactions

To facilitate active parent participation in meetings, teams should select a time and location with the family and confirm the time beforehand. Well before the meeting, team members should address issues such as the meeting agenda, transportation, and presence of an interpreter. Friend and Cook (2003) and Dabkowski (2004) recommended that professionals wait for family members to arrive and talk a little before sitting in the meeting area. The most familiar school staff should act as host, sit near the family members, and provide a folder of the student's work, copies of relevant forms, and paper and pens. Meetings should be structured to give family members frequent opportunities to participate. Team members can ask for parents' ideas or opinions, seek specific information, and request parent approval. To be sure parents are informed in their decision-making, team members should give them relevant information (e.g., special education procedures, program options, specific instructional approaches) and answer their questions well before the meeting. Professionals should avoid the barriers to parent participation that often creep into a meeting under the guise of "efficiency" (e.g., too short meeting times that prevent serious discussion; IEPs written before the meeting coupled with comments such as "Do you want to add anything?").

Adopt a home–school notebook system of communication

1. At the start of the school year in your letter home to parents, introduce the traveling notebook system for fostering communication.
   - Describe the system: a simple spiral notebook, personalized for every student and parent, that travels between home and school in the student's backpack (frequency per week to be determined)
   - Identify that your main interest is in helping students make progress in school
   - Tell what can be done to make it work (by you the teacher, by the parent, and by the student)
   - Seek parents' interest in the process
2. Send postcards to students welcoming them to the class and telling them about the notebook system.
3. Reinforce the idea in your first parent–teacher conference.
4. Write informative comments about each student's day, keeping the tone positive and honest; minimize the "bad news." Reassure parents, and treat them with respect. Consider their educational level before writing comments. Write in ways that can be understood. Adjust the procedure if parents cannot read to include siblings or neighbors who might assist. Address parents with titles in your communication. Send the notebook home; encourage but, particularly at first, don't "require," parents' responses.
5. Be persistent, be positive, and gradually help parents participate more actively. Know that it takes time to establish rapport or to "undo" poor past relationships with schools.

Figure 5.5. Establishing a home–school notebook of communication. (From: "Passing Notes to Parents," by V.L. Williams and G. Cartledge. Teaching Exceptional Children, vol. 30:1, pages 30–34. The Council for Exceptional Children, Copyright 1997. Reprinted with permission.)

Team members should also be sensitive to the families' feelings about disability and potential when discussing diagnostic evaluations. They should meet with family members in a private setting with only necessary professionals and start by seeking parents' views of their child. Test results should be given with examples and without jargon. Team members should share the limits of the diagnosis and let parents take the information in, think about it, and clarify their questions before moving to education planning. They should supplement test information with team and family knowledge about the student's abilities so that the overall focus of the meeting is on capability. Finally, teams should work through conflicts that may arise by identifying the issues of concern and resolving them.

Chapter 6

Teaching Collaboratively

Student Snapshot

Walter often benefits from having directions restated and reminders to look as teachers give instructions. Sometimes repetition and demonstrations help. Although liked by his peers, he does not always interpret social feedback. Walter is often paired with peers who can model appropriate behavior.

Ms. Burton meets weekly with Walter's basic English teacher, Ms. Hill. They plan the content and the approaches they will take together and how they will support students with IEPs. For the unit on Greek myths, they decide to use one of the simpler co-teaching approaches involving the whole group and Ms. Hill as lead teacher. While Ms. Hill leads whole-class activities and discussions, Ms. Burton circulates among the students, using short, intensive instructional sessions to review or extend concepts and paying particular attention to several students who have IEPs. Later, for math, Walter receives pull-in support, but on set days, he gets pull-out support in the academic lab where Ms. Burton works with a small group of eleventh graders. Walter and other classmates receive needed support in geometry from Ms. Burton, who also co-teaches with Ms. Washington in one of her geometry classes.

This chapter addresses how teachers work together in the general education classroom to meet the educational needs of a diverse group of students. *Collaborative teaching* (i.e., co-teaching or team teaching) is a broad umbrella term with many variations; its generic meaning is two or more professional team members teaching together in the same setting to provide effective instruction to a group of students with a range of learning abilities. Its narrower meaning is stated more explicitly by Vaughn, Bos, and Schumm:

> The special education and the general education teacher are both in the classroom during the same lesson and both participate in the instruction. The roles of both teachers vary according to the goals of the lessons and the needs of the students. (2000, p. 107)

A less traditional use of the term includes other professionals who co-teach with the general education teacher (e.g., occupational therapist co-teaches a unit on good positioning in keyboarding class; school nurse assists when teaching third graders about nutrition).

Co-teaching is more complex than simply sharing instruction because it also involves:

- Designing teaching roles to reflect the expertise and interests of both teachers

- Preserving regular time periods to plan together

- Expanding teacher roles and skills to enhance student outcomes

- Assessing and considering both the student and teacher outcomes of the collaborative partnership and exploring improvements

- Communicating and resolving conflicts together

- Using processes that help teachers work together cooperatively (e.g., regular feedback and planning, peer coaching, role release)

Chapter 1 discusses two terms that are related to collaborative teaching: pull-in and pull-out service delivery. *Pull-in* involves team members (e.g., special education teacher, paraprofessional, related services staff) bringing special education supports that are consistent with team planning into the classroom for one or more students. Supports include instruction with or without adaptations, as well as behavior monitoring, cuing, and supervising. *Pull-out*, or *alternative activities*, involve the same team members providing special education support in an environment apart from the general education classroom, such as a resource room, study hall, or community training site. Ideally, pull-out service delivery is provided in ways that are consistent with team planning and involve ongoing collaboration.

Technically, collaborative teaching is also "the pulling in of special education." In both approaches, special education staff members provide support to identified students at scheduled times in the same location as their peers. There are, however, several differences. First, pull-in services are primarily limited to special education staff or related services personnel who work with the target student(s) in the same room, area, or group alongside peers without disabilities. Pull-in does not include a shared responsibility for teaching other class members. Therefore, although pull-in does involve collaborative planning with the classroom teacher, the planning only addresses the student(s) with special needs, not the whole class. Second, pull-in arrangements involve a more traditional separation of roles between the special educator and the classroom teacher. Third, co-teaching involves professionals, typically the special educator, working with the classroom teacher. Having professional training and credentials means the two individuals are peers and can better fill a partnership (Friend & Cook, 2003). Fourth, the two strategies differ in the amount of collaboration they require. Although some co-teaching approaches require less planning, most approaches call for significant planning between the special and general education teachers and result in a softening of role boundaries, as the two teachers teach all students cooperatively. A collaborative teaching approach is not for all teachers and classrooms; some general education teachers prefer to have special education services pulled into the classroom according to team planning but do not want to involve the special education teacher in whole- or small-group instruction on a routine, scheduled basis.

RATIONALE FOR COOPERATIVE TEACHING

The primary rationale for collaborative teaching is to "meet the educational needs of students with diverse learning abilities" in inclusive classrooms (Friend & Cook, 2003, p. 176). Having a specialist plan and teach alongside a generalist means better instruction of a diverse group of learners. Special educators know about making and using adaptations in curriculum and instruction and addressing motivation and behavioral issues that affect learning. Middle and high school teachers have specialized knowledge in subject areas.

Co-teaching avoids pulling students with disabilities out of the classroom for instruction, which is disruptive to learning and teaching. (Figure 6.1 provides one general education teacher's views of this rationale.) Co-teaching includes rather than separates students with disabilities. It eliminates the stigma of being segregated in school, allows membership in general education classrooms, gives more class options, provides typical peer models, and facilitates a variety of peer interactions and friendships.

Voices from the Classroom

"Before we started co-teaching, I basically didn't know what my children were doing outside my room; they just went somewhere and did something. They would miss whatever was going on in my class. I wouldn't schedule a test at that time, but they missed the lesson that hour or sometimes they even missed story time, the fun part. They had to miss something. Now [with co-teaching] I'm able to expand on what the children have learned. . . ." (Nowacek, 1992, p. 263).

Figure 6.1. A general education teacher on co-teaching.

BENEFITS OF CO-TEACHING

The benefits and effects of collaborative teaching have been examined by a number of researchers (Austin, 2001; Fennick & Liddy, 2001; Gerber & Pop, 1999, 2000; Nowacek, 1992; Pugach & Wesson, 1995; Walther-Thomas, 1997; Weiss & Lloyd, 2002; Welch, 2000). Because co-teaching has many variations and researchers have examined a range of approaches, it is difficult to draw simple conclusions about its effectiveness. In a meta-analysis of six quantitative research studies of co-teaching classrooms, Murawski and Swanson concluded that "co-teaching is a moderately effective procedure for influencing student outcomes" (2001, p. 264), with good effect sizes for reading and language arts and moderate effect sizes for math. However, neither this meta-analysis of actual student outcomes nor teacher opinion survey research (Austin, 2001) has shown strong support for social outcomes (peer acceptance, friendship, self-concept). Given the small amount of data, the authors urged cautious interpretation. Although the data they analyzed addressed both primary grades and high school and reading and math scores, there was not enough data to know if certain approaches had better outcomes for different ages, grades, disabilities, or curriculum areas. In summary, these findings substantiate the use of co-teaching approaches within supportive school settings as a way to achieve good student learning outcomes.

In addition to the potential advantages for both students and teachers, some challenges do exist, many of which mirror the challenges of collaborative teams: having adequate planning time and administrative assistance; helping teachers get accustomed to working together; and providing appropriate training, mentoring, and sustained support. Given the fairly consistent support for co-teaching, it is important that schools continuously evaluate their own student and staff outcomes and make improvements when these are lacking.

COLLABORATIVE TEACHING APPROACHES

Collaborative teaching approaches vary from less to more collaboration between teachers. Those with less collaboration also usually mean less mutual planning, less time together in the classroom, and less teaching by the special educator or co-teacher. Many special educators use a variety of approaches in any given year of teaching, selecting the approach that suits both the general educators' preferences and their own, matches their caseload and its distribution, and is related to the support given by the school administration for collaborative teaching and inclusion. Figure 6.2 describes commonly used co-teaching approaches and within-school and outside-school pressures affecting the use of co-teaching.

Student Snapshot

In Walter's basic English class, Ms. Hill and Ms. Burton have agreed to use the co-teaching approach of one group/one lead teacher, one teacher "teaching on purpose." They decided on this approach because Ms. Burton's specialized skills were not being used in the "drift and support" approach. Each week, they plan and note where students are in their understanding of class concepts and who might need mini-lessons to reinforce or extend understanding. When Ms. Burton "teaches on purpose," she gives students 1- and 2-minute mini-lessons individually or in pairs, and she notes their performance in the log she keeps with Ms. Hill. For instance, she helps Walter get started on an in-class writing assignment by asking him to organize his thoughts and start a story map diagram: "Think about the characters in Catcher in the Rye. Which one will you choose to write about? I'll be back." Then, Ms. Burton moves across the room to check the work of two other students with IEPs and gives one mini-lesson on using periods. From a distance, she monitors a student who has a notetaker (paraprofessional) to whom he dictates his sentences. She then returns to Walter and checks

Influencing pressures from inside and outside the school affecting co-teaching
Logistical and scheduling issues
• Special educator caseload, caseload distribution, general education class size, priority for co-teaching, diversity of student need, teacher school assignment[1,2]
Content understanding by special educator
• How much of the general classroom content did the special educator know well enough to teach? Is the class content pertinent to state-mandated test performance and diploma requirements?[2]
Acceptance by general educators
• Does the classroom teacher agree that the special educator's skills and teaching style are a complement to his or her own and believe that this individual will improve classroom outcomes?[2]
Skill needs of the students with disabilities and others in the class
• What is the range of student ability in the classroom in the content area? What is the range of behavioral needs and social/study skills of the students in the classroom?[2] What do parents and students want?

Co-teaching approaches	Potential problems/benefits
One group/one teacher, one supporter (one teaching, one drifting)[1,2,3] Little or no joint planning; general educator teaches; special educator provides support for instruction and behavior, but no teaching.	Special educator's skills underused; special educator often feels less valued; support can be provided by paraprofessional; more like pull-in than co-teaching.
One group/one teacher at a time (tag-team teaching)[3] May jointly plan but teach separately, one teacher first, other teacher follows.	Inefficient use of teachers as support that can be provided by paraprofessional; use if special educator must leave class early.
One group/one lead teacher, one teacher "teaching on purpose"[3] Joint plan; lead teacher varies, other teacher gives 1-, 2-, or 5-minute lessons (approach student, check understanding, give mini-lesson) to individuals, pairs, or small groups to reinforce or extend instruction; written log to keep track.	Better alternative to first two approaches. If both teachers alternate in the two roles, approach is more collaborative.
Two groups/two teachers teach same content (parallel instruction)[1,3] Jointly plan but teach separately; each teach half group same content.	Students with disabilities need not and should not always be in same group with special education teacher.
Two groups/one teacher re-teaches, one teaches alternative information (flexible grouping)[3]	Students with disabilities need not and should not always be in same group with the special education teacher.
Alternative teaching[1] Jointly plan but teach separately; small group gets instruction that is different from rest of class.	Students with disabilities need not and should not always be in same group with the special education teacher.
Two or more groups/two teachers monitor/teach; content varies (station teaching)[1,3] Jointly plan but teach separately; each teaches content to a groups that rotate across teachers; may include independent work station.	Non-teaching teacher can monitor student progress, provide mini-lessons to single students or groups, or work with one group while other monitors.
One group/two teachers teach same content (team teaching)[1,2,3] Jointly plan and teach content together; may use creative teaching roles (debate, explainer/demonstrator), use multiple grouping formats.	Although both teachers present content in planned ways at the same time, the special educator can also provide strategies to assist in better recall and organization of information presented.

Figure 6.2.   Different approaches for co-teaching and influencing pressures. [1]Friend and Cook (2003); [2]Weiss and Lloyd (2002); [3]Vaughn, Schumm, and Arguelles (1997).

his story map. Once Walter verbalizes the character he has chosen to write about, she does a mini-lesson reinforcing his use of the story map, then prompts him to start writing. Later, Ms. Burton checks back. Soon, students move into small groups to edit their writing; Ms. Burton works with Walter, another student with special needs, and two classmates while other small groups work under Ms. Hill's supervision.

It is not unusual for collaborative classrooms to bustle with activity, be noisier than other classrooms, or have more misbehavior. There are many ways to address these issues: 1) scheduling independent work at the same time when using a multiple group approach; 2) reducing the size of the class; 3) adding a paraprofessional to float and lend support; 4) strengthening classroom management or student motivation; or 5) changing the classroom arrangement so small groups are at opposite ends, study carrels are available for independent work groups, or heterogeneous small groups move for part of the class to a non–special education setting that suits the specific purpose of the group's focus or lesson (e.g., library, computer lab, outside nature trail).

Student Snapshot

Ms. Golder, the seventh-grade science teacher, co-teaches with Mr. Gaines, the special educator. Five students with IEPs, including Vanessa, are part of the class. The teachers frequently use a stations approach to co-teaching, and the class divides into two or three groups and rotates. Mr. Gaines has a bachelor's degree in science and a master's degree in special education, so he is qualified in the content area. He plans lab activities on the same topic for every lecture/discussion Ms. Golder gives. Often, they move outdoors where they make measurements and observations or gather specimens; other times they use the science room, the gym, or the home economics room for experiments. This helps hold the noise level down and allows the kids to move about during the 90-minute class period.

PLANNING AT THE SCHOOL LEVEL

Adequate time, cooperation from others, and workload are three obstacles to collaborative teaching (Bauwens, Hourcade, & Friend, 1989; Karge et al., 1995). Administrators need to be involved in creating ways to overcome these obstacles, such as the following (Walther-Thomas, Bryant, & Land, 1996):

1. Discussing the purposes and characteristics of collaborative teaching and identifying potential participants

2. Addressing logistical factors (e.g., realistic class sizes, pragmatic special educator caseloads and distribution, options for mutual planning time)

3. Creating classroom rosters that reflect heterogeneous groups, hand-scheduling students with special needs into classes, and not grouping students by test scores alone (Dawson, 1987)

4. Proving parents with information regarding the planned changes, obtaining parent input, and addressing parent concerns

5. Educating teachers about co-teaching and the approaches

6. Defining the roles and responsibilities of teaching partners

7. Ensuring that students' IEPs reflect skills that are needed in general education classrooms

8. Exploring the use of one or several classrooms to pilot the approach chosen and make improvements based on the outcomes

Because school scheduling has a major impact on co-teaching, principals have to stand behind the approach by including it in their schedule planning for classes, students, and staff. Other issues that impact co-teaching arrangements are class size and enrollment, teacher preferences, special educator's school assignment, caseload, and caseload distribution. When building administrators buy into co-teaching and initiate it in the school, they

Issue	Impact
Special educator caseload	With a caseload of 20 or fewer students, co-teaching can be feasible. If the special educator is responsible for too many students (e.g., more than 30), it may be nearly impossible to arrange for co-teaching.
Caseload distribution	If students on the special educator's caseload are clustered in classes (but not making up more than 33% of the class group), delivering services is a reasonable expectation. If students are widely distributed, or the special educator is expected to co-teach in six or more classes each day, difficulties arise.
General education class size	Co-taught classes should have approximately the same number of students as classes without this service. If several extra students are assigned because "after all, two teachers are there," the effectiveness of co-teaching is diminished.
Priority for co-teaching	As a service delivery option, co-teaching occurs in lieu of other services students receive. If special educators are expected to provide resource or other pull-out services to most or all of the students on their caseloads, co-teaching becomes a luxury that cannot be afforded because it is added onto those other services. In schools in which this dilemma occurs, educators often note that they cannot co-teach without additional staff being hired. Also, special educators may contend that in-class services can only be offered by paraprofessionals because teacher time must be spent delivering instruction in the special education setting.
Diversity of student need	Some special educators have a single student who needs a significant amount of pull-out service while all of the other students could be served in co-teaching. Unless special education staff and other professional collaborate to find a way to deliver the range of services needed by every student, co-teaching will not be feasible.
Teacher school assignment	In small school districts, special education teachers and other professional staff may be itinerant, serving two, three, or even more schools. In such instances, co-teaching can be only a small part of their jobs, often in a single location where it can be justified based on student numbers and needs.

Figure 6.3. Logistical issues that affect co-teaching. (From Friend, Marilyn And Cook, L. Interactions: Collaboration Skills for School Professionals, 4/e. Published by Allyn and Bacon, Boston, MA. Copyright © 2003 by Pearson Education. Reprinted by permission of the publisher.)

also need to communicate co-teaching as a standard practice in which all teachers may be asked to participate. Figure 6.3 gives an excellent summary of the logistical issues that have an impact on all co-teaching approaches.

Teacher Compatibility

Collaborative teaching partnerships must be entered into with some caution (Trent, 1998; Walther-Thomas et al., 1996). Potential teaching partners must first determine whether they are compatible enough to teach together (e.g., personality, teaching styles, knowledge) and clarify their purposes for co-teaching (Keefe, Moore, & Duff, 2004). Trent (1998) observed that incompatible teachers in a high school environment had differences in teaching styles, communication patterns, organization and operational methods, amount of planning and preparation, and reliability or follow-through. He found that both teachers in a strong co-teaching partnership take turns stepping into the roles of "expert" and "help-seeker" throughout any given day or week. A single pair of teachers use a variety of co-teaching approaches over a given semester of co-teaching.

Preparatory Steps

When an interest exists among teachers to learn about and apply a co-teaching approach and to extend or supplement pull-in services with co-teaching, teachers need to take several preparatory steps. Before teachers start a co-teaching partnership, they should know themselves, their partners, their students, and their talents (Gately & Gately, 2001; Keefe et al., 2004; Murawski & Dieker, 2004; Trent, 1998). Figure 6.4 sets forth some guidelines that teachers may use for 1) determining whether co-teaching will work for them, 2) implementing co-teaching, and 3) assessing its success at the end of a semester or school year (DeBoer & Fister, 1994).

Co-teaching arrangements need not be exclusive or extend across the whole day or year. Teachers typically limit their collaborative teaching to part of the day (e.g., certain subjects, certain teaching periods) or part of the year (e.g., particular grading periods, special units) (DeBoer & Fister, 1995–1996; Walther-Thomas et al., 1996). Multiple co-teaching plans can mesh nicely with the schedule of a special educator or related services staff member for lending team-planned support to several classrooms.

- Limited collaborative teaching arrangements (i.e., one or several periods or activities a day) are more common than co-teaching arrangements that take place all day, every day.

- Because special education teachers often support students in several general education classrooms, they work with multiple classrooms and teachers; this often makes it necessary to limit the co-teaching arrangement with any given teacher to part of the day.

- Because teams decide on a variety of supports for the students whom they serve, special education teachers often use a combination of ways to deliver services to students and teachers: collaborative teaching, pull-in, and, depending on student needs and team decisions, perhaps some pull-out with collaborative teaming.

- If two teachers do not think co-teaching will work, they can always plan, as a team, for special education supports to be pulled into the classroom.

Student Snapshot

In Ms. Skrincosky's seventh-grade English class, Mr. Gaines provides monitoring for Vanessa, supplies daily pull-in support for three students, and oversees two teaching assistants who carry out team-generated support plans for two other students; however, because he teaches an instructional group of students during another of Ms. Skrincosky's English classes, he also co-teaches with her. She is an active team member on the seventh-grade team and on the individual student teams. During social studies with Mr. Smith, Mr. Gaines provides only pull-in support but checks in weekly to plan and address any issues. Mr. Gaines operates a reading/writing lab for a small group of students, most of whom have IEPs (pull-out with collaborative teaming). He frequently touches base with Vanessa's English teacher so that his pull-out tutoring efforts are coordinated with her English class content and objectives.

Transition to Collaborative Teaching

Schools who have made the decision to begin using collaborative teaching should do so slowly. Teachers who have experience with collaborative teaching can serve as teaching partners for others who have no experience or as coaches for co-teaching partners. During the transition away from pull-out services, DeBoer and Fister (1995–1996) suggested that special education teachers initially de-

Before you start

- Identify who wants to teach collaboratively and with whom you might be compatible.
- Determine your rationale and objectives for co-teaching.
- Identify the resources/talents you both bring.
- Describe the supports/resources you may need.
- Discuss the content areas that will be co-taught.
- Decide on the time frame for planning and starting.
- Determine the formal approvals/support you will need from school administration.
- Study the class makeup and analyze the students' needs.
- Decide how student outcomes will be monitored.
- Decide how teaching outcomes will be monitored.
- Identify the daily/weekly time period that will be reserved for planning.
- Determine your roles and responsibilities in collaborative teaching.
- Decide how you will explain this arrangement to parents.
- Identify a coach/mentor who can provide you with critical feedback and guidance.
- Formalize your agreement between yourselves and with your administrator/supervisor.

As you implement

- Explain co-teaching to your students.
- Use planning times; reevaluate length of time needed.
- Get in the habit of dynamically communicating with each other; check perceptions, ask questions, reinforce each other, and provide feedback regularly.
- Extend your dynamic communication to administrators and facilitators/mentors.
- Monitor student and teacher outcomes, compare with goals, and ask if progress is adequate or if improvements are needed.
- Confer with your coach.
- If improvements are needed, identify improvements, develop a plan to make the improvements, and implement the plan.
- If additional training/support is needed, identify what it is and generate ways to obtain it.

At the end of the semester/year

- Continue communication and coaching.
- Monitor student and teacher outcomes, compare with goals, and ask if progress is adequate or if improvements are needed.
- Confer with your coach.
- Share student/teacher outcome data with colleagues and administrators.
- Celebrate accomplishments.
- If improvements are needed, confer with your coach, identify improvements, develop a plan to make the improvements, and implement the plan.
- Determine your collaborative teaching arrangements for the next year.

Figure 6.4. Guidelines for making collaborative teaming work. (From DeBoer, A., & Fister, S. [1994]. *Strategies and tools for collaborative teaching: Participant's handbook.* Longmont, CO: Sopris West; adapted by permission.)

sign their schedules to use pull-in services one third of the time or more, collaborative teaching one third of the time or more, and pull-out with collaboration one third of the time or less. This may require support staff to schedule multiple arrangements for delivering special education support; however, some support staff who prefer one type of arrange-ment may use that arrangement exclusively or primarily. Therefore, in the same school, one special educator might teach collaboratively on a full-time basis across grades and classrooms if and when it is suitable; another special educator might only provide pull-in services (consulting teacher role) across grades; and a third teacher, more experienced with resource or self-contained instruction models, might be responsible for any student needing a period of pull-out services with collaboration (e.g., community-based instruction, tutoring, writing labs, study hall support). Ultimately, team decisions regarding individual student needs, not staff preferences, should determine the way in which special education supports are delivered and also the way in which special education and related services staff will schedule their times to provide supports.

In the 1980s, many schools used team teaching models in which two general education teachers combined classes for certain subject areas. Teachers who have experience with general education team teaching are aware of the importance of compatibility between teaching partners and the ongoing need for communication; coordination in planning; and collaboration on teaching content, evaluation methods, and schedules. Some schools, particularly high schools, hire consulting special education teachers to coordinate other special education teachers, oversee procedures (eligibility and IEP meetings), troubleshoot, and serve as the liaison between administration and student. Because of their overview of the school's general and special education program and their experience with many teachers, consulting teachers often can be effective coaches to general and special educators learning to teach collaboratively.

ROLE EXCHANGE STRATEGY

Kenna Colley, a special education consultant, describes role exchange as a variation of role release that enables teachers to coach or model for each other while they develop new routines that all staff will implement with one or several target students. First, the team member who has the most experience with the developing teaching procedure models the teaching routine in an actual classroom situation while other team members observe. Team members give their input during or

after the demonstration and then adjust the procedure. Then, during the next natural opportunity to use the teaching routine, the teaching role shifts to another team member (e.g., classroom teacher, paraprofessional, related services staff) who tries it out in front of other team members who can coach or provide input as appropriate. Once team members discuss the success of the procedure, needed improvements are added to the teaching routine. The routine continues to rotate to other team members who will be using the procedure, and the same coaching, teaming, and refinement process is applied.

Student Snapshot

 In January, Melanie's team wanted to expand her schedule to include the fourth-grade writing-to-read computer lab; however, they knew they would need consistency across team members in implementing this schedule change. Melanie posed significant behavioral challenges whenever her schedule was changed to include new routines. Her teachers started the change by planning the routine with the computer teacher. Next, the teaching assistant and special education teacher accompanied Melanie and her classmates to computer lab for the first week. The special education teacher modeled the targeted routine by walking Melanie through the steps (e.g., sitting down at the computer that displayed her name card, typing in her name and date, redirecting her back to the computer when she got up and left). Following the suggestions of the special education teacher, the teaching assistant tried taking Melanie through the routine the next day. The special education teacher tried it again the following day with suggestions from the assistant. The general education teacher observed all week as she supervised Melanie's classmates in computer lab and offered ideas. Finally, after 5 days of this process, a set routine was written down at the team meeting with the input of the two teachers and the assistant. The following week, the general education teacher implemented the procedure in the presence of either the special education or the assistant. In

this example, role exchange and coaching allowed team members to both try out their ideas as they developed them and to model them for each other during collaborative teaching.

COMPLEMENTARY INSTRUCTION

Several authors have used the term *complementary instruction* in reference to the division of labor used by collaborative teachers to teach a classroom of diverse students efficiently and effectively. For example, the special education teacher might 1) prepare study guides; 2) keep a notebook of class notes; 3) organize students into working pairs and facilitate their active teamwork to review facts or complete application activities and worksheets; 4) teach half of the class part of a lesson and then rotate groups; 5) teach a smaller group that requires more adaptations; 6) teach organizational skills to the whole class; 7) model note-taking on an overhead while the general education teacher lectures or leads a class discussion regarding assigned reading; 8) modify the class worksheets for some or all students; and 9) adapt written tests or read exam questions to some students. These teaching duties, however, need to complement the classroom teacher's role; therefore, co-teachers need to think through their complementary roles for every lesson.

Planning is used to determine the complementary roles a team of two teachers will use in any given class; when teachers are experienced and comfortable in co-teaching roles, they adopt complementary routines for certain class topics or formats which require less precise planning. Figure 6.5 sets forth the complementary co-teaching tasks used by two teachers during the first 30 minutes of a ninth-grade English class and mimics a similar example that Walther-Thomas et al. (1996) described for a middle school classroom. In this ninth-grade English class, a team of a general education and a special education teacher co-taught 29 students, 6 of whom re-

ceived special education services. The teachers used a "one group/one lead teacher, one teacher 'teaching on purpose'" approach (see Figure 6.2). The classroom teacher maintained primary responsibility for teaching the subject matter and the special education teacher filled a complementary role: She assumed "primary responsibility for students' mastery of the academic survival skills necessary to acquire the subject content" at the time they were needed (Bauwens et al., 1989, p. 19). The special educator also increased her individualized direct instruction role by using the "teaching on purpose" approach of giving 1- to 5-minute mini-lessons to one, two, or three students at a time (Vaughn, Schumm, & Arguelles, 1997).

SUPPORTIVE LEARNING ACTIVITIES

Supportive learning activities are a version of co-teaching (Bauwens et al., 1989) that is very similar to complementary instruction. The classroom teacher introduces the primary academic content of a lesson while the special educator plans and teaches activities that supplement and enhance the primary academic content. Other supportive learning activities that could be taught by special educators include teacher-led group discussions; cooperative learning groups, labs, or experiments; or drill and practice using a classwide peer tutoring method.

Student Snapshot

 During a unit on plant life in Melanie's class, Ms. Ramirez addressed photosynthesis using explanation, overhead pictures, and a video. Afterward, Ms. Pitonyak conducted a lab designed to enrich the content on photosynthesis. Students organized into cooperative groups examined plants that they had placed to grow under different amounts of light and measured their growth.

English teacher	Special education teacher
• Reviews the past 2 days	• Takes roll silently
• Introduces discussion of questions completed on homework	• Assists student in locating materials
• Locates materials for a student	• Walks around room to check for completed homework; makes record in grade book
• Leads discussion of each question, including reading the question, calling on students for the answers, probing for more in-depth responses, reinforcing students for their comments, and writing responses on the board	• Restates several questions for clarification while checking work
	• Records class notes and answers on overhead projector
	• Prompts student to read aloud
• Moves around room continuing to question	• Prompts student to attend to discussion
• Questions a detail that requires students to locate an answer in book	• Adds details to discussion
	• Walks around room with eyes on students' books to be sure all are on correct page
• Calls on student to reread for clarification	• Helps a student find the correct page
• Continues to lead discussion of questions, reinforcing students for their answers	• Continues overhead notetaking; quietly reinforces student
• Prompts a student to behave	• Quietly prompts Sam to used his behavior self-monitoring procedure when he talks out
• Tells students when to expect a turn to answer when several students want to answer a question	• Checks student's notes for clarity
• Continues to lead class discussion	• Restates point from a different perspective
• Wraps up discussion, reinforces everyone's effort	• Rechecks Sam's work and gives thumbs up
• Announces the reading of "Old Demon" for homework	• Writes assignment on overhead
• Divides the class into small heterogeneous groups and gives discussion options and directions	• Gives student 2-minute mini-lesson on her self-management objective of recoding assignment and quiz in planner
	• Gives 1-minute mini-lesson with two students who will do alternate assignments to replace missed assignments
• Circlulates, spending 5 minutes with three groups, listening and acknowledging their work	• Circlulates, spending 5 minutes with three other groups listening and acknowledging their work

Figure 6.5. Co-teaching complementary roles in a high school English class using the approach of one group/one lead teacher, one teacher "teaching on purpose." (Contributed by Johnna Elliott.)

VARIATIONS FOR TEAMING ACROSS GRADE LEVELS

Numerous possibilities exist for applying co-teaching with or without pull-in services across different age groups. Regular team planning must take place with the classroom teacher for content, co-teaching approaches, and timing. Teacher stress is lowest and student learning highest when the classroom flow of traffic is nondisruptive and predictable.

Elementary Schools

Ms. Pitonyak, Daniel's special education teacher, teaches a reading group two times a week in Daniel's classroom. There are six students in this group, two of whom have IEPs. Ms. James knows that Ms. Pitonyak is working on the same skills with this group that she teaches to the rest of the class; however, each lesson is not co-planned in detail. When the two teachers meet weekly and touch base on-the-fly during the day, they relate their progress. In kindergarten, Ms. Pitonyak also teaches small groups and co-plans her reading readiness activities weekly with the two kindergarten teachers, all of which overlap with kindergarten or pre-kindergarten objectives; the small groups rotate through Ms. Pitonyak's "teaching station" just as they rotate through the other adult-directed activities.

Secondary Schools

As in elementary and middle schools, variations of pull-in services and co-teaching (as well as some pull-out with collaboration) are used at the high school level. One high school that practices inclusion has approximately 1,100 students enrolled, 11% (120 students) of whom qualify for special education services. This caseload is divided among seven special education teachers, most of whom are responsible during the day for managing their caseload of students and for teaching by means of pull-in and co-teaching approaches. Four of the seven special education teachers work in partnership with general education teachers for four or five periods out of the seven-period day. Each teacher provides direct instruction in a resource environment for one or two periods and has a planning period.

Student Snapshot

 Ms. Dowling, a special educator at Sam's school, begins her day with a planning period. During second period, she provides pull-in services to Sam in world geography while monitoring several other students in the class. During third period, she goes to the study hall and checks on four students who often require assistance with studying or may need to complete tests for other classes. During fourth and sixth periods, Ms. Dowling provides pull-in support in two tenth-grade English classes. During fifth and seventh periods, she co-teaches in English 9. Therefore, Ms. Dowling's day consists of providing pull-in support during general education classes and study hall and co-teaching for two of the seven periods. Because Ms. Dowling studied English literature (along with special

education) in college, she was the logical person to support students in those classes and team with the English department. Early in the year, Ms. Dowling assessed classroom activities and then discussed needed adaptations with each teacher. Ms. Dowling planned her support to reflect their needs.

At the same high school, one special education teacher (the consulting teacher) provides resource support and maintains a pull-out option for students who require or request one-to-one instruction in adapted content, direct instruction in reading, or intensive short-term behavioral support. Another special education teacher coordinates and supervises several alternative, noninclusive options for one or more periods of the day for students who, with parental approval, have elected these activities. These options include 1) community-based instruction, 2) supported employment, and 3) self-contained academic instruction. The consulting special education teacher, who manages a smaller caseload, oversees the entire program; she coordinates the teaching assistants and teachers, reviews all paperwork, provides emergency support to students and teachers, and chairs eligibility and child study committees. Finally, five teaching aides lend support by attending scheduled classes and assisting identified students with their accommodations (e.g., one teaching aide serves as a notetaker for a student in earth science). Assistants monitor each student's progress and then consult with the student's case manager.

PLANNING BETWEEN COLLABORATIVE TEACHERS

The obvious foundation for co-teaching is collaboration within the core team for each student with special needs who is enrolled in the classroom. Collaborative teachers implement team-generated plans for individual students. Extended team members, including occupational therapists, physical therapists, speech-language pathologists, and guidance counselors, may also pair up with a classroom teacher, though they are more likely to provide pull-in services in the classroom for specific students. Other collaborative teams that address the needs of groups of students (e.g., grade-level or department teams) can contribute support to teachers who pair together to teach, particularly in middle school where students often rotate among a team of teachers.

Collaborative Planning of Classroom Practices

Using pull-in arrangements for support often means that the special education teacher is more like a visitor to a number of classrooms rather than part of an actual teaching team. Special education teachers often need to work hard to fit into existing classroom practices by implementing team-designed modifications or adding supplementary instructional practices to the existing programs for students with special needs. Under pull-in support arrangements, the classroom teacher may initially regard the target student as the "special education teacher's student" (or the paraprofessional's student) and yield to that person on what is "best." This viewpoint usually changes once the classroom teacher becomes familiar with the student and his or her needs, gains confidence, and uses methods modeled by the special education teacher (Giangreco et al., 1993).

Teachers' efforts are more fully integrated when they follow the planning steps for co-teaching than when they follow the steps for a pull-in approach. Both teachers must learn about the other's practices and probably will influence each other a great deal as they blend their teaching ideas. Although both pull-in services and collaborative teaching require the contributing team members to understand the classroom teacher's practices, collaborative teaching goes a step further than pull-in: Teachers must reach consensus on classroom practices, as both will actively use them. These practices include class rules and consequences, homework procedures and

policy, in-class participation, grouping, teaching methods (e.g., lecture, discussions), practice options (e.g., independent work, cooperative groups, labs), approaches for monitoring and evaluating progress, and approaches for communicating with families. Another book in this series, *Modifying Schoolwork, Second Edition* (Janney & Snell, 2004), explains this part of the process as an assessment of the general education classroom activities and spells out steps for doing so. The General Assessment of Classroom Activities (see Figure 6.6 for a completed form for Sam) is particularly helpful to co-teachers in this initial stage of defining the general education classroom. Additionally, collaborative teaching requires that both teachers share their ideas and philosophies regarding these practices with one another and, through teaming, learn new approaches from each other as they design the shared portions of the day.

Collaborative Planning of Instruction

Once teachers and administrators have successfully navigated the steps leading to collaborative teaching, the team of teachers jointly addresses two broad questions about instruction:

1. What should we teach?
2. How should we teach this content so that all students learn what they need to learn?

Janney and Snell (2004) also described in detail the collaborative planning of instruction within the framework of designing modifications to school work.

Student Snapshot

 Daily during third period, Mr. Gaines co-teaches with Ms. Golder in the seventh-grade general science class. Five students with IEPs are enrolled in science: Three students have learning disabilities (one is Vanessa), one student has multiple

General Assessment of Classroom Activities

Subject/grade level: <u>*World Geography/9th*</u> Date: <u>*9/2004*</u>

Student: <u>*Sam*</u> Teacher: <u>*Ms. Sailor*</u>

Instructional activities		
Typical activities	**Frequently used student responses/tasks**	**Adaptations?**
Whole class		
· Lecture/discussion	*Take notes from board and overhead projector; raise hands to volunteer answers to questions (daily)*	*Yes*
· Maps	*Locate places, describe/discuss geographic features (almost daily)*	*No*
· Films	*Take notes, discuss (approximately 1x/week)*	*No*
· Oral reading of text	*students volunteer to read (2–3x/week)*	*No*
Small group		
· Cooperative projects	*Research, writing reports in groups of 4 (1–2x/week)*	*Yes (minimal)*
Independent		
· Silent reading	*(1–2x/week)*	*Yes*
· Seatwork	*Answer chapter questions, look up vocabulary words, map worksheets (2–3x/week)*	*Yes*
Homework (frequency and approximate duration) *Monday through Thursday, 20–30 minutes; usually have a few minutes at end of period to start*		*Yes*
Textbooks, other frequently used materials *World geography text* *Atlas, globe, wall maps*		*Yes* *No*
General education teacher assistance provided to all students *Teacher circulates throughout room, providing opportunities to ask questions; checks frequently for understanding. Students are encouraged to ask each other questions.*		*Yes*
Evaluation/testing • Test/quiz format *Unit tests: multiple choice, matching, true/false* *Vocabulary quiz for each unit: fill in the blank* • Sources of information for tests *Textbook, lecture notes, worksheets* *Review 1 day prior to test: good opportunity for students to prepare study guide*		*Yes to all*
Classroom rules and contingencies *Must bring textbook, paper, pencil* *Strict enforcement of school conduct code re: attendance, appearance, language* *Students responsible for making up missed work within 2 days of absence or no credit* **Norms for student interaction and movement** *Raise hand during lecture/discussion; talking okay while working in groups* *May move around to sharpen pencils, get atlases, etc., except during lecture or test* **Procedures for routines** *Student at front of each row hands out/collects papers* *Folder on teacher's desk with previous day's handouts for students who are absent*		*Yes to all*

Figure 6.6. General assessment of classroom activities in Sam's ninth-grade world geography class. (From Janney, R., & Snell, M.E. [2004]. *Modifying schoolwork* [2nd ed., p. 64]. Baltimore: Paul H. Brookes Publishing Co.; reprinted by permission.)

Collaborative Teaching Planning Form			
Subject: _____ **Period:** _____ **Prepared by:** _____			
Lesson overview		Education standards assessment	
Lesson element	**General educator's reponsibilities**	**Special educator's reponsibilities**	**Additional notes and comments**
Tasks to be completed			
Criteria for student success			
Learning strategies			
Strategies to implement positive behavior support			

Figure 6.7. Collaborative teaching planning form (From: "The Four 'Knows' of Collaborative Teaching," by E.B. Keefe, V. Moore, & F. Duff, *Teaching Exceptional Children*, vol. 36:5, page 40. The Council for Exceptional Children. Copyright 2004. Reprinted with permission.)

disabilities, and the fifth student has cognitive disabilities. Along with their principal, the two teachers arranged for a day and a half of planning time during the summer. First, even though familiar with each others' teaching styles and general outlook on education, they shared their own teaching philosophies. Second, they identified the roles and responsibilities each teacher would fill in science class. (See Figures 3.6 and 6.7 for examples of forms useful in completing this planning step.) Third, they reviewed Ms. Golder's class characteristics by completing the *classroom assessment form. Fourth, they identified who might need curricular adaptations. Then, using a unit plan form (see Figure 6.8), they outlined the units they would use during the school year. Next, they designed activity-based science lessons for each unit to provide active learning for all students. Finally, they discussed the co-teaching approaches they liked best and also determined how cooperative learning would allow them to make use of peer support in heterogeneous groups of students. After this initial planning, they felt ready to start*

Unit Plan

Unit theme: _____   Teachers: _____

Dates and times: _____

Unit goals: "big ideas" (Concepts, principles, and issues)	Minimal competencies (Essential facts, skills, and processes)
Extended/advanced objectives	**Adapted objectives**

Tasks/activities

_____ Lecture: _____

_____ Reading: _____

_____ Discussion: _____

_____ Library research: _____

_____ Writing: _____

_____ Building/creating: _____

_____ Solving: _____

_____

Major unit projects (Note adaptations)	Supplementary activities
Evaluation measures	**Adapted evaluation measures**
Materials needed	**Adapted materials needed**

Figure 6.8.   Unit plan form.

a year of collaborative teaching for the general science class; their weekly planning period, along with regular communication before school on an as needed basis, would provide them with the time they would need to adjust this planned structure over time.

Multilevel Curriculum and Curriculum Overlap

Students who are included in general education often have curriculum objectives that do not differ from their typical classmates; however, their IEPs may also specify objectives that differ in complexity from their classmates' or that are drawn from different subject or skill areas. The term *multilevel curriculum* refers to lessons involving objectives of varying degrees of difficulty for various students; *curriculum overlap* refers to lessons for which students' objectives are drawn from different subject or skill areas (Giangreco & Putnam, 1991). Both types of objectives involve the provision of individualized adaptations to enable students with IEPs to participate in learning activities with their classmates. Multilevel instruction (instruction at different levels of difficulty) is regarded by most teachers as simpler, more ordinary, and less special than curriculum overlap. Therefore, multilevel curriculum objectives are preferred if they enable social and instructional participation for the target students. If improved participation can be obtained for a given student through the use of curriculum overlap, then teachers should use this type of curriculum adaptation.

Collaborative Planning of Lessons and Instructional Units

Thematic units that integrate several curriculum areas (e.g., reading, writing, science) under an organizing topic can be easily applied for a class of students who have a wide range of abilities and interests. Teachers work to identify the unit's "Big Ideas" (i.e., concepts, principles, and issues that it will address) and minimal competencies (i.e., facts, skills, and

processes that are regarded as essential for all students to learn; see Figure 6.8). Then, considering the range of students in the class, the teachers identify extended or advanced learning objectives (for those whose capabilities exceed the minimal competencies) and simplified or adapted objectives for those students who need them. Next, teachers identify the tasks and the activities for the unit, making sure to use as many input modes (i.e., ways to present material) and output modes (i.e., ways for students to respond) as possible. The major projects and activities planned for the unit are listed, and needed adaptations are noted. A listing or folder of supplementary activities for students to complete as alternatives to the major activities is created for each unit. Teachers plan their methods for evaluating the students, with notes regarding adapted measures for those students who need them. Finally, unit materials are listed, and any needed adaptive materials are noted. An alternate form for planning lessons over several days can be found in Figure 6.9.

Activity-Based Lessons

Activity-based lessons are those lessons that involve a "hands on" activity through which teachers instruct students or provide them with practice of previously taught skills. In place of a worksheet on liquid measurement equivalencies, middle school students might fill the class aquarium using several equivalent measures or make Kool-Aid or concentrated juice for the class.

Activity-based lessons are prevalent in inclusive classrooms because they 1) provide practical meaning to abstract concepts, 2) make it easier to present material in several ways (e.g., visual, kinesthetic, auditory, tactile), and 3) follow a structure that facilitates the use of a variety of curriculum objectives in a single lesson. Activity-based instruction does not and should not replace skill-based instruction; instead, it is often supplemented with direct instruction on specific skills in addition to drill and practice in the use of those skills and the application of the acquired knowledge.

Co-teaching Daily Lesson Plans

General educator: *Harriett Golder*   **Special educator:** *Dean Gaines*   **Class:** *Basic Science 7*

Date	Subject	Approach	Specific tasks of both teachers	Materials	Evaluation of learning	Students who need follow-up
10/5	Roots and stems	Two or more groups/two teachers monitor/teach; content varies	HG: Monitor the other groups DG: Work with one group	Celery stalks, carrots, colored water, lab notebook, short video	Completion of lab report Following procedures	Raul: Have Raul paraphrase steps before beginning procedures
10/6	Photo-synthesis	Two groups/two teachers teach same content	Each teacher works with one group of students	Various types of plants, library books on plants, colored transparencies	Weekly quiz Learning logs	John and Julie: Review vocabulary words one-to-one or with partner Sarah: Reread library book to improve fluency Vanessa: more time on quiz in resource
10/7	Leaves: transpiration and water regulation	One group/one lead teacher, one teacher "teaching on purpose"	HG: Lead DG: Teach on purpose - - - - - - - - - - - HG: Alternative information DG: Re-teach	Textbook: Broad-leaf plants, Vaseline, lab notebook, colors	KWL sheet Diagram of observation Lab report	Julie: Retype lab report on computer using spell check to assist with handwriting and spelling

Figure 6.9.   Co-teaching daily lesson plans for a seventh-grade basic science class. (From: "The ABCDEs of co-teaching," by S. Vaughn, J.S. Schumm, & M.E. Arguelles. Teaching Exceptional Children, vol. 30:2, page 6. The Council for Exceptional Children, Copyright 1997. Adapted with permission.)

Cooperative Learning Groups

Teachers should make use of cooperative learning groups because of their proven effectiveness in promoting social and academic learning within mixed ability classrooms. To ensure success, teachers should identify cooperative learning activities that mesh with the unit being studied and teach their students the cooperative skills required for these

groups to be productive. Cooperative learning has five essential components that teachers will need to implement:

- Positive interdependence among students

- Individual accountability

- Heterogeneous grouping

- Direct instruction of necessary social skills

- Group processing methods that enable
  groups to examine their cooperation and
  learning

Student Snapshot

*After studying the records of
the students in the third-period
science class, Ms. Golder and
Mr. Gaines made a preliminary
list of cooperative groups. Although the students had worked in cooperative groups before, the teachers felt that they
should schedule the first 3 weeks to review or
teach the concepts of positive interdependency, individual accountability, group processing, and the required social skills. They
decided to use cooperative group activities
twice a week.*

Scheduling

When special education teachers provide
pull-in services and co-teach, they usually rotate among classrooms, rather than work
with only one classroom. Some researchers
recommend concentrating students with disabilities in a smaller number of classes,
thereby reducing the number of classrooms
in which the special education teachers must
co-teach. Although this approach may make
the special education teacher's job easier and
more efficient, students with special needs
should be assigned to classrooms with their
peers without disabilities in proportions similar to their natural proportions in a neighborhood school.

Student Snapshot

*Because 11% of students at
Vanessa's rural middle school
have special needs, approximately 3 students in each class
of 30 will have identified special needs; however, the proportion may be
less in advanced courses. In Ms. Golder's basic
science class there are five students with IEPs,
whereas there are two students with IEPS in her
advanced science class.*

Scheduling classes so students are enrolled
in what they want to take and classes are heterogeneous and balanced is challenging. The
school administrator must work closely with
guidance counselors and special and general
educators at each grade level to assess teachers' talent for and interest in having students
with disabilities in their classroom and to provide necessary training and support.

Student Snapshot

*Mr. Gaines's schedule is a good
illustration of balance. He rotates among seven classes
using pull-in services for three
to five students in social studies, reading, math, and language arts; co-
teaches in science; and uses pull-out services
for five students in the form of an academic
lab geared primarily toward three students
with special needs.*

Ideally, special education teachers in inclusive schools will have broader training and
experience that allows them to adequately
serve all or most of the children with identified needs for a single grade level (e.g., eighth-
grade team), multiple grade levels (e.g.,
kindergarten through second grades), or high
school department depending on the size
of the school (e.g., science, math, English).
Those students with more extensive support
needs may require services from a special education teacher who rotates across all grade
levels to consult with the classroom teachers

and to support these students directly. When only a few children with severe disabilities are present in a school and teachers with specialized training in severe disabilities are not on staff, the school's central office might assign a teacher from a nearby school to support these students on a consultative basis or may assign specialized teachers to work on a regional basis (e.g., one teacher serves all students with severe disabilities enrolled in schools in the southern feeder pattern).

The organizing schedules that teachers develop are crucial to the implementation of needed individualized supports. Teams will modify these schedules over time when new students enroll, students move, staff and semesters change, and schedule complications arise. These schedule changes should be generated, or at least approved, by the team(s) involved.

EVALUATING OUTCOMES

Teachers who co-teach will want to evaluate their interpersonal effectiveness as a teaching team (e.g., comfort, shared decision-making, compatibility) and their impact on students (e.g., attitudes, knowledge and skills, behavior, friendship and group skills, referrals). Evaluations should be conducted regularly year's end (e.g., DeBoer & Fister, 1995–1996; Trent, 1998). Teachers should develop a plan and a regular schedule for evaluating their co-teaching. If problems do arise between teachers or with the success of collaborative teaching, these evaluation plans will provide teachers with a previously determined opportunity to examine data and to make modifications.

Evaluating the Effects of Collaborative Teaching on Students

Collaborative teaching can be evaluated in many ways. Data can be gathered from dif-

ferent sources (students, teachers, parents) using a variety of methods (informal discussion, interviews, self-ratings, observation). In addition, school records can be examined before and after the use of co-teaching to assess its impact on student performance (attendance records, grades, number of office referrals). This information can be used to assess and improve the impact that a shift to collaborative teaching has had in a school.

Student Snapshot

 At the end of their first seventh-grade science unit in October, Ms. Golder and Mr. Gaines used a questionnaire to assess the effect that their collaborative teaching had on the class. They read 10 questions aloud and asked students to circle one of five ratings, depicted by smiley face (liked very much), neutral face (was okay), and sad face (didn't like at all) symbols and two in-between ratings, to rate the new teaching methods they had used. After they collected the questionnaires (without student names on them), they held an open discussion regarding the questions and other issues that came up.

Processing Together Between Teachers

Similar to processing within collaborative teams (see Chapters 3 and 7), teachers who are involved in collaborative teaching should take a few minutes after each co-taught lesson to compare notes regarding their impressions of the session and to explore ways they might improve less-successful areas. Figure 6.10 provides a teacher reflection questionnaires by DeBoer and Fister (1995–1996); however, teachers should develop their own questionnaires based on the shared values and ground rules they developed with their collaborative team(s). They should also add items regarding the specific roles and responsibilities identified early in co-teaching to their listing of interpersonal skills.

Item	Not at all ◄————————► Completely
1. I feel that my knowledge and skills are valued.	1 2 3 4 5 6 7 8 9
2. I believe that information and materials are freely shared.	1 2 3 4 5 6 7 8 9
3. I believe that I am an equal partner in the decisions that are made.	1 2 3 4 5 6 7 8 9
4. I am frequently acknowledged and reinforced by my partner.	1 2 3 4 5 6 7 8 9
5. I believe we are using sound instructional practices.	1 2 3 4 5 6 7 8 9
6. I am learning as a result of our roles and responsibilities.	1 2 3 4 5 6 7 8 9
7. My time is used productively when I am in the classroom.	1 2 3 4 5 6 7 8 9
8. I am satisfied with our roles and responsibilities.	1 2 3 4 5 6 7 8 9
9. I am satisfied with the way we communicate with and coach each other.	1 2 3 4 5 6 7 8 9

Figure 6.10.   Questionnaire for teachers to reflect on collaborative teaching. (From DeBoer, A., & Fister, S. [1994]. *Strategies and tools for collaborative teaching: Participant's handbook.* Longmont, CO: Sopris West; adapted by permission.)

Chapter 7

Improving Communication
and Handling Conflict

Student Snapshot

Ms. Brown is late once again to Walter's team meeting—this time by 20 minutes—and the meeting is almost over. Ms. Hill reacts, "How do you expect us to work together if you are never here on time?" "You always blame me," Ms. Brown retorts and stomps out of the room in tears.

To make matters worse, Walter's mom refuses to sign his IEP, even after the lengthy process his teachers used to involve her. Team members are disappointed and angry. "What does she want anyway? We put everything in his program!" "She doesn't know how good that IEP is!"

Even good teams experience lapses in trust, negative stereotyping, miscommunication, and impasse. No team can operate without having some internal conflict. A team's members, experiences, and outcomes are dynamic and changing, as is a team's relationship with its supporting school environment. This chapter addresses the characteristics of strong and effective teams: establishing team trust, promoting accurate and unambiguous communication, being sensitive to diversity and avoiding stereotyping, fostering positive staff–family interactions, and addressing disagreement. These interrelated characteristics contribute to the interpersonal relationships and communication among team members, both of which are essential for creative and cooperative work conditions. Inevitably, even when these characteristics are in place, most teams periodically experience problem behavior from one or more team members and nonconstructive conflict within the group. The last section of this chapter discusses strategies for addressing these threats to team effectiveness.

ESTABLISHING TEAM TRUST

Establishing trust among team members is not a simple process; it requires both trusting others and being trustworthy (Johnson &

Johnson, 2000). When each team member trusts his or her fellow team members, several qualities are realized:

- *Interdependency*—Team outcomes depend on others as well as on oneself.

- *Shared risk*—Team outcomes can be good or bad and can result in gains or losses for oneself, the student, and/or the team.

- *Confidence*—Team outcomes will be good and will yield benefits (Deutsch, 1962).

Interdependency, for example, involves a willingness on the part of each team member to contribute to the achievement of team goals by 1) sharing their resources for group gain (e.g., talents, materials, ideas, time, energy), 2) giving help to others (e.g., modeling skills, volunteering for tasks in team action plans), 3) receiving help from each other (e.g., learning from one another's demonstrations; seeking and listening to the viewpoints, advice, or information of other team members), and 4) dividing the team's work. These interdependent behaviors are associated with team members' open expression of ideas, feelings, reactions, opinions, and information (Johnson & Johnson, 2000).

Student Snapshot

Ms. Wilson wonders whether there will be harmful or beneficial outcomes if she confesses her frustrations with Sam to her teammates: "As Sam's teacher in English 9, I am a member of Sam's team. I contributed to the design of his support plans, which were drawn up in August. However, after 2 months of using these plans, I'm very frustrated by the way in which other students seem to push his buttons, which almost always causes him to get upset; then I get upset and off task. Co-teaching with Ms. Elliott is working well; however, she seems much more able to ignore these interactions, to let them just go, or to prompt him (like we agreed in the action plan) to say things such as, 'get off my back' or, 'lay off.' I get tense and fearful that Sam will

explode, I won't know what to do, and the whole class will fall apart. I've decided to say something, even though I'm concerned that the problem might really be my problem, but I worry: If I openly express myself, will you use it against me? Will you think I'm less capable or that I'm not trying?"

The way in which Ms. Wilson's teammates respond to her trusting and open expression will have a lasting influence on her comfort with the team as well as on her eventual ability to be successful in supporting Sam.

How Team Members Gain Trust

DeBoer (1995) identified three basic strategies for facilitating trust among co-workers and team members:

1. Empathy toward other team members occurs when one team member is able to take the perspective of others.
    "You know I feel the same way sometimes," says another teacher. "I see Sam a lot every day, and he's not the first challenging student I have had; however, I remember that same fearful feeling when I first met Sam!" Ms. Elliott adds.

2. Acceptance of the other team members for what they are means showing genuine positive regard for another person's capacity, experiences, talents, and unique viewpoints.
    "I can understand how scary it can be—you've seen one of his worst explosions," says a counselor, who remembers Sam's anger in English during the first week of classes. "He exploded the day he forgot to take his medication; school had just started, high school was brand new for him, and he was confused about his schedule. He has not fallen apart like that since, thank goodness—and I think it's because of all of our supports, including his parents' help with the medication schedule!" the counselor adds.

3. Credibility means that team members perceive each other as compatible or similar and competent (i.e., having talents to bring to the team that others value) and as someone who openly speaks his or her mind and takes the group's interest to heart.
    Ms. Wilson and her teammates have many years of high school teaching experience among them. They have strong respect for each other's talents. Each team member interacts with Sam regularly, and, for the most part, their team-generated action plan for supporting him has been highly successful.

Trust is built when an individual takes a risk in initiating an interaction with another person and is affirmed, which leads to team members' open sharing (disclosure).

Although trust is essential to team effectiveness, there are limits to trust. Trust in another team member is appropriate only when the potential for benefit is greater than the potential for harm. This requires "sizing up" the situation and initiating or reacting accordingly.

PROMOTING ACCURATE AND UNAMBIGUOUS COMMUNICATION

Team members who want their messages to be understood have to meet three rudimentary requirements (Johnson & Johnson, 2000):

1. Phrase the message in a way that listeners can understand. Avoid acronyms and technical terminology, use examples, and adjust language to the audience (see Figure 7.1).

2. Be a credible message sender. Receivers must regard your messages as trustworthy.

3. Ask others for feedback regarding their understanding of and reaction to what was communicated.

Communicators have credibility when they are viewed as being knowledgeable about the content under discussion, when their motives

Sending messages effectively	Receiving messages effectively
• Own your messages by using first person (i.e., "I" and "My").	• Check your understanding of the message by paraphrasing as accurately as possible, without any judgment of the sender's message or feelings. To do this,
• Use complete and specific messages (as needed, communicate your frame of reference, assumptions, and intentions).	• Restate the message in your own words.
• Be congruent in your verbal and your nonverbal messages.	• Do not communicate any approval or disapproval.
• Repeat your message in more than one way and through another channel to be clear.	• Do not add to or take away from the message.
• Seek feedback from teammates on your message.	• Step into the speaker's "shoes" to understand the meaning of his or her message.
• Match the message to listeners' frame of reference (e.g., student, another teacher, parent, administrator).	• Communicate that you want to fully understand before you make an evaluation.
• Be unambiguous by describing your feelings (e.g., name them, use figurative speech, or state actions): "I feel happy!" "I'm down in the dumps!" or, "I want to run away from this."	• Check your perceptions of the sender's feelings by describing them:
	• Describe tentatively; seek confirmation.
• Describe the behavior of others but do not evaluate or interpret it (e.g., "You keep interrupting" not, "You are a horrible listener").	• Do not communicate any approval or disapproval or try to interpret or explain your perceptions (e.g., "It seems like you are worried about Jennifer being in sixth-grade classes. Am I right?").
	• Talk to the sender and negotiate the interpretation of his/her message until you both agree on the meaning.

Figure 7.1. Being effective senders and receivers of messages. (*Source:* Johnson & Johnson, 2000.)

are not suspect, when their tone and style are friendly, when listeners regard them as trustworthy, and when they are assertive and emphatic in communicating their messages.

The skill of listening to or receiving a message has two fundamental requirements: 1) communicating, primarily through nonverbal behavior, that you want to understand the speaker's message and feelings, and 2) actually understanding the speaker's message and feelings (Johnson & Johnson, 2000). Communicating intent is achieved mainly through the receiver's nonverbal behavior (e.g., facing the speaker, establishing eye contact, looking interested, not interrupting).

When a receiver makes immediate judgments regarding a speaker's message without first confirming his or her understanding of the message, he or she often stops listening

or leaps to conclusions based on a premature or erroneous evaluation of the message. Trust is consequently eroded. Premature evaluations by receivers also cause senders to be defensive, closed, and less able to explain or expand on their message.

Student Snapshot

 In Melanie's school system, transition to middle school occurs at the end of fourth grade because middle schools house grades 5 through 8. When Melanie's team met with her future team members at the middle school in March, trust had not developed between both groups. Ms. Ramirez and Ms. Pitonyak narrated the video that Melanie's peers had made of class activi-

ties that showed off many of Melanie's talents. The two teachers described the various ways the team supported Melanie (e.g., small group pull-in, co-teaching, peer tutoring) and emphasized that pull-out was rarely needed anymore. Two of the fifth-grade teachers started frowning; one shook her head but said nothing. Ms. Ramirez, who had been happily sharing Melanie's successes, felt judged and angry, as if her ideas were being discredited. She abruptly stopped talking; the meeting room became quiet and was filled with tension.

After Ms. Ramirez abruptly stopped, one of the fifth-grade teachers sensed the tension and misunderstanding. She said, "It seems as if you and Ms. Pitonyak have experienced a lot of success in teaching Melanie alongside her fourth-grade classmates. This makes your whole team feel successful."

"That's right," beamed Ms. Ramirez, happy that one of the listeners understood her message. "It was hard at first because I had never had someone like Melanie in my classroom, and it took some creative team problem-solving to make it work as well as it has. Melanie, however, has met all of her IEP goals, her family is happy with her success, she never misses school anymore, she has friends, and, as you saw in the video, her classmates have positive things to say about having her as a classmate."

The fifth-grade teacher who had spoken up added, "We might need your help . . ."

Ms. Ramirez spoke up: "We'd like to help . . . and we know that middle school is not elementary school. You might have to change our strategies to fit middle school a little better, and you probably will think up lots of new ideas that work better with your class schedules. We'd be very willing, however, to show you all that we have learned about fourth-grade academic work and social issues."

The expressions on the faces of all three fifth-grade teachers brightened.

Tough listening times occur when a speaker sends a message that takes a judgmental position (DeBoer, 1995). Often, the message conflicts directly with strongly held beliefs or values of the listener, but the listener should still listen to what the speaker is saying during these situations before responding or waiting until a later time to make a reasoned response. Figure 7.2 provides examples of these situations, in addition to guidance on how to listen.

If a team's comfort level is low in seeking clarification of a message through questioning each other, they might want to 1) devise interesting exercises to practice the skill (e.g., give incomplete directions, tell a story/joke but leave out a key line), 2) modify their ground rules ("Listen and understand me before you judge my ideas"), and 3) recall examples of their own tough listening situations and discuss alternative ways they might have used effective listening strategies.

Giving and Receiving Feedback Effectively

Any improvement that results from constructive feedback given to a teammate depends equally on the talents of the person giving and the one receiving the feedback. Givers must be sensitive to the receptivity of the receiver, only provide credible feedback, tailor their wording to suit the individual, and have positive motives. Receivers must be able to listen, seek clarification without being defensive, explore suggestions regarding change, take steps to self-improve, and seek feedback from teammates on their behavior (see Figure 7.3). The process of giving and receiving positive and constructive feedback may be the best way to prevent conflict among team members and to improve effectiveness in collaboration.

BEING SENSITIVE TO DIVERSITY AND AVOIDING STEREOTYPING

Cultural diversity, when combined with intercultural knowledge, communication, and positive experiences, is always an asset; however, misunderstanding, stereotypes, prejudices, and even racism can result when knowledge, communication, and experiences are lacking (Harry, 1997). Ignorance often is due to a lack of experience with the minority culture/group in a particular environment or

When team members are in tough situations, it is critical that they hear what others are saying. Only then do they have any hope of influencing the beliefs, feelings, or behaviors of their co-workers. The following are examples of tough listening:

- A teammate who was absent from a meeting tears apart the team's carefully developed action plan, which you had a big part in developing; to makes things worse, some of her strongest complaints seem to have some validity. You listen.

- A colleague openly cuts down your values on inclusion, hitting on many things you hold dear. You listen, although only because you know that if you try to defend yourself now, she will not pay attention later.

- In the presence of others in the teachers' lounge, a fellow teacher severely berates a student whom you know well and care for greatly. Several teachers who are listening agree with the complainer and sympathize with her miseries of having him as a student. Your admiration for that student is great; however, given the negative and heated climate, you decide not to say anything now but to listen to her message and plan your response for a less emotional opportunity.

- As the team focuses on several teaching challenges, you are brimming with ideas that you think are brilliant and could resolve all the challenges. You resist jumping in and dominating the discussion and sending messages of your impatience with their contributions. Although you think you could outline the entire action plan, you know it would be your plan and not the team's plan. Instead, you take your turn, contributing the best of your ideas, listening to others' ideas, and looking for chances to integrate the team's ideas into a creative plan that is truly team-generated.

All of these tough listening situations involve team members sending clear messages about their feelings and their needs. The nonverbal behaviors that speakers and listeners use—facial expressions, gestures, physical stance, voice volume and tone, and eye contact—are the primary ways such messages are sent. While it is not easy to listen under these tough conditions, it is essential to do so; *"until people feel certain you have heard their message, it is impossible for them to listen to you"* (DeBoer & Fister, 1995–1996, p. 71).

   To gain a complete understanding of other team members' messages, skilled listeners can use facilitative listening skills: 1) attending, 2) responding (e.g., by paraphrasing, clarifying, reflecting, and checking perceptions), and 3) using leading strategies (e.g., interpreting, explaining, encouraging, assuring, suggesting, agreeing/disagreeing, challenging, humoring) (see Chapter 3).

Figure 7.2. Good listening is tough listening. (From DeBoer, A., & Fister, S. [1995–1996]. *Working together: Tools for collaborative teaching.* Longmont, CO: Sopris West; adapted by permission.)

inadequate knowledge of the practices, beliefs, and characteristics of the members of that culture/group. Stereotypes reflect false beliefs about causal connections between two unrelated, and often negative, factors (e.g., being poor and being lazy). They are dangerous because they guide thinking about groups of people and are highly resistant to change. Trent (1997) found that teachers' sociocultural stereotypes regarding students' abilities and their home life were negatively associated with their reduced expectations for students with disabilities and for students' lack of progress. Johnson and Johnson (2000, pp. 463–466) listed the ways that stereotypes are perpetuated:

- Stereotypes influence what people perceive and remember about the actions of nondominant group members.

- Stereotypes create an oversimplified picture of nondominant group members; the larger the nondominant group, the more likely oversimplifications are to occur.

- Individuals tend to overestimate the similarity of behavior among nondominant group members.

- People tend to have a bias toward false consensus: They believe that most people share their stereotypes.

- Stereotypes tend to be self-fulfilling.

Providing positive feedback	Providing constructive feedback for improvement	Receiving constructive feedback for improvement
Goal: To help another realize the way that his or her behavior has had a positive influence on a person, group, or issue; to encourage the person to continue or to expand the behavior. The team trait that is most often cited for enhancing teamwork is positive communication conducted in flexible ways; it is characterized by honesty, positive tone, and tactfulness (Dinnebeil, Hale, & Rule, 1996).	*Goal: To help another receive information about improving or changing his or her behavior; reaching this goal depends on the receptivity of the recipient, the capability of the sender at giving feedback, and the credibility of the feedback*	*Goal: To hear what is being offered nondefensively and to consider feedback as an opportunity for self-improvement. Lundy (1994) noted, "Those who defend their weaknesses can keep them, and probably will; the greatest weakness is the awareness of none."*
Mention specific behaviors, acts, or events so that the person will understand more clearly.	Be perceptive to the recipient's readiness for feedback.	Keep your mind open and listen; absorb as much as you can.
Tell why you think the behavior had a positive impact (e.g., your feelings, others' reactions).	Word your feedback in ways that do not hurt or damage.	Listen for understanding, quell judgments, and focus totally on what is being said.
Give only sincere praise; undeserved praise can have bad effects, and insincere praise can threaten relationships.	Identify specific behaviors and situations; be unambiguous and do not generalize beyond the specific or exaggerate.	Do not interrupt to maximize your understanding. Make notes to help clarify your understanding later.
Sincere praise is easy to give and goes a long way.	Address behavior and actions, not personality traits.	Hold your desire to react in check. Take a deep breath, be quiet, and think through your questions.
Find appropriate opportunities to give public credit that is due—orally or in written reports.	Tell how you feel, but omit any judgments or speculations on the recipient's motives.	Confirm your understanding of the message with the sender right away or later if you need time to gain self-control; sooner is better than later because you may misunderstand the feedback.
	Give feedback promptly; time erodes our memory of events.	
	Make your feedback brief and avoid unneeded repetition; this helps minimize defensiveness.	Seek clarification—ask about confusing aspects, request illustrations, and avoid being defensive in the process.
	Confirm understanding by listening to the person's reaction or thoughts regarding self-improvement.	Size up the situation: what the sender is saying reflects how he or she feels—his or her reality.
	Preface your suggestions with introductory questions: Have you considered? Do you suppose? Would it help?	State your appreciation, even if you do not agree; try to regard feedback as a "gift of information" (1994, p. 164).
	Suggest, but do not dictate.	Seek more information to clarify whether the viewpoint is shared by other teammates. If so, or if you agree with the criticism, continue the steps below.
	"Look forward to opportunity, not backward to blame" (Lundy, 1994, p. 162). Suggest alternatives for the future.	
	Check back with the person on his or her comfort level with suggestions.	Discuss ways to improve; those giving feedback may be good sources for ideas.
	Make the person's needs the focus, not your needs as the helper.	Focus on changing your behavior; seek the assistance of teammates.
		Ask for feedback on progress.

Figure 7.3. Giving and receiving feedback from team members. (Reprinted with permission from *Dartnell's T.E.A.M.S: Together Each Achieves More Success*, copyright 1994 by Dartnell Corporation, 360 Hiatt Drive, Palm Beach Gardens, FL 33418. All rights reserved. For more information on our training products, please call 1-800-621-5463, ext. 563 or visit our Web site at www.dartnellcorp.com.)

- Stereotypes lead to scapegoating.

- People often develop a rationale and explanation to justify their stereotypes and prejudices.

Collaborative teams must be vigilant in identifying, discussing, confronting, and eradicating the conditions that breed or perpetuate stereotypes:

- When one or several team members' cultures are different from that of the rest of the team, the familiarization phase should involve time for the team member to share information about his or her culture. This might include learning vocabulary, recognizing a holiday, sharing ethnic food, or learning personal information about the individual.

- When the dominant culture of the professional staff differs from that of the paraprofessional staff and the students in a school, the effort to educate dominant and nondominant groups must be extensive and ongoing.

- Schools should prepare staff and students to understand the background of the nondominant group(s) in ways that do not over-generalize the information. Consider, as an example, the large range of linguistic and intracultural differences among people often identified as Hispanic, including Cubans, Puerto Ricans, Central and South Americans, Spaniards, and Mexicans (Harry, 1992a; Mardinos, 1989). Likewise, individuals who are recent immigrants often differ in their cultural practices and language from first- and second-generation immigrants.

- Professionals must recognize their own cultural values prior to developing a sensitivity to the diversity in language, culture, customs, and attitudes of the students and families with whom they work (Harry, 1992b, 1997; Salisbury & Dunst, 1997).

When family members are from a nondominant culture, several steps should be taken to

make members' styles more congruent (Sileo, Sileo, & Prater, 1996). First, differences in team members' regard for time might mean that the team needs to allow more time to think aloud together and not just aim for a "quick fix." Second, when there are conflicts in beliefs concerning the target student's independence, professionals should encourage extended family members to join the team to design programs that reflect their home practices of shared child rearing responsibility. Finally, when the equity beliefs of team members differ from those of the student's family, professionals should regard the target student's family's view of itself as an expert view in its own right.

FOSTERING POSITIVE STAFF–FAMILY INTERACTIONS

The initial meetings that family members attend—evaluation and identification, IEP planning, and placement—are the most critical and often the most difficult for several reasons: 1) Parents and professionals usually do not know each other (especially when a child is first considered for special education); 2) team membership has not yet been established because eligibility, program planning, or placement have not yet been determined; and 3) family members are presented with information about their child that is often new, complex, confusing, unpleasant, and scary.

Staff members on collaborative teams can foster family members' involvement in the teaming process through the attitudes they communicate and the teaming procedures they use (Losen & Losen, 1994; Turnbull & Turnbull, 2000).

- Teams can be cognizant of, sensitive to, and respectful of the family's culture, values, and viewpoints.

- Teams can communicate repeatedly that the family's knowledge, information, concerns, hopes, and opinions about their child are very valuable.

- Teams can be sensitive to communicating doubt or superiority; members should question for clarity, not accuracy.

- Teams can accept that there is no standard measurement for family involvement. For some families, just getting the child dressed, fed, and to school on time is a major undertaking (Carney & Gamel-McCormick, 1996).

- Teams can be vigilant about not feeding into any parental guilt over a child's disability or learning or behavioral challenges.

- Teams can communicate that they share the responsibility for designing and implementing programs to support the student's learning and behavior.

- Teams can examine any forms that will be used during a meeting (e.g., permission to test, IEP, transition plan) and review the procedural steps with the parents.

Although family members typically are not present at every team meeting and rarely are present for on-the-fly interchanges between staff members during the school day, their role as team members must not be forgotten. Teams should guarantee that family members will be able to contribute their input on every issue and every action plan. Members can seek the family's ideas beforehand, include them in the meeting process, and check team decisions with them before assuming team consensus.

Though it is their right, parents rarely bring legal counsel to team meetings. It is more common for parents to bring advocates or parent advisors with them. Public law encourages parents to invite trusted friends, advisors, or family members to attend team meetings with them to lend support and assist in their understanding and their articulation of concerns. The presence of these individuals, however, can be adversarial for professional staff. Lawyers rarely feel obligated to follow a team's procedure, as their dedication is to their client; therefore, the presence of lawyers may be not only psychologically, but also procedurally, disruptive (Losen & Losen, 1994).

Legal council is more often sought by parents because of a dispute with program administrators than a dispute with specific team members; the controversy, however, often seeps into the team as well and may be impossible to ignore. Recognizing the rightful presence of these outsiders and acknowledging their right to interrupt, the team facilitator can appeal to the group for cooperation and request their help in avoiding confrontation:

> We should acknowledge, before we begin, that Mr. Lagiano is here to represent the Clarks as their attorney. He may be helpful to all of us in our proceedings, but since most of us are unaccustomed to working with lawyers present, we will need to be sure that our discomfort does not lead us to be overly cautious in what we say or how we say it. (Losen & Losen, 1994, p. 129)

The team facilitator needs to remind the team members that *their focus must remain on the student*. The agenda, processing steps (e.g., celebrate, examine team relationships), and team procedures should not be forgotten even though they may be difficult to carry out. Well-established teamwork routines can help overcome a difficult atmosphere and allow the important day-to-day decision making to get done. Although the team facilitators will not want to alienate parents by limiting the guest's participation in the team meeting, facilitators should interrupt when a guest's comments are out of place, premature, or not suited to the team's current task. Facilitators can remind the guest and the other team members to follow the agenda and to focus on their purpose: meeting the student's educational needs.

ADDRESSING DISAGREEMENT

Even the best collaborative teams run into communication blocks and get side-tracked by conflict. The best prevention for uncooperativeness and competition among team members is routine self-evaluation or team processing. This section describes three elements of team processing: 1) taking time to process, 2) assessing group functioning, and 3) observing the behavior of team members (Thousand & Villa, 2000).

Take Time to Process

Teams often begin their meetings by celebrating their successes, an activity that contributes to team building. Teams also will often stop halfway through their agenda, and again at the end of the meeting, to process interpersonal dynamics and meeting progress. Processing often consists of posing questions such as the following:

- How are we doing?

- Are we making progress?

- Do we need to adjust our agenda to reflect what now seems to be the priority?

- Do we have interpersonal problems that are blocking our progress?

- If we do, what can we do differently?

When teams learn to schedule and then pose processing questions, they briefly shift their attention to themselves during the meeting, thereby increasing the probability that interpersonal channels will operate more smoothly (Johnson & Johnson, 2000).

Assess Group Functioning

Regular self-assessment of team health is a good preventative measure for serious conflict. Procedures teams use to process group functioning include effective ways to give feedback to team members (Thousand & Villa, 2000). One member is designated to be the group observer; this person not only contributes to work on agenda items but also watches interactions among members and helps team members self-examine in a number of ways:

- Team members each self-evaluate against a checklist of teaming skills (see Figure

7.4) or their own ground rules and then reflect as a group.

- Teams target one or several areas on which to focus in the next meeting.

- At the next meeting, the team observer reminds team members of the targeted areas, observes these areas, and then shares the observations with other members while giving feedback to each member.

- Team members comment on the observations.

- The observer shares incidents of positive teamwork and encourages others to contribute their observations.

- Team members discuss the observations and then identify or refine goals for improvement at individual and group levels.

Feedback can be better absorbed by team members if observers are positive and direct in their reports. Observers should establish eye contact with team members, present them with objective data, and be honest (Thousand & Villa, 2000). Figure 7.3 provides suggestions for giving constructive feedback, for more guidance.

Student Snapshot

 Mr. Martin, a member of the "Energizer Team" at Vanessa's school, reports that each member of this team regularly appraises their team, from high to low, on 25 questions concerning how they are operating together. In their first evaluation, one teacher combines the anonymous ratings, and the team reviews them by celebrating their high scores and discussing their lower scores. They reach consensus on areas of need and create a plan for improvement. The Energizer Team discovered that they needed work in several areas: using their time better, improving communication with parents, and striving to integrate separate subject areas while coordinating major assignments and units. They scheduled time to tackle each area and later reevaluated themselves.

Team profile

Reflect on your team as a whole. For each item, circle the appropriate number that best corresponds with your view/opinion.

Our team as a whole	Almost never	Completely never	Often	Very often	Almost always
1. Team members are clear on their roles.	1	2	3	4	5
2. Team members listen to one another.	1	2	3	4	5
3. Team members check to understand what others are saying.	1	2	3	4	5
4. Team members understand and could identify group norms.	1	2	3	4	5
5. Goals and objectives are set by the whole team.	1	2	3	4	5
6. Timelines (due dates) are set for each team goal.	1	2	3	4	5
7. Goals are accomplished within set timelines.	1	2	3	4	5
8. All members are encouraged to participate.	1	2	3	4	5
9. Differences of opinion are expressed face-to-face.	1	2	3	4	5
10. The usual reaction to disappointment is a willingness to listen and problem-solve.	1	2	3	4	5

Our team meetings	Almost never	Completely never	Often	Very often	Almost always
11. Start on time	1	2	3	4	5
12. Have an agenda	1	2	3	4	5
13. Face a facilitator	1	2	3	4	5
14. Have time limits for agenda items	1	2	3	4	5
15. Include a plan for "who will do what by when"	1	2	3	4	5
16. Are summarized in writing at the end of the meeting	1	2	3	4	5
17. Are evaluated by members for effectiveness	1	2	3	4	5
18. Have a recorder who writes down outcomes	1	2	3	4	5
19. Are productive and an efficient use of time	1	2	3	4	5
20. End on time	1	2	3	4	5

21. To what extent do I feel a real part of the team? *(circle below)*

1	2	3	4	5
Not really part of this team	Generally outside, except for one or two short periods	Sometimes in, Sometimes out	Part of this team most of the time	Completely part of this team

Figure 7.4. Team profile. (From Self-assessment: A key process of successful team development, J. Olson & C.L. Murphy, *Young Exceptional Children*, 2[3], 1999, 4–5; reprinted by permission.)

(continued)

Figure 7.4.   *(continued)*

22. How safe is it in this team to be at ease, relaxed, and myself?

1	2	3	4	5
It would be foolish to be oneself on this team.	I am fearful about being myself.	Generally, I feel I have to be careful about what I say and do.	Most people accept me if I am myself.	I feel perfectly safe to be myself

23. To what extent do I keep my opinions "under wraps" (i.e., have ideas and feelings that I do not bring to the open)?

1	2	3	4	5
Almost completely under wraps	Fearful about being myself	Sometimes free and expressive	Free and expressive most of the time	Almost completely free and expressive

24. How effective is the team in including all members in making decisions?

1	2	3	4	5
We do not encourage everyone to share ideas.	Only ideas of a few members are used in making decisions.	We hear the views of most members before making decisions.	A few are hesitant about sharing opinions, but we have good participation.	Everyone's ideas are heard before decisions are made.

25. How clear are the goals that the team is working toward?

1	2	3	4	5
I do not understand the goals of the team.	Much of what we are doing is not clear.	Sometimes I am clear on the team's goals.	I understand most of what we are doing.	I am well aware of all team goals.

26. How well does the team progress toward its goals and related tasks?

1	2	3	4	5
Coasts, loafs, makes no progress	Makes little progress, most members loaf	Has slow spurts of effective work	Has above average progress and pace of work	Works well, achieves definite progress

27. The way the team operates is influenced largely by:

1	2	3	4	5
One team member	A clique or group	Shifts from one person or clique to another	Shared by most members	Shared by all members

28. Who accepts responsibility for most of the tasks of the team?

1	2	3	4	5
Nobody assumes responsibility for work done.	Only a few assume responsibility for work done.	About half assume responsibility for work done.	Most members assume responsibility for work done.	All members assume responsibility for work done.

29. How are differences or conflicts handled by the team?

1	2	3	4	5
They are denied suppressed, or avoided.	They are recognized but discussed outside of the team.	They are recognized, and some members try to work through them.	They are recognized, and most members try to work through them.	They are recognized, and the team works through them.

30. What is the typical style of leadership on the team?

1	2	3	4	5
The leader dominates the team.	The leader controls the team, although people generally agree.	There is some give and take between the leader and team members.	Team members relate easily to the leader and give input.	No one dominates; team members respect the leader.

Please list items or areas that you would like to see your *team* work on.

_____

_____

_____

_____

Observe the Behavior of Team Members

A more structured observation approach can be useful to teams that need an objective check on specific interpersonal difficulties. When there is clear evidence of problems in listening, communicating, practicing shared values and ground rules, or reaching consensus, teams may select a group member or seek an outsider to observe their interactions. When definitive signs of difficulty have been noted and discussed by team members, it is good to have team members select one or several specific collaborative skills to observe that are closely linked to the signs of difficulty. When skills—not people or problems—are the focus of observation, then teams are less likely to experience blame, accusations, hurt feelings, and anger.

Once the specific skills of concern have been identified, teams are advised to

- Have the team observer check on members' understanding of the targeted skills.

- Use an observation process that the team agrees on (see Figure 7.5).

- Have the observer record the frequency of team members' skill performance.

- Record positive examples of members using the skill and other relevant teaming interactions that are not related to the target skills.

- Have the observer summarize the observations for the team.

- Take time to discuss these observations and to explore ways to improve team skills.

- Use team processing in later meetings to check team progress.

When teams take a short amount of time on a regular basis to directly address the quality of their interactions, members can develop a sensitivity to their own interactions and assume more responsibility for maintaining effective listening and communication. Teams that learn to focus on themselves in this way can expect better results when they shift their focus to students.

RESOLVING CONFLICT CONSTRUCTIVELY

When disagreements or conflicts arise within a team, they must first be identified. Once identified, teams need to decide whether they want to address them. Some conflicts are best handled by being ignored, especially if they are minor. Other conflicts are best just acknowledged, particularly when their open recognition is adequate to sensitize members (e.g., "Gosh, you can tell by the way we are picking at each other that we are really ready for spring break!").

Identify the Conflict

Although some unaddressed conflicts will diminish over time, others have a way of festering. Many team conflicts involve school staff on one side and family members on the other side (Snell & Janney, 2000):

- *Disagreement about student goals and problem identification*—A lack of consensus on student goals sometimes leads to disagreement regarding what is or is not a problem.

- *Coordination problems*—Conflict sometimes arises while making or implementing plans that results from logistics (e.g., class schedules, available equipment, movement of students) and fragmentation of services and time.

- *Implementation and evaluation problems*—These problems often concern the skill of the person implementing the solution, the lack of team consensus in developing a solution, inadequate solutions, or a failure to improve and refine solutions over time.

Observer: _____   **Date:** _____

Team meeting: _____

Target skills	Carla (GE)	Kenna (SE)	Joy (SLP)	Brenda (Parent)	Mary (TA)
Waits for team member to finish speaking before talking					
Follows team ground rules					
Avoids arguing but expresses disagreement by seeking clarification or stating an alternate viewpoint					

+   indicates an instance of the behavior/skill

−   indicates a need for the behavior/skill

Anecdotal record of "good" examples of skill performance (note member)
Other relevant observations that are related to target skills

Figure 7.5.   Grid for observing cooperative skills used by team members. (From Thousand, J.S., & Villa, R.A. [2000]. Collaborative teaming: A powerful tool in school restructuring. In R.A. Villa & J.S. Thousand [Eds.], *Restructuring for caring and effective education: Piecing the puzzle together* [2nd ed., pp. 254–291]. Baltimore: Paul H. Brookes Publishing Co.; adapted by permission.)

- *Communication problems*—These problems are due to inadequate time to fully discuss supports and include second-hand reporting, and lack of trust.

When problems seem to be associated primarily with one team member, a subset of the team (often the core teachers) may discuss the concern separately from the rest of the team. Although this method is usually the best way to explore the problem initially, any action will ultimately need to involve the target team member.

Nonconfrontational Solutions

At times, a simple, indirect intervention will diminish the problem enough for the team to once again function normally. If ground rules are being broken, teams might review these rules and discuss potential changes. In other cases, team members might choose to work around the problem instead of confronting it.

Student Snapshot

 When Mr. Marcie was an itinerant special education teacher working with many classrooms at two different elementary schools, communication was too infrequent, and it was difficult to build trust. For Daniel's team in particular, there was a role conflict between the classroom teacher and Mr. Marcie, which made it difficult to be a team. A preventive plan was formulated with other team members who recognized the conflict. To avoid conflict, these team members directed their focus to Daniel and tried to accomplish one small but important child-focused task during each weekly meeting. Whenever there was a hint of conflict with the classroom teacher, team members used a mediation strategy to refocus the group and prevent a reaction to that team member. This experience taught Mr. Marcie that one of the biggest enemies of team trust is time. The next year, the system Mr. Marcie worked in stopped assigning teachers to more than one school, and the problem disappeared.

Indirect or "Gentle" Confrontation

Team problems frequently stem from one person's failure to follow team procedures (e.g., always late, often absent, doesn't follow through on team solutions) or from the behavior of a team member during meetings (e.g., overly negative or critical, interruptive, dominating, frequently off-task). Other problems stem from philosophical and methodological disagreement. When these problems cannot be ignored and do not respond to modeling and shaping and an exploration of their cause seems unhelpful, indirect or direct confrontation may be pursued.

Indirect confrontation involves calling attention to the troublesome behavior in a meeting but without identifying the person who engages in that behavior. Such confrontation is sometimes followed by team problem-solving but often involves defusing rather than resolving the conflict directly. Team members can use humor to call attention to the difficulty (e.g., "How many strong personalities can we fit into one room?") or suggest an alternative to the problem behavior. They can turn the unfavorable behavior into a favorable behavior without confrontation. "Have the 'joker' be responsible for starting each meeting with a funny story; ask the person who always wanders off task to give a signal when others get off task" (Thousand & Villa, 2000, pp. 94–95). They can also make the difficult member an "expert" on certain team needs: A faculty member who is viewed as "always critical" may be the only one who has taken a specialized reading course and learned new approaches for grouping and adaptation that the team could use. That person can offer some of his or her ideas during the next brain-storming session. Finally, as Thousand and Villa suggested, turn the individual's problem into an asset: ". . . assign an 'aggressor' the role of devil's advocate for certain issues . . . assign a 'dominator' the role of 'encourager' or 'equalizer'" (2000, pp. 94–95).

Teams can also encourage self-assessment

- "Why do we engage in (the problem behavior)?" "What function does it serve?"

- "How might our team procedures be changed to help reduce the problem behavior?"
- "When someone engages in this behavior, what do the rest of us do to encourage it?"
- "In what other ways can we behave toward this person to help change the problem behavior?"

Direct Confrontation and Problem-Solving

When indirect confrontation strategies do not work, a more direct approach should be considered (Johnson & Johnson, 2000; Thousand & Villa, 2000). *Direct confrontation* involves several steps: describing the problem behavior to the person who engages in it, finding a solution, implementing the solution, and assessing satisfaction. These steps mirror the problem-solving approaches discussed in Chapter 4, and the same steps (problem identification, brainstorming, action plan) can be adapted for use with team conflict. When direct confrontation is the first and last step, mutual resolution is less likely.

A face-to-face confrontation may mean that one team member decides or is "elected" to confront the dysfunctional member but only if the problem occurs regularly and cannot be ignored. This approach must be taken with care. Team members may want to plan who should undertake the task. Sometimes it helps to have the confrontor be someone who knows the receiver well and can relate personally to him or her. Confrontation in private is often preferable to confrontation in front of the entire team, especially if it is likely that the person will be unhappy, embarrassed, or angered by the feedback. The approach one uses to confront another must be carefully thought through, address issues not people, and avoid anger and blame.

When confronting a person, it is often best to describe the troublesome behavior to the individual in objective terms in addition to describing its effect on the team and possible solutions. I-messages are an effective way to confront without attacking (DeBoer, 1995). You-messages should be avoided because they often sound condescending, abrasive, and judgmental (e.g., "It sounds as if you are angry . . ." "You're late all the time," "You need to . . . ," "You did not understand my question"). I-messages have four parts and require some practice to use:

1. Describe the *behavior* that is not acceptable or causes you stress (e.g., "When someone interrupts me, I cannot think straight . . ."). Do not use "you."

2. Describe the *effect of this behavior* on you (e.g., "I get distracted by my anger, which makes it difficult for me to focus on the complexities of Sam's special needs").

3. Address the effect that the behavior has on *how you feel* (e.g., "I feel angry").

4. Describe the *preferred behavior* and specifically state what is you need from the person in place of the problem behavior (e.g., "What I need is for you to wait until I finish what I am trying to say") (see Figure 7.6).

The following examples involve all four elements:

- "When I am not involved in a decision about Daniel's school program, I feel devalued in my role as a professional, and I am hurt and wonder why my opinion was not consulted. I need to be consulted before changes are made to Daniel's program, and I need to have my viewpoints heard before a final decision is made."
- "When I see students we share are primarily on a punishment system, I feel sad because I see the debilitating side effects. I need for us to mutually design a positive system that meets both our needs" (DeBoer, 1995, p. 106).
- "I feel a little peeved when we agree to an action plan and everyone doesn't do their

---

Use I-messages to confront conflict that gentle approaches have not resolved

I-messages are:

- Messages that you own (*I* and *my,* not *you* and *your*)
- Straightforward, open, and honest statements
- Statements that communicate how something is affecting you and what you need

Use I-messages when:

- You need to communicate to someone that their behavior is unacceptable or is creating a problem for you.
- You need to be assertive so a solution can be found.

Four elements of I-messages:

1. Your true feelings about the behavior
2. Brief description of the behavior that is unacceptable/causing you stress
3. Concrete effects/outcomes of that behavior on you personally
4. A description of the behavior that is preferred

"I feel (state how you feel) when (describe the behavior) because (tell how it affects you)"

"What I need is (describe/invite a solution)"

Figure 7.6.   I-messages.

part . . . because that means the plan won't work and Melanie gets the short end. What I need is for us to make realistic action plans. If we can't do what we promise, I need to find out before it is too late."

Although I-statements are less offensive than you-statements, they are still very difficult to deliver and somewhat unnatural to construct. The giver should practice confronting the dysfunctional team member ahead of time; he or she may even write out the statement and check for the four needed elements.

One of the biggest challenges of direct confrontation is getting the person to be part of the problem-solving. That person may be feeling a variety of emotions: angry, embarrassed, defensive, guilty, or surprised. Once an I-statement has been used to confront a teammate, the giver should shift from the speaker role to the listener role. DeBoer suggested that active listening be conducted "with an attitude of empathy for the person's situation and an acceptance of them as an individual," which does not mean that the per-

son confronting the team member must agree with the troublesome behavior (1995, p. 108). The confronting team member could ask the person what his or her thoughts and feelings are and what might be done. From the problem-solving discussion, which may best take place at a second meeting when emotions are lower, should come mutually generated suggestions for reducing the problem during future team sessions. Sometimes, after listening to the confronted team member's perspective, it may be necessary for the confronting team member to restate the original I-message or rephrase the message in order to remind the person of his or her viewpoint and move toward a resolution.

In addition to the problem-solving methods described in Chapter 4, two additional approaches that have been used to address conflict between team members are 1) principled negotiation and 2) building a bridge between this parent's point of view and mine. Principled negotiation, or "negotiating agreement without giving in" (Fisher & Ertel, 1995; Fisher & Ury, 1983), is a frequently used approach to resolving conflicts in the business world. It uses a creative problem-solving process that has been successfully applied by many teams to address conflict between teachers and family members (Carney & Gamel-McCormick, 1996), but its use is hardly limited to teacher–parent conflict! The first basic element of principled negotiation is to identify the problem, with the added requirement that the problem be separated from the person. Figure 7.7 lists and illustrates the elements of principled negotiation. This approach allows teams to confront conflict directly by identifying the issues "stalemated by conflict" (1996, p. 454) and dealing with them.

Building a bridge between this parent's point of view and mine is a five-step approach described by Harry (1997) and Kalyanpur and Harry (in press). Often, the issues of disagreement between professionals and family members (e.g., amount of services, these services and not those services, location of schooling, this label not that one) are only part of the picture. When the issues of disagreement become the only focus, however, both parties are trapped in conflict. Harry's message is that an individual's underlying beliefs and values provide the logic for the person's position. Harry gives examples of differing beliefs, stereotypes, or values we hold about 1) groups of people, 2) the meaning of disability, 3) parenting styles, and 4) goal setting. These differences may relate to one's culture, background, upbringing, heritage, language, religion, and education. The process for resolving conflict is to bridge that gap between the two viewpoints by first identifying the issues of disagreement and then understanding the underlying beliefs and values supporting each viewpoint. The process for resolving conflict involves:

1. Identify the issues.
    Walter is in the eleventh grade and has had an IEP for most of his school career with a label of mental retardation. At the most recent IEP meeting, his mother, Mrs. Smith, refused to sign his IEP. The teachers were confused because she had always signed it before and agreed to the goals

and objectives, saying she wanted him to graduate and get a good job. The team knew that they needed the mother's approval to move forward with his transition-to-work plan. As Walter and his mother left the meeting, it was clear that Mrs. Smith was upset. Ms. Elliott heard her say, "You all think Walter's a retard, but he's not!" Ms. Elliott realized that Walter's mother was angry about the label of mental retardation that appeared on his IEP.

2. Identify the professionals' underlying values.
    The teachers met to discuss their beliefs behind their views. Walter needed a disability label to qualify for special education. His tests since elementary school met the criteria for mild mental retardation. Walter had a good history of learning and was likely to graduate with a job if he could complete his transition plan, but without a signed IEP, he could not continue.

3. Identify the parent's underlying values
    Ms. Elliott knew Walter and his mom pretty well and called to see if she could drop by to talk. Mrs. Smith agreed. When they were seated over coffee, Ms. Elliott asked if Mrs. Smith was worried about the label of mental retardation on Walter's IEP. Without answering the question, Mrs. Smith quickly responded: "Walter's not stupid or crazy. He can do lots of things. He's worked at the farm, mowed the lawn, and helped at the garage, but he won't get a job if you call him a retard!"

4. Discuss both sets of beliefs.
    As Ms. Elliott and Mrs. Smith talked, they explored what was on the transition plan for Walter's last year at school. Mrs. Smith knew that Walter was excited about the training he would get at the automotive shop near their house. She learned that Walter would be paid after a few weeks of training. Ms. Elliott told her that Walter's school records could not be seen by anyone without her permission and that his diploma would be an "IEP diploma" just like many other kids in special education. It would not be a "mental retardation diploma."

5. Collaborate by focusing on values shared with the parent

Basic elements	Applied	Results
1. Separating the people from the problem	*The problem is confused with the people:* Parents' failure to participate in IEP meetings means they are not concerned about their child's education. *The problem is separated from the people:* In what ways might we obtain information from parents that will help in planning?	"By transcending personality differences, parties involved in conflict can begin to view one another as allies in the effort to solve a difficult problem" (Carney & Gamel-McCormick, 1996, p. 455).
2. Focusing on interests, not positions	*Position, or something you have decided on:* Parents argue for direct occupational therapy for their son, saying that integrated therapy will not be intensive enough. *Interests, or what causes one to decide:* Parents really want their son to learn to manage snaps and zippers, not to be dependent on others to do these things. If the parents' real interest is understood, the team can problem-solve ways to accomplish the goal with involvement from other services and supports while still addressing the parents' position.	Focusing on interests helps both parties in conflict find a common ground. Then, both parties can identify different paths to the desired end.
3. Creating options for mutual gain	All parties participate in brainstorming solutions. They select criteria by which to evaluate these ideas, work together to select the most promising ideas, and improve the ideas until all agree on the solution(s).	Brainstorming lets groups look through the eyes of different experts and develop a solution from team-generated ideas.
4. Using objective criteria to evaluate outcomes	Team members identify and select objective criteria by which they will evaluate the outcomes of their decision. These criteria might include • Whether student outcomes have been reached • Whether interests of team members have been met	Team-defined criteria provide an impartial means to determine whether team interests have been met. If interests are met, then negotiation is successful. If they are not met, the team simply engages in more problem-solving.

Figure 7.7.   Basic elements of principled negotiation. (From Carney, I.H., & Gamel-McCormick, M. [1996]. Working with families. In F.P. Orelove & D. Sobsey [Eds.], *Educating children with multiple disabilities: A transdisciplinary approach* [3rd ed., pp. 451–476]. Baltimore: Paul H. Brookes Publishing Co.; adapted by permission.)

As the two talked, they both realized that they each took pride in Walter's accomplishments at school and had high hopes for his future. They agreed that his last year of school and the job training planned in his IEP was important. Ms. Elliott wrote a letter that Mrs. Smith signed to go in Walter's file saying that his IEP and all of his other educational records were not open to anyone beyond the IEP team without Mrs. Smith's or Walter's approval. Mrs. Smith then signed the IEP.

CONCLUSION

Without the work of collaborative teams, inclusive schools cannot succeed. Effective teamwork rests on a foundation of mutual trust and equity, with team members coordinating their efforts through face-to-face interactions involving problem-solving to achieve a common goal. Although team-based decision making is clearly a part of all special education procedures, there is no guarantee that teams will operate in this manner. Educators may have to learn these strategies and administrators may need to support them in this process. We hope this book serves as a useful guide to collaborative teaming.

References

Amrein, A.L., & Berliner, D.C. (2002, March 28). High-stakes testing, uncertainty, and student learning. *Education Policy Analysis Archives, 10*(18). Retrieved September 28, 2003, from http://epaa.asu.edu/epaa/v10n18/

Amrein-Beardsley, A.A., & Berliner, D.C. (2003, August 4). Re-analysis of NAEP math and reading scores in states with and without high-stakes tests: Response to Rosenshine. *Education Policy Analysis Archives, 11*(25). Retrieved September 24, 2003, from http://epaa.asu.edu/epaa/v11n25/

Appl, D.J., Troha, C., & Rowell, J. (2001). Reflections of a first-year team: The growth of a collaborative partnership. *Teaching Exceptional Children, 33*(3), 4–8.

Austin, V.L. (2001). Teachers' beliefs about co-teaching. *Remedial and Special Education, 22*(4), 245–255.

Bahr, M.W., Whitten, E., Dieker, L., Kocarek, C.E., & Manson, D. (1999). A comparison of school-based intervention teams: Implications for educational and legal reform. *Exceptional Children, 66*(1), 67–83.

Bambara, L.M., Gomez, O., Koger, F., Lohrmann-O'Rourke, S., & Xin, Y.P. (2001). More than techniques: Team members' perspectives on implementing positive supports for adults with severe challenging behaviors. *Journal of The Association for Persons with Severe Handicaps, 26*(4), 213–228.

Bateman, B.D., & Linden, M.A. (1998). *Better IEPs: How to develop legally correct and educationally useful programs* (3rd ed.). Longmont, CO: Sopris West.

Bauer, A.M., & Shea, T.M. (1999). *Inclusion 101: How to teach all learners.* Baltimore: Paul H. Brookes Publishing Co.

Bauwens, J., Hourcade, J., & Friend, M. (1989). Cooperative teaching: A model for general and special education integration. *Remedial and Special Education 10*(2), 17–22.

Beck, R. (Ed.). (1997). *PROJECT RIDE: Responding to individualized differences in education.* Longmont, CO: Sopris West.

Briggs, M.H. (1993). Team talk: Communication skills for early intervention teams. *Journal of Childhood Communication Disorders, 15*(1), 33–40.

Brownell, M.T., Yeager, E., Rennells, M.S., & Riley, T. (1997). Teachers working together: What teacher educators and reserachers should know. *Teacher Education and Special Education, 20,* 340–359.

Buck, G.H., Polloway, E.A., Smith-Thomas, A., & Cook, K.W. (2003). Prereferral intervention processes: A survey of state practices. *Exceptional Children, 69*(3), 349–360.

Carney, I.H., & Gamel-McCormick, M. (1996). Working with families. In F.P. Orelove & D. Sobsey (Eds.), *Educating children with multiple disabilities: A transdisciplinary approach* (3rd ed., pp. 451–476). Baltimore: Paul H. Brookes Publishing Co.

Cook, B.G., Semmel, M.I., & Gerber, M.M. (1999). Attitudes of principals and special education teachers tworad the inclusion of students with mild disabilities: Critical differences of opinion. *Remedial and Special Education, 20*(4), 199–207.

Cook, L., & Friend, M. (1993). Interpersonal and procedural considerations of collaborative teams and problem-solving. In R. Beck (Ed.), *Project RIDE: Responding to individual differences in education* (p. 44). Longmont, CO: Sopris West.

Dabkowski, D.M. (2004). Encouraging active parent participation in IEP team meetings. *Teaching Exceptional Children, 36*(3), 34–39.

Darling-Hammond, L. (1996). What matters most: A competent teacher for every child. *Phi Delta Kappan, 78*(3), 193–200.

Davern, L. (2004). School-to-home notebooks: What parents have to say. *Teaching Exceptional Children, 36*(5), 22–27.

Dawson, M.M. (1987). Beyond ability grouping: A review of the effectiveness of ability grouping and its alternatives. *School Psychology Review, 16,* 348–369.

DeBoer, A. (1995). *Working together: The art of consulting and communicating.* Longmont, CO: Sopris West.

DeBoer, A., & Fister, S. (1994). *Strategies and tools for collaborative teaching* (Participant's handbook). Longmont, CO: Sopris West.

DeBoer, A., & Fister, S. (1995–1996). *Working together: Tools for collaborative teaching.* Longmont, CO: Sopris West.

Deutsch, M. (1962). Cooperation and trust: Some theoretical notes. In M.R. Jones (Ed.), *Nebraska symposium on motivation* (pp. 275–320). Lincoln: University of Nebraska Press.

Dinnebeil, L.A., Hale, L.M., & Rule, S. (1996). A qualitative analysis of parents' and service coordinators' descriptions of variables that influence collaborative relationships. *Topics in Early Childhood Special Education, 16,* 322–347.

Dinnebeil, L.A., & Rule, S. (1994). Variables that influence collaboration between parents and service coordinators. *Journal of Early Intervention, 18*(4), 349–361.

Dole, E.L. (2004). Collaborating successfully with your school's physical therapist. *Teaching Exceptional Children, 36*(5), 28–35.

Downing, J.E. (2002). *Including students with severe and multiple disabilities in typical classrooms: Practical strategies for teachers* (2nd ed.). Baltimore: Paul H. Brookes Publishing Co.

Downing, J.E., Ryndak, D.L., & Clark, D. (2000). Paraeducators in inclusive classrooms: Their own perceptions. *Remedial and Special Education, 21*(3), 171–181.

Doyle, M.B. (2002). *The paraprofessional's guide to the inclusive classroom: Working as a team* (2nd ed.). Baltimore: Paul H. Brookes Publishing.

Doyle, M.B., York-Barr, J., & Kronberg, R.M. (1996). *Creating inclusive school communities: Module 5. Collaboration: Providing support in the classroom, facilitator guide.* Baltimore: Paul H. Brookes Publishing Co.

Duhaney, L.M.G. (1999). A content analysis of state education agencies' policies/position statements on inclusion. *Remedial and Special Education, 20*(6), 367–378.

Dunst, C.J., Johanson, C., Rounds, T., Trivette, C.M., & Hamby, D. (1992). Characteristics of parent-professional partnerships. In S.L. Christenson & J.C. Conoley (Eds.), *Home–school collaboration: Enhancing children's academic and social competence* (pp. 157–174). Silver Spring, MD: National Association of School Psychologists.

Educational Resources Information Center. (2003, Spring). Paraeducators: Providing support to students with disabilities and their teachers. *Research Connections in Special Education, 12.*

Elliott, D., & McKenney, M. (1998). Four inclusion models that work. *Teaching Exceptional Children, 31*(4), 54–58.

Etscheidt, S.K., & Bartlett, L. (1999). The IDEA amendments: A four-step approach for determining supplementary aids and services. *Exceptional Children, 65*(2), 163–174.

Fennick, E. (2001). Coteaching: An inclusive curriculum for transition. *Teaching Exceptional Children, 33*(4), 60–66.

Fennick, E., & Liddy, D. (2001). Responsiblities and preparation for collaborative teaching: Coteachers' perspectives. *Teacher Education and Special Education, 24,* 229–240.

Fisher, R., & Ertel, D. (1995). *Getting ready to negotiate: The getting to yes workbook.* New York: Penguin Books.

Fisher, R., & Ury, W. (1983). *Getting to yes.* New York: Penguin Books.

Foley, R.M., & Lewis, J.A. (1999). Self-perceived competence in secondary school principals to serve as school leaders in collaborative-based educational delivery systems. *Remedial and Special Education, 20*(4), 233–243.

Ford, A., Messenheimer-Young, T., Toshner, J., Fitzgerald, M.A., Dyer, C., Glodoski, J., & Laveck, J. (1995, July). *A team planning packet for inclusive education.* Milwaukee: The Wisconsin School Inclusion Project.

French, N.H. (2001). Supervising paraprofessionals: A survey of teacher practices. *Journal of Special Education, 35*(1), 41–53.

French, N.H., & Chopra, R.V. (1999). Parent perspectives on the role of the paraprofessional in inclusion. *Journal of The Association for Persons with Severe Handicaps, 24*(4), 1–14.

Friend, M. (2000). Myths and misunderstandings about professional collaboration. *Remedial and Special Education, 21*(3), 130–132.

Friend, M., & Cook, L. (1990). Collaboration as a predictor for success in school reform. *Journal of Educational and Psychological Consultation, 1*(1), 69–86.

Friend, M., & Cook, L. (2003). *Interactions: Collaboration skills for school professionals* (4th ed.). New York: Longman.

Fullan, M.G., (1991). *The new meaning of educational change* (2nd ed.). New York: Teachers College Press.

Garner, H.G., Uhl, M., & Cox, A.W. (1992a). *Interdisciplinary teamwork* [videotape]. Richmond: Virginia Commonwealth University, Virginia Institute for Developmental Disabilities.

Garner, H.G., Uhl, M., & Cox, A.W. (1992b). *Interdisciplinary teamwork: A guide for trainers and viewers.* Richmond: Virginia Commonwealth University, Virginia Institute for Developmental Disabilities.

Gately, S.E., & Gately, F.J. (2001). Understanding coteaching components. *Teaching Exceptional Children, 33*(4), 40–47.

Gerber. P.J., & Pop, P.A. (1999). Consumer perspectives on the collaborative teaching model: Views of students with and without LD and their parents. *Remedial and Special Education, 20,* 288–296.

Gerber. P.J., & Pop, P.A. (2000). Making collaborative teaching more effective for academically able students: Recommendation for implementation and training. *Learning Disability Quarterly, 23,* 229–236

Giangreco, M.F. (1993). Using creative problem-solving methods to include students with severe disabilities in general education classroom activities. *Journal of Educational and Psychological Consultation, 4*(2), 113–135.

Giangreco, M.F. (1996). *Vermont interdependent services team approach (VISTA): A guide to coordinating educational support services.* Baltimore: Paul H. Brookes Publishing Co.

Giangreco, M.F. (1998). *Ants in his pants: Absurdities and realities of special education.* Minnetonka, MN: Peytral Publications.

Giangreco, M.F. (1999). *Flying by the seat of your pants: More absurdities and realities of special education.* Minnetonka, MN: Peytral Publications.

Giangreco, M.F. (2000). *Teaching old logs new tricks: More absurdities and realities of education.* Minnetonka, MN: Peytral Publications.

Giangreco, M.F., Broer, S.M., & Edelman, S.W. (1999). The tip of the iceberg: Determining whether paraprofessional support is needed for students with disabilities in general education settings. *Journal of The Association for Persons with Severe Handicaps, 24*(4), 281–291.

Giangreco, M.F., Cloninger, C.J., Dennis, R.E., & Edelman, S.W. (1994). Problem-solving methods to facilitate inclusive education. In J.S. Thousand, R.A. Villa, & A.I. Nevin (Eds.), *Creativity and collaborative learning: A practical guide to empowering students and teachers* (pp. 321–346). Baltimore: Paul H. Brookes Publishing Co.

Giangreco, M.F., Cloninger, C.J., & Iverson, V.S. (1998). *Choosing options and accommodations for children (COACH): A guide to educational planning for students with disabilities* (2nd ed.). Baltimore: Paul H. Brookes Publishing Co.

Giangreco, M.F., Dennis, R., Cloninger, C.J., Edelman, S., & Schattman, R. (1993). "I've counted Jon": Transformational experiences of teachers educating children with disabilities. *Exceptional Children, 59*(4), 359–372.

Giangreco, M.F., Dennis, R., Edelman, S., & Cloninger, C. (1994). Dressing your IEPs for the general education climate: Analysis of IEP goals and objectives for students with multiple disabilities. *Remedial and Special Education, 15*(5), 288–296.

Giangreco, M.F., Edelman, S.W., Broer, S.M., & Doyle, M.B. (2001). Paraprofessional support of students with disabilties: Literature from the past decade. *Exceptional Children, 68,* 45–63.

Giangreco, M.F., Edelman, S.W., & Dennis, R.E. (1991). Common professional practices that interfere with the integrated delivery of related services. *Remedial and Special Education, 12*(2), 16–24.

Giangreco, M.F., Edelman, S.W., Luiselli, T.E., & MacFarland, S.Z.C. (1997). Helping or hovering? Effects of instructional assistant proximity on students with disabilties. *Exceptional Children, 64*(1), 7–18.

Giangreco, M.F., & Putnam, J.W. (1991). Supporting the education of students with severe disabilities in regular education environments. In L.H. Meyer, C.A. Peck, & L. Brown (Eds.), *Critical issues in the lives of people with severe disabilities* (pp. 245–270). Baltimore: Paul H. Brookes Publishing Co.

Giangreco, M.F., & Ruelle, K. (2002). *Absurdities and realities of special education: The best of ants . . . , flying . . . , and logs.* Minnetonka: MN: Peytral Publications.

Gunter, P.L., Miller, K.A., Venn, M.L., Thomas, K., & House, S. (2002). Self-graphing to success: Computerized data management. *Teaching Exceptional Children, 35*(2), 30–34.

Hall, T.E., Wolfe, P.S., & Bollig, A.A. (2003). The home-to-school notebook: An effective communication strategy for students with severe disabilities. *Teaching Exceptional Children, 36*(2), 68–73.

Hargreaves, A. (1994). *Changing teachers, changing times.* New York: Teachers College Press.

Harry, B. (1992a). An ethnographic study of cross-cultural communication with Puerto Rican-American families in the special education system. *American Educational Research Journal, 29*(2), 471–494.

Harry, B. (1992b). *Cultural diversity, families, and the special education system: Communication and empowerment.* New York: Teachers College Press.

Harry, B. (1997). Leaning forward or bending over backwards: Cultural reciprocity in working with families. *Journal of Early Intervention, 23*(1), 62–72.

Harry, B., Kalyanpur, M., & Day, M. (1999). *Building cultural reciprocity with families: Case studies in special education.* Baltimore: Paul H. Brookes Publishing Co.

Hennen, L., Hirschy, M., Opatz, K., Perlman, E., & Read, K. (1996). *From vision to practice: Ideas for implementing inclusive education.* Minneapolis: University of Minnesota, Institute on Community Integration.

Henriques, D.B. (2003, September 2). Rising demands for testing push limits of its accuracy. *The New York Times,* pp. A1, 6.

Hunt, P., Doering, K., Hirose-Hatae, A., Maier, J., & Goetz, L. (2001). Across-program collaboration to support students with and without disabilities in a general education classroom. *Journal of The Association for Persons with Severe Handicaps, 26*(4), 240–256.

Hunt, P., Soto, G., Maier, J., & Doering, K. (2003). Collaborative teaming to support students at risk and students with severe disabilities in general education classrooms. *Exceptional Children, 69*(3), 315–332.

Idol, L. (1990). The scientific art of classroom consultation. *Journal of Educational and Psychological Consultation, 1*(1), 3–22.

Idol, L. (1997). Key questions related to building collaborative and inclusive schools. *Journal of Learning Disabilities, 30*(4), 384–394.

Individuals with Disabilities Education Act (IDEA) of 1990, PL 101-476, 20 U.S.C. §§ 1400 *et seq.*

Individuals with Disabilities Education Act Amendments of 1997, PL 105-17, 20 U.S.C. §§ 1400 *et seq.*

Isaksen, S.G., & Parnes, S.J. (1992). Curriculum planning for creative thinking and problem solving. In S.J. Parnes (Ed.), *Source book for creative problem-solving* (pp. 422–440). Buffalo, NY: Creative Education Foundation Press.

Jackson, C.W., & Larkin, M.J. (2002). Teaching students to use grading rubrics. *Teaching Exceptional Children, 35*(1), 40–45.

Janney, R.E., & Snell, M.E. (2000). *Teachers' guide to inclusive practices: Behavioral support.* Baltimore: Paul H. Brookes Publishing Co.

Janney, R.E., & Snell, M.E. (2004). *Teachers' guides to inclusive practices: Modifying schoolwork* (2nd ed.). Baltimore: Paul H. Brookes Publishing Co.

Janney, R.E., Snell, M.E., Beers, M.K., & Raynes, M. (1995). Integrating students with moderate and severe disabilities into general education classes. *Exceptional Children, 61*, 425–439.

Johnson, D.W., & Johnson, F.P. (1997). *Joining together: Group theory and group skills* (6th ed.). Boston: Allyn & Bacon.

Johnson, D.W., & Johnson, F.P. (2000). *Joining together: Group theory and group skills* (7th ed.). Boston: Allyn & Bacon.

Johnson, L.J., Zorn, D., Tam, B.K.Y., Lamontagne, M., & Johnson, S.A. (2003). Stakeholders: Views of factors that impact successful interagency collaboration. *Exceptional Children, 69*(2), 195–109.

Kaczmarek, L., Pennington, R., & Goldstein, H. (2000). Transdiciplinary consultation: A center-based team functioning model. *Education and Treatment of Children, 23*(2), 156–172.

Kalyanpur, M., & Harry, B. (in press). *Cultural underpinnings of special education policy and practice.* Baltimore: Paul H. Brookes Publishing Co.

Karge, B.D., McClure. M., & Patton, P.L. (1995). The success of collaboration in resource programs for students with disabilities in grades 6 through 8. *Remedial and Special Education, 16*(2), 79–89.

Katzenbach, J., & Smith, D. (1993). *The wisdom of teams.* Cambridge, MA: Harvard Business School Press.

Keefe, E.B., Moore, V., & Duff, F. (2004). The four "knows" of collaborative teaching. *Teaching Exceptional Children, 36*(5), 36–42.

Lipsky, D.K., & Gartner, A. (1997). *Inclusion and school reform: Transforming America's classrooms.* Baltimore: Paul H. Brookes Publishing Co.

Losen, S.M., & Losen, J.G. (1994). Teamwork and the involvement of parents in special education programming, In H.G. Garner & F.P. Orelove (Eds.), *Teamwork in human services: Models and application across the life span* (pp. 117–141). Newton, MA: Butterworth-Heinemann.

Lundy, J. (1994). *T.E.A.M.S: Together each achieves more success.* Chicago: Dartnell.

Mabry, L., Poole, J., Redmond, L., & Schultz, A. (July 18, 2003). Local impact of state testing in southwest Washington. *Education Policy Analysis Archives, 11*(21). Retrieved September 24, 2003, from http://epaa.asu.edu/epaa/v11n22/

Mardinos, M. (1989). Conception of childhood disability among Mexican-American parents. *Medical Anthropology, 12*, 55–68.

Marks, S.U., Schrader, C., & Levine, M. (1999). Paraeducator experiences in inclusive settings; Helping, hovering, or holding their own? *Exceptional Children, 65*, 315–328.

Mattingly, D.J., Prislin, R., McKenzie, T.L., Rodrigues, & Kayzar, B. (2002). Evaluating evaluations: The case of parent involvement programs. *Review of Educational Research, 72*(4), 549–576.

McLaughlin, M.J., & Warren, S.H. (1992). *Issues and options in restructuring schools and special education programs.* College Park: University of Maryland and Westat.

McWilliam, R.A. (1996). How to provide integrated therapy. In R.A. Mcwilliam (Ed.), *Rethinking pull-out services in early intervention* (pp. 147–184). Baltimore: Paul H. Brookes Publishing Co.

Minondo, S., Meyer, L.H., & Xin, J.F. (2001). The role and responsibilities of teaching assistants in inclusive education: What's appropriate? *Journal of The Association for Persons with Severe Handicaps, 26*(2), 114–119.

Munk, D.D., & Bursuck, W.D. (2001). Preliminary findings on personalized grading plans for middle school sudents with learning disabilitites. *Exceptional Children, 67*, 211–234.

Murawski, W.W., & Dieker, L.A. (2004). Tips and strategies for co-teaching at the secondary level. *Teaching Exceptional Children, 36*(5), 52–58.

Murawski, W.W., & Swanson, H.L. (2001). A meta-analysis of co-teaching research: Where are the data? *Remedial and Special Education, 22*(5), 258–267.

National Association of State Boards of Education (NASBE). (October, 1992). *Winners all: A call for inclusive schools.* Alexandria, VA: Author.

National Center for Children and Youth with Disabilities (NICHCY). (July 1995). Planning for inclusion. *NICHCY News Digest, 5*(1), 1–31.

Nelson, J. (1987). *Positive discipline.* New York: Ballantine Books.

No Child Left Behind Act of 2001, PL 107-110, 115 Stat.1425 (2002).

Noell, G.H., Witt, J.C., LaFleur, L.H., Mortenson, B.P., Rainer, D.D., & LeVelle, J. (2000). Increasing intervention implementation in general education following consultation: A comparison of two follow-up strategies. *Journal of Applied Behavior Analysis, 33,* 271–284.

Nowacek, J.E. (1992). Professionals talk about teaching together: Interviews with five collaborating teachers. *Intervention in School and Clinic, 27,* 262–276.

Olson, J., & Murphy, C.L. (1999). Self-assessment: A key process of successful team development. *Young Exceptional Children, 2*(3), 2–8.

Parett, H.P., & Petch-Hogan, B. (2000). Approaching families: Facilitating culturally/linguistically diverse family involvement. *Teaching Exceptional Children, 32*(2), 4–10.

Parnes, S.J. (1992). Creative problem-solving and visionizing. In S.J. Parnes (Ed.), *Source book for creative problem-solving* (pp. 133–154). Buffalo, NY: Creative Education Foundation Press.

Parsons, M.B., & Reid, D.H. (1999). Training basic teaching skills to paraeducators of students with severe disabilities: A one-day program. *Teaching Exceptional Children, 31*(4), 48–55.

Parsons, M.B., Reid, D.H, & Green, C.W. (1996). Training basic teaching skills to community and institutional support staff for people with severe disabilities: A one-day trianing program. *Research in Developmental Disabilities, 17,* 467–485.

Pemberton, J.B., (2003). Communicating academic progress as an integral part of assessment. *Teaching Exceptional Children, 35*(4), 16–20.

Porter, G.L., Wilson, M., Kelly, B., & Den Otter, J. (1991). Problem-solving teams: A thirty-minute peer-helping model. In G.L. Porter & D. Richler (Eds.), *Changing Canadian schools: Perspectives on disability and inclusion* (pp. 219–238). North York, Ontario, Canada: The Roeher Institute.

Praisner, C. (2003). Attitudes of elementary school principals toward the inclusion of students with disabilities. *Exceptional Children, 69,* 135–145.

Pugach, M.C., & Johnson, L.J. (2002). *Collaborative practitioners: Collaborative schools* (2nd ed.). Denver, CO: Love.

Pugach, M.C., & Wesson, C.L. (1995). Teachers' and students' views of team teaching and general education and learning-disabled students in two fifth-grade classes. *Elementary School Journal, 95*(3), 279–295.

Rainforth, B., & England, J. (1997). Collaborations for inclusion. *Education and Treatment of Children, 20,* 85–104.

Rainforth, B., & York-Barr, J. (1997). *Collaborative teams for students with severe disabilities: Integrating therapy and educational services* (2nd ed.). Baltimore: Paul H. Brookes Publishing Co.

Riggs, C.G. (2004). Top 10 list to teachers: What paraeducators what you to know. *Teaching Exceptional Children, 36*(5), 8–12.

Riggs, C.G., & Mueller, P.H., (2001). Employment and utilization of paraeducators in inclusive settings. *Journal of Special Education, 35,* 54–62.

Roach, V. (1995, May). *Winning ways: Creating inclusive schools, classroom, and communities.* Alexandria, VA: National Association of State Boards of Education.

Russ, S., Chiang, B., Rylance, B.J., & Bongers, J. (2001). Caseload in special education: An integration of research findings. *Exceptional Children, 67,* 161–172.

Salend, S.J., & Duhaney, L.M.G. (1999). The impact of inclusion on students with and without disabilities and their educators. *Remedial and Special Education, 20,* 114–126.

Salend, S.J., & Duhaney, L.M.G. (2002). Grading students in inclusive settings. *TEACHING Exceptional Children, 34*(3), 8–15.

Salisbury, C.L., & Dunst, C.J. (1997). Home, school, and community partnerships: Building inclusive teams. In B. Rainforth & J. York-Barr (Eds.), *Collaborative teams for students with severe disabilities: Integrating therapy and educational services* (2nd ed., pp. 57–87). Baltimore: Paul H. Brookes Publishing Co.

Salisbury, C.L., Evans, I.M., & Palombaro, M.M. (1997). Collaborative problem-solving to promote the inclusion of young children with significant disabilities in primary grades. *Exceptional Children, 63,* 195–209.

Salisbury, C.L., & McGregor, G. (2002). The administrative climate and context of inclusive elementary schools. *Exceptional Children, 68,* 259–274.

Salisbury, C.L., & Palombaro, M.M. (Eds.). (1993). *No problem: Working things out our way.* Pittsburgh: Allegheny Singer Research Institute, Child and Family Studies Program.

Senge, P., Roberts, C., Ross, R., Smith, B., & Kleiner, A. (1994). *Learning to work together: The fifth discipline fieldbook.* New York: Doubleday.

Sileo, T.W., Sileo, A.P., & Prater, M.A. (1996). Parent and professional partnerships in special education: Multicultural considerations. *Intervention in School and Clinic, 31,* 145–153.

Snell, M.E. (2002, May). *Inclusion of children with high and low support needs in upper elementary class-*

rooms. Paper presented at the meeting of the American Association on Mental Retardation, Orlando, FL.

Snell, M.E., & Janney, R.J. (2000). Teachers' problem solving about young children with moderate and severe disabilities in elementary classrooms. *Exceptional Children, 66,* 472–490.

Snell, M.E., Lowman, D.K., & Canady, R.L. (1997). Parallel block scheduling: Accomodating students' diverse needs in elementary schools. *Journal of Early Intervention, 20,* 266–278.

Snell, M.E., & Macfarland, C.A. (2001, November). *Inclusion in upper elementary classrooms: "A lot of it falls apart without the planning."* Paper presented at the meeting of The Association for Persons with Severe Handicaps, Anaheim, CA.

Snell, M.E., Raynes, M., Byrd, J.O., Colley, K.M., Gilley, C., Pitonyak, C., Stallings, M.A., VanDyke, R., William, P.S., & Willis, C.J. (1995). Changing roles in inclusive schools: Staff perspectives at Gilbert Linkous Elementary. *Kappa Delta Pi Record, 31,* 104–109.

Soodak, L.C. (1998). Parents and inclusive schooling: Advocating for and participating in the reform of special education. In S.J. Vitello & D. Mithaug (Eds.), *Inclusive schooling: National and international perspectives* (pp. 113–131). Mahwah, NJ: Lawrence Erlbaum Associates.

Stamps, J., Anda, M.C., Perez, C., & Drummond, H. (2002). Collaborative tactics for nestsite selection by pairs of Blue Footed Boobies. *Behaviour, 139,* 1383–1412.

Stanovich, P.J. (1996). Collaboration: The key to successful instruction in today's inclusive schools. *Intervention in School and Clinic, 32,* 39–43.

Talbert, J.F. (1993). Constructing a schoolwide professional community: The negotiated order of a performing arts school. In J.W. Little & M.W. McLaughlin (Eds.), *Teachers' work: Individuals, colleagues, and contexts* (pp. 164–184). New York: Teachers College Press.

Thomas, C.C., Correa, V.I., & Morsink, C.V. (1995). *Interactive teaming: Consultation and collaboration in special education.* Upper Saddle River, NJ: Prentice-Hall.

Thousand, J.S., & Villa, R.A. (2000). Collaborative teaming: A powerful tool in school restructuring. In R.A. Villa & J.S. Thousand (Eds.), *Restructuring for caring and effective education: Piecing the puzzle together* (2nd ed., pp. 254–293). Baltimore: Paul H. Brookes Publishing Co.

Trent, S.C. (1997). Teaching urban African American students with learning disabilities in inclusive classrooms: Using study groups to facilitate change. *Learning Disabilities Research and Practice, 12*(2), 132–142.

Trent, S. (1998). False starts and other dilemmas of a secondary general education collaborative teacher: A case study. *Journal of Learning Disabilities, 31,* 503–513.

Turnbull, A.P., Rothstein-Fisch, C., Greenfield, P.M., & Quiroz, B. (2001). *Bridging cultures between home and school: A guide for teachers.* Mahwah, NJ: Lawrence Erlbaum Associates.

Turnbull, A.P., & Turnbull, H.R. (2000). Fostering family-professional partnerships. In M.E. Snell & F. Brown (Eds.), *Instruction of students with severe disabilities* (5th ed., pp. 31–66). Upper Saddle River, NJ: Merrill/Prentice-Hall.

U.S. Department of Education. (1994). Sixteenth annual report to Congress on the implementation of the Individuals with Disabilities Education Act. Washington, DC: Author (ERIC Documentation Reproduction Service No. ED373531)

Vaughn, S., Bos, C.S., & Schumm, J.S. (2000). *Teaching exceptional, diverse, and at-risk students in the general education classroom* (2nd ed.). Boston: Allyn & Bacon.

Vaughn, S., Schumm, J.S., & Arguelles, M.E. (1997). The ABCDEs of co-teaching. *Teaching Exceptional Children, 30*(2), 4–10.

Villa, R.A., & Thousand, J.S. (Eds.) (2000). *Restructuring for caring and effective education: Piecing the puzzle together* (2nd ed.). Baltimore: Paul H. Brookes Publishing Co.

Villa, R.A., Thousand, J.S., Meyers, H., & Nevin, A. (1996). Teacher and administrator perceptions of heterogeneous education. *Exceptional Children, 63,* 29–45.

Vitello, S.J., & Mithaug, D.E. (1998). *Inclusive schooling: National and international prespectives.* Mahwah, NJ: Lawrence Erlbaum Associates.

Wadsworth, D.E., & Knight, D. (1996). Paraprofessionals: The bridge to successful full inclusion. *Intervention in School and Clinic, 31,* 166–171.

Wallace, T., Shin, J., Bartholomay, T., & Stahl, B.J. (2001). Knowledge and skills for teachers supervising the work of paraprofessionals. *Exceptional Children, 67,* 520–533.

Walther-Thomas, C.S. (1997). Co-teaching experiences: The benefits and problems that teachers and principals report over time. *Journal of Learning Disabilities, 30,* 395–407.

Walther-Thomas, C., Bryant, M., & Land, S. (1996). Planning for effective co-teaching: The key to successful inclusion. *Remedial and Special Education, 17,* 255–265.

Washburn-Moses, L. (2003). What every special educator should know about high-stakes testing. *Teaching Exceptional Children, 35*(4), 12–15.

Weiner, H.M. (2003). Effective inclusion: Professional development in the context of the classroom. *Teaching Exceptional Children, 35*(6), 12–19.

Weiss, M.P., & Lloyd, J.W. (2002). Congruence between roles and actions of secondary special education educators in co-taught and special education settings. *Journal of Special Education, 36*(2), 58–68.

Welch, M. (2000). Descriptive analysis of team teaching in two elementary classrooms: A formative experimental approach. *Remedial and Special Education, 21*(6), 366–376.

West, J.F., & Idol, L. (1990). Collaborative consultation and the education of mildly handicapped and at-risk students. *Remedial and Special Education, 11*(1), 22–31.

Williams, V.L., & Cartledge, G. (1997). Passing notes to parents. *Teaching Exceptional Children, 30*(1), 30–34.

Wisniewski, L., & Gargiulo, R.M. (1997). Occupational stress and burnout among special educators: A review of the literature. *Journal of Special Education, 31*(3), 325–346.

Wood, M. (1998). Whose job is it anyway? Educational roles in inclusion. *Exceptional Children, 64*(1), 181–195.

York-Barr, J. (Series Ed.). (1996). *Creating inclusive school communities: Modules 1–5.* Baltimore: Paul H. Brookes Publishing Co.

Appendix

Blank Forms

Issue-Action Planning Form

Team/student/group: _____ Date: _____

Team members present: _____

_____

Issue	Planned action	Person(s) responsible

Collaborative Team Meeting Worksheet

Date: _____

Members present	Members absent	Others who need to know
_____	_____	_____
_____	_____	_____
_____	_____	_____
_____	_____	_____
_____	_____	_____

Roles:

	This meeting	Next meeting
Timekeeper	_____	_____
Recorder	_____	_____
Facilitator	_____	_____
Jargon buster	_____	_____
Processor or observer	_____	_____
Other: _____	_____	_____

Agenda

Items   **Time limit**

1. Celebrations _____
2. _____
3. _____
4. _____
5. Process: How are we doing? _____
6. _____
7. _____
8. _____
9. Process: How did we do? _____

Action plan

Action items	Person responsible	By when?
1. Telling others who need to know		
2.		
3.		
4.		
5.		

Agenda building for the next meeting

Date: _____

Expected agenda items

Time: _____   1. _____   3. _____

Location: _____   2. _____   4. _____

SAM Problem-Solving Form

Objective-finding and Problem-finding: _____?

In what ways might we address the educational needs of _____ in _____

                                             (student's name)   (class/activity)

Fact-finding		Idea-finding	
Facts about student's needs 1	Facts about class/activity 2	Direct Ideas 3	Indirect Ideas 4

(From Giangreco, M.F., Cloninger, C.J., Dennis, R.E., & Edelman, S.W. [1994]. Problem-solving methods to facilitate inclusive education. In J.S. Thousand, R.A. Villa, & A.I. Nevin [Eds.], *Creativity and collaborative learning: A practical guide to empowering students and teachers* (pp. 321–346). Baltimore: Paul H. Brookes Publishing Co.; adapted by permission.)

Collaborative Teaming (2nd ed.) Snell & Janney, © 2005 Paul H. Brookes Publishing Co.

SAM Problem-Solving Form (page 2)

Solution-finding Potential solutions	Criteria				
	Addresses student need	Neutral or positive for students without disabilities	Likely to support valued life outcomes	Perceived as usable by users (e.g., teacher, student, parent)	Other: _____ _____ _____ _____
1.					
2.					
3.					
4.					
5.					
6.					
7.					
8.					
9.					
10.					
11.					
12.					

Acceptance-Finding: What needs to be done? Who is going to do it? When is it going to be done? How can the ideas be improved? Where will it be done?

Issue	Action	By whom?	When?

(From Giangreco, M.F., Cloninger, C.J., Dennis, R.E., & Edelman, S.W. [1994]. Problem-solving methods to facilitate inclusive education. In J.S. Thousand, R.A. Villa, & A.I. Nevin [Eds.], *Creativity and collaborative learning: A practical guide to empowering students and teachers* (pp. 321–346). Baltimore: Paul H. Brookes Publishing Co.; adapted by permission.)

Index

Page numbers followed by *f* indicate figures.